Beyond the Information Commons

Beyond the Information Commons

A Field Guide to Evolving Library Services, Technologies, and Spaces

Second Edition

Edited by
Charles Forrest
Martin Halbert

ROWMAN & LITTLEFIELD
Lanham • Boulder • New York • London

Published by Rowman & Littlefield
An imprint of The Rowman & Littlefield Publishing Group, Inc.
4501 Forbes Boulevard, Suite 200, Lanham, Maryland 20706
www.rowman.com

6 Tinworth Street, London, SE11 5AL, United Kingdom

Selection and editorial matter © 2020 by The Rowman & Littlefield Publishing Group, Inc.
Copyright of individual chapters held by respective authors.

All rights reserved. No part of this book may be reproduced in any form or by any electronic or mechanical means, including information storage and retrieval systems, without written permission from the publisher, except by a reviewer who may quote passages in a review.

British Library Cataloguing in Publication Information Available

Library of Congress Cataloging-in-Publication Data

Names: Forrest, Charles, 1953- editor. | Halbert, Martin, editor.
Title: Beyond the information commons : a field guide to evolving library services, technologies, and spaces / Charles G. Forrest, Martin Halbert.
Description: Second edition. | Lanham : Rowman & Littlefield, [2020] | Includes bibliographical references and index. | Summary: "This new book updates this review of current practice in the Information Commons and other new kinds of facilities inspired by the same needs and intents. This book is an attempt to answer the question: 'What might be the next emerging concept for a technology-enabled, user-responsive, mission-driven form of the academic library?'"—Provided by publisher.
Identifiers: LCCN 2020003469 (print) | LCCN 2020003470 (ebook) | ISBN 9781538141137 (cloth) | ISBN 9781538141144 (epub)
Subjects: LCSH: Information commons. | Academic libraries—Information technology. | Information commons—United States—Case studies. | Academic libraries—United States—Case studies.
Classification: LCC ZA3270 .B49 2020 (print) | LCC ZA3270 (ebook) | DDC 027.7—dc23
LC record available at https://lccn.loc.gov/2020003469
LC ebook record available at https://lccn.loc.gov/2020003470

∞™ The paper used in this publication meets the minimum requirements of American National Standard for Information Sciences—Permanence of Paper for Printed Library Materials, ANSI/NISO Z39.48-1992.

Dedicated to the memory of Susan K. Nutter (1944-2019),
library leader, innovator, and visionary

Contents

Foreword   xi
Susan K. Nutter

Acknowledgments   xv
Charles Forrest and Martin Halbert

Introduction   xvii
Charles Forrest and Martin Halbert

Part I: The Information Commons

Chapter 1   **Origin and Evolution of the Commons in Academic Libraries**   3
Liz Milewicz

Chapter 2   **Surveying the Landscape**   23
Joan Lippincott

Chapter 3   **Twenty-First-Century Library Service Design**   32
Elliot Felix and Matthew Swift

Chapter 4   **Integrating Technology into the Information Commons**   41
Parke Rhoads

Chapter 5   **Designing Flexible Spaces**   53
Summer Cook and Betsy Maddox

Chapter 6   **Tying It All Together**   62
Kelly Brubaker

Part II: The Field Guide
Kristi Burns

Field Guide   75
Claremont Colleges Library (CA)   75
   Collaborative Commons
Dartmouth College (NH)   78
   Jones Media Center

Duke University (NC) — 82
The Ruppert Commons for Research, Technology and Collaboration ("The Edge")
Emory University (GA) — 88
Learning Commons, Student Digital Life
Indiana University (IN) — 92
Learning Commons
Jackson State University (MS) — 95
JSU Innovate
Kansas State University (KS) — 97
K-State InfoCommons
North Carolina State University (NC) — 100
Lake Raleigh Learning Commons
Ohio University (OH) — 104
Learning Commons
Pennsylvania State University (PA) — 106
Knowledge Commons
Simon Fraser University (BC, Canada) — 109
Student Learning Commons
Texas Christian University (TX) — 112
Information Commons
Trinity University (TX) — 114
Information Commons
University of Cape Town (South Africa) — 118
Knowledge Commons, Research Commons, & Learning Commons
University of Central Florida (FL) — 120
Knowledge Commons
University of Illinois at Urbana-Champaign (IL) — 124
Scholarly Commons
University of Iowa (IA) — 129
Learning Commons
University of Maryland (MD) — 134
Terrapin Learning Commons
University of Minnesota Twin Cities (MN) — 137
SMART Learning Commons
University of North Carolina at Greensboro (NC) — 141
Digital Media Commons
University of North Texas (TX) — 144
Collaboration & Learning Commons
University of North Texas (TX) — 148
The Factory
University of Oklahoma (OK) — 151
Helmerich Collaborative Learning Center
University of Tennessee at Chattanooga (TN) — 154
Studio
University of Texas (TX) — 157
PCL Learning Commons
Virginia Commonwealth University (VA) — 162
Multimedia Collaboration Room
Virginia Tech University (VA) — 164
Learning Commons

Afterword	**169**
Marie S.A. Sorensen, AIA	
Appendix A: Field Guide Entry Survey Form	**185**
Appendix B: Timeline	**191**
Index	195
About the Editors and Contributors	201

Foreword

Susan K. Nutter

"What is unique about the Hunt Library is its conception of what a twenty-first-century learning environment should be. It transitions from being a place you go to take away information in book form to a place that provides an intellectual home for you to deeply experience the knowledge that you are interacting with. It encourages hands-on capabilities to take the knowledge that you might find in conventional libraries and apply it in creative, interactive, innovative ways to explore what knowledge can do."—R. Michael Young, Professor of Computer Science, North Carolina State University

A host of factors continues to drive the development and evolution of the services, technologies, and spaces of the academic and research library, both from within the library profession and higher education, as well as from the larger society. A generation ago the information commons emerged as a unifying concept for a new service program in academic libraries that responded to these changes. The information commons featured an integrated suite of desktop applications to support productivity and enhance learning, combined with a robust infrastructure enabling fast and responsive connectivity to a full range of resources both on campus and off campus, managed and supported by a service program based on collaboration between the library and a growing list of campus partners. This book, *Beyond the Information Commons*, will summarize the development of the commons from inception to maturity and suggest new directions for the continuing evolution of learning spaces, services, and programs in academic libraries.

In order to keep pace with these changes in the nature of contemporary research, teaching, and learning, the new James B. Hunt Jr. Library at North Carolina State University had to be a departure from a traditional library building. For it to serve not only as a catalyst for, but an integral component of the academic infrastructure of our campus, it needed to house a variety of integrated technology environments, various public and private collaborative spaces, and a comprehensive suite of services. These could only be achieved through a few crucial design solutions.

The first was an automated retrieval system, now affectionately known as the bookBot. With the ability to store up to 2 million volumes, it condenses our collection down to one-ninth the size of a normal stacks solution, providing us the square footage necessary to create the spaces our user community needed. The second was the consolidation of all of our services points into the singular Ask Us service point. But another critical decision was our handling of the commons concept.

Rather than being a central information commons, the Hunt Library is home to four commons areas—the NextGen Learning Commons on Level 3, the Graduate Student Commons on Level 4, the Lake Raleigh Learning Commons also on Level 4, and the Faculty Research Commons on Level 5. These spaces are certainly active and popular with faculty and graduate and undergraduate students alike. But while each may serve as a minihub of sorts, they are anything but central. Scattered throughout the building, they are customized to serve different constituents and their various working styles.

In fact, a cross section of Hunt would reveal students and faculty working in any number of specialized, technology-rich spaces. From creating 3-D models in our makerspaces to analyzing data on large-scale visualization walls, these spaces reflect the changing ways students and faculty work and expose how potent a library that offers a diverse array of collaborative, high-tech environments can be for a campus.

Increasingly, students and researchers produce and showcase scholarship via emerging technologies. Assignments or research projects may require a smartphone, tablet, or whiteboard on one end and specialized computing or large-scale visualization presentation spaces on the other end. With the ubiquitousness of mobile and consumer-grade technologies, the development of new niche spaces, and the maturation of technology lending services, the need for desktop computing has naturally decreased. Since this had been a cornerstone feature of the information commons, it's time to reevaluate the very elements of an information commons and the role it plays in an academic library.

With the new paradigm for learning spaces that has emerged in the past decade—one that emphasizes collaboration, exploration, and engagement, and recognizes the importance of good design—libraries are experimenting with at least the second generation of the "learning commons" model in order to effectively meet the needs of today's connected learners. By offering a variety of inviting spaces for both individual and collaborative work, academic libraries are catering to students' participatory culture, one in which everybody creates and shares, and where informal, peer-to-peer learning is supported. In combination with our expertise in discovery tools, libraries are well-positioned to expand the learning commons paradigm to accommodate emerging technologies—interactive computing, virtual and augmented reality, as well as machine learning and AI.

Instead of serving as the central hub of the library, the learning commons (or multiple commons in our case) is becoming one option among any number of more specialized spaces. In addition to computing, printing/scanning, group study, and presentation practice spaces, we are finding it necessary to offer additional spaces that allow for the collaborative use of digital and analog technologies. A makerspace is a kind of learning commons, as is a music production studio, as is the immersive environment a large-scale visualization wall enables.

While some of the technologies offered in these spaces were incubated in specific departments around campus, the democratic access that housing them in the library affords has been a paradigm shift for the NC State community. "Desiloization" in general has been an intentional cultural change on our campus supported at the highest levels of administration, and recent strategic plans have emphasized support for interdisciplinarity.

The spaces we have designed in support of this shift satisfy either a dormant need on campus for different modes of academic output or showcase new possibilities for those who hadn't previously been exposed to such resources. In either case, not only do these spaces enable students and faculty the opportunity to produce nontraditional scholarship, they also expose that work to nontraditional audiences. Our visualization walls are seen by thousands of visitors each day, and prototypes from the makerspace are inexpensive, safe, and durable, so a researcher doesn't have to think twice about bringing her materials into a classroom setting. Since these are exactly the kind of outreach opportunities grant-giving institutions are now calling for, it makes sense that libraries should be evolving to provide them.

But providing these opportunities is just the first step. While there will be some initial buy-in from researchers whose work was being held back by not having access to such tools and spaces, a vast majority of users will need to be exposed to the ways in which these emerging technologies can enhance their work. A robust slate of diverse programming is crucial to exhibiting the capabilities of these spaces.

For example, to spur engagement with our visualization spaces, we've developed a series called Coffee & Viz in which researchers and practitioners share how large-scale visualization expands the possibilities for their particular line of inquiry. These presentations are free and open to the public, and bagels and coffee are provided. Inevitably, newcomers to these spaces are inspired, seeing how they can adapt the presenter's techniques to their own work. The Q&As are active and exciting and often end up with "Let's talk more after" and an exchange of contact information. This is how mentorships, peer-to-peer professional development, and collaborations are born.

For spaces that are traditionally dominated by a narrower demographic, more intentional and strategic approaches are required. For example, to ensure that our makerspace program serves a more diverse user community, we've developed the Making Space program, a series of public talks and workshops that raises awareness among women about access to tools and technology, lowers barriers to entry for first-time users of makerspaces, and serves as a networking opportunity for women in the NC State community.

As a result, developing and executing these events has become an essential and significant portfolio element for our staff and is part of a larger shift in hiring and professional development. In order to deliver on the promise of these innovative spaces, staff must have the creative and technical skills it takes to help users navigate them. It would be irresponsible to think that new kinds of spaces and services wouldn't require a new kind of librarian.

One example of this professional development is our creation of the Data Sciences and Visualization Institute for Librarians—an immersive, week-long course that focuses on developing the knowledge, skills, and confidence needed in order to communicate effectively with and provide consultancy for faculty and student researchers about their data visualization. This sort of intentional opportunity is critical in preparing staff to be vital participants in these new kinds of research, teaching, and learning.

It should be said that our particular approach to the commons—the fragmenting of it and the specific technologies we feature in each—is a campus-specific solution. By no means should this be used as a one-size-fits-all concept for commons moving forward. In fact, the ways in which Hunt Library has influenced the renovations to our older main library, D. H. Hill, might be a better example. It is a more iterative, space-by-space approach based on the success of such spaces at Hunt. In the four years since Hunt opened, a Graduate Student Commons, a Faculty Research Commons, Music Booths, a Visualization Studio, and a makerspace—all spaces piloted at Hunt—have opened in D. H. Hill.

Whatever the approach, it should be arrived at with a heavy dose of user input. Whether it's through regular communication with key members of student government, a university-driven standing committee like our University Library Committee, or a more homegrown group like our Student Advisory Forum, knowing how faculty and students work and what tools they need to optimize that work is invaluable. This user-centered approach not only leads to successful designs, it fosters early buy-in and garners support from university administrators. Only with this confluence of results can a space truly be embraced and become the campus resource you envisioned it to be.

Acknowledgments

Thank you to Joan Lippincott and Liz Milewicz for returning to review and update their own work. Likewise, for returning to review and update the work of their colleagues, thank you to Kelly Brubaker and Parke Rhoads. And a big thank you to those who join us for the first time: Summer Cook, Elliot Felix, Betsy Maddox, Susan K. Nutter, Marie Sorensen, and Matthew Swift. We have enjoyed working with all our contributors, old and new, and are grateful for many interesting, informative, and lively conference calls and conversations. The conceptual foundation and the detailed analysis benefitted immensely from your engaged conversation, and breadth and depth of experience. Thank you to the editor, Martin Dillon, for agreeing to go another round with us, and best wishes for a happy retirement. Special thanks to Kristi Burns for her gentle, persistent work to keep us on task and on schedule (at least most of the time). And finally, many thanks to our spouses and families for coming along for another ride on this roller coaster.

Introduction

Charles Forrest and Martin Halbert

In the closing decades of the twentieth century, academic libraries responded to rapid changes in their environment by acquiring and making accessible a host of new information resources, developing innovative new services and collaborative partnerships, and building new kinds of technology-equipped spaces to support changing user behaviors and emerging patterns of learning. The "information commons" or "InfoCommons" blossomed in a relatively short amount of time in libraries across North America and around the world, particularly in Europe and the British Commonwealth.

This book is the second edition of *A Field Guide to the Information Commons*, a 2009 monograph that sought to document and describe the information commons trend. The motivation for the first edition originally came from our own curiosity as we wondered, "What is this phenomenon, and what accounts for its rapid, and more or less simultaneous, widespread appearance?" The motivation in issuing a second edition arose from our observation that the trend has continued to evolve and, in fact, the InfoCommons may have matured as an innovative service model, and that we are moving into a new and different landscape of technologies, facilities, and services.

The first edition of the *Field Guide* attempted to document the emergence of a range of facilities and service programs that called themselves "Information Commons." Our aim was not to comprehensively document every occurrence of every form of the commons, but rather, through representative entries, to describe and understand how the information commons was actually implemented in libraries across the country and around the world.

With this second edition we attempt to update this review of current practice in the information commons and other new kinds of facilities inspired by the same needs and intents. This book will describe the continued evolution of the commons since the compilation of the first edition over a decade ago, in an attempt to answer the question: "What might be the next emerging concept for a technology-enabled, user-responsive, mission-driven form of the academic library?"

Like its predecessor, *Beyond the Information Commons* is structured in two parts. First, a brief series of essays explore the information commons from historical, organizational, technological, and architectural perspectives. The second part is once again composed of more than two dozen representative entries describing various information commons using a consistent format that provides both perspective on issues and useful details about actual implementations.

Pennsylvania State University, Knowledge Commons
Source: Forrest/Halbert

Contributed Chapters

The essays in the first section bring together a range of perspectives on the emergence of the information commons. Our contributors span many types of professional backgrounds and interests, each offering a different lens on the evolution of the information commons (see "About the Editors and Contributors").

Susan K. Nutter gets things started in her "Foreword" by describing the planning and design of the James B. Hunt Jr. Library at North Carolina State University, with its customized commons spaces scattered throughout the building on multiple floors—NextGen Learning Commons, Graduate Student Commons, Lake Raleigh Learning Commons, and Faculty Research Commons. With their combination of new kinds of technologies, new kinds of expert assistance, and public programming and outreach, the Hunt Library's commons are decentralized to the point of fragmentation, offering a glimpse into the user-centered approach that informs the development of the Library's services in response to the changing needs of this academic community.

Liz Milewicz updates her essay, "Origin and Evolution of the Commons in Academic Libraries," documenting the shift from shared access, especially to digital resources and information, to shared creation and dissemination, pointing to a more active role for the library in the production of knowledge, and the reaffirmation of the importance of library as place and learning space. She concludes with a discussion of trends that are leading to the differentiation and segmentation of commons spaces, such as the increase in the use of personal, portable devices; the need to support individual, focused (undistracted) work as well as collaborative, group productivity; and the emergence of the library as an important partner and center for technology-enabled making and scholarly production.

Why The Edge at Duke University?
Liz Milewicz

We had the space—a large, open floor on the first level of Bostock Library, a crowd of computers and scanners, surrounded by bookshelves and tables. Students were there, it was being used, but was it being effectively utilized? More importantly, what were the growing research needs of the Duke community, and how could the Libraries better anticipate and address them? We had the space, what would we do with it?

In 2011, after interviewing administrative and faculty stakeholders on campus as part of the DLF E-Science Institute, conducting ethnographies of different academic departments, studying the research needs of undergraduate students, and visiting and researching commons environments at various academic libraries, we identified a program of services: scholarly communication, digital curation, data services, digital tools and training, and digitization that would better meet the emerging digital research needs of our campus and that could build on and accentuate our libraries' growing expertise in supporting innovative research. Although not all of these services are located within The Edge, it has served as a focal point for publicizing these services and for staff to train in them.

One of the guiding principles that we took in our intense research on the campus community was that research—what it looks like and its outputs—are changing dramatically. More and more undergraduates are conducting original research, research is becoming more collaborative and team-based, and the products of research are changing drastically. We were no longer serving users by providing only space for single-study or support for traditional research outputs.

Before building the space that would become The Edge, the architects led a visioning workshop with different campus stakeholders, to determine the guiding principles for the design. Following are some ideas that emerged in that workshop and that continue to color our thinking about the purpose of this space as well as guide our thinking of how to measure success:

- Expand the role of the Library as partners, scholars, and teachers
- Create an environment that encourages researchers to take risks and acts as a catalyst for innovation
- Foster discovery, serendipity, and inter/transdisciplinary collaboration
- Provide a resource rich environment with "grab-able" people, spaces, and tools
- Maintain flexibility for future changes and continued experimentation

For us, success meant not merely that users were in the space. We wanted to actually hear and see their work in progress—teams working together, writing on boards, reserving and using project rooms. We also saw success in our ability to bring different groups together (disciplinary

(continued)

> researchers and support units), ideally working on projects or questions alongside library staff. To do this, we also had to get more comfortable with ceding control of how the space looked and sounded at any particular time, so we could better witness and respond to how researchers made the space work for them.
>
> This focus on users has also extended to our programming in The Edge. We've sought to provide space and support for students interested in creating exhibits and sharing work and expertise, both with staff and with each other. This has meant giving up some of the control we typically enjoy with workshops and presentations, but this shift has been beneficial. In many ways, we, as library staff, had to take to heart the goals of The Edge: to push ourselves to our limit, to lean in, to try something that is a bit beyond our comfort zone.

In her chapter, "Surveying the landscape," Joan Lippincott notes the widespread adoption of the commons in the last twenty years under a variety of terms and models. Characterized by technologies that promote seamless access to information, the commons also delivers user services for both technology as well as content. Features of the commons run the gamut from workstations for individual and group use, spaces for presentation practice and videoconferencing, and consultation areas and classrooms, to exhibit and event spaces, and vending areas and cafes. The library commons will continue to play an important role in the learning community it serves.

> **Relatively New, Relatively Big**
>
> - Most of the commons in this sample were established fairly recently, about a decade-and-a-half ago. The average year was 2006.
> - Most of the facilities were renovated or overhauled one or more times in the last decade.
> - While there is a lot of variation in size, the average is 16,000 square feet, or for a conceptual gross space picture, a square roughly 125 feet on a side.

In their chapter, "Twenty-First-Century Library Service Design," Elliot Felix and Matthew Swift discuss the need for libraries to go beyond simple access to information, to creating and connecting people, technology, and resources. New and emerging user needs compel libraries to rethink their services, and their organizational structures, processes, and cultures. Drawing on their work with nearly fifty academic libraries, the authors describe a process for thinking systematically about library service philosophy and delivery, redesign of work process, and organizational restructuring, based on a user-driven perspective.

Parke Rhoads addresses one of the core elements of the Library Commons in "Integrating Technology into the Information Commons." Focusing on first principles such as mission, community needs, and overall trends, he discusses technology integration, innovation, lifecycle planning and budgeting, and the nuts and bolts of power, data, networking, wayfinding, and security. His discussion of trends covers everything from rapid prototyping and sandboxes, through digital asset management and software/virtualization, to "technology convergence," the movement toward a unified digital platform that will enable the commons to continue to remain central to the library's mission.

> **Extended Hours, Service Points, Computers**
>
> - These commons are open on average roughly 120 hours per week, over 70% of the time in a week—fairly long hours.
> - They were staffed on average around 100 hours per week—again, long hours.
> - Most of them had more than one service point.
> - There was extreme variation in the number of desktop computers, but most had dozens.
> - On average they had about half as many laptops as desktop computers.

Summer Cook and Betsy Maddox address the place where all this happens in "Designing Flexible Spaces." They underscore the need for constant innovation and change in the library commons in order to effectively support the faculty, staff, and students they serve. In a series of case studies they describe rapid design processes, and lightweight renovation and construction, that enabled libraries to quickly implement projects that produced flexible and attractive spaces in response to institutional growth and change.

Kelly Brubaker concludes the contributed chapters with "Tying It All Together." Designed in response to the needs of the end-user, the research- and learning-focused space that is the successful information commons offers an experience based on available devices, inspiring physical spaces, virtual connections, and a host of services not typically associated with libraries of the past. Moving through a range of planning themes that include the overall experience, services and partnerships, tools for creation and dissemination, technology, and identity, the evolution of the commons is traced from the destination commons, through the distributed commons, to the idea that the library is the commons. The commons of the future will reach out beyond the walls of the library, crossing disciplinary boundaries as a hub for innovation designed to foster productive collaboration, promote interdisciplinary learning, and support groundbreaking research across campus.

> **Heavy Transactional Usage**
>
> - These facilities are heavily used, with tens of thousands of entries per month.
> - On average, roughly half of the entries seem to have had an associated service transaction.
> - On average, roughly 75% of the entries seem to have had an associated logon to a computer.

The last word is given to Marie Sorensen, who in her "Afterword" takes us on a guided tour of a range of facilities and landscapes exemplifying and showcasing seven "memes" that point toward a set of big ideas that could inform and shape the design of the next generation of services, technologies, and spaces in academic libraries.

Part II: Commons Entries

Some twenty-seven entries in the current volume feature facilities that are relatively new and relatively big. Most of the commons in this sample were established fairly recently, about a decade-and-a-half ago; the average year was 2006. Most of the facilities were renovated or overhauled one or more times in the last decade. While there is a lot of variation in size, the average size is 16,000 square feet (picture a square roughly 125 feet on a side). There was wide variation in the number of desktop computers, but most had dozens. On average the commons discussed here had about half as many laptops as desktop computers.

These commons are open on average about 120 hours per week, over 70% of the time—fairly long hours. They were staffed on average around 100 hours per week—again, long hours, with staffing roughly 80% of the time they were open. Most of them had more than one service point. These facilities are heavily used, with tens of thousands of user entries per month; typically, half of the entries seem to have had an associated service transaction. On average, roughly 75% of the entries seem to have had an associated logon to a computer.

Libraries continue to innovate and adapt their services and facilities to the changing landscape of new technologies. The longstanding use of the root word "commons" (information, learning, digital, etc.) has now begun to expand to wholly new terms like makerspace, digital scholarship center, and so on. The complexity of developing, managing, and staffing these new services and facilities is a central challenge facing all institutions. Layering these new services and facilities on top of legacy programs and spaces confronts us with decisions about priorities, including decisions about what to let go of, to stop doing.

Beyond the Information Commons

While the phrase "information commons" (as well as "learning commons," "digital commons," "research commons," and the like) is still compelling and evocative to many, we find both practical and conceptual reasons to support the view that the field has moved beyond the information commons. The powerful historical connotations of the word "commons" are a fundamental part of the trend (a point that several of the contributors to this book allude to). It is worth noting the diversification and divergence of the "commons" in libraries, both in the form of both a "strong" identity as a central, named service and organizing principle, and also in the form of a "weak" identity, characterized by a convergence of "library" and "commons," in which the entire library *is* the commons. We see signs that the latter perspective is increasingly becoming active throughout the field and becoming assimilated into the basic understanding of what constitutes an academic library in the twenty-first century.

As this innovative service model enters the mainstream, we can trace its adoption and evolution over a 30-year span, from an initial period of innovation and excitement, through a second decade of maturity and productivity, followed by a third decade of growing restlessness and exploration, culminating in asking (and answering) the driving question, "What's next?" The initial period of introduction, adoption, and operation produces a need for segmentation and diversification (continually driven by changes in technology and user expectations, as well as staff and institutional learning), resulting in the next big cycle of intervention, innovation, and investment.

As information commons concepts are assimilated into the core idea of the library (instead of being a separate destination within, the commons grows and expands until in some cases the library *is* the commons), makerspaces, digital scholarship centers, and various facilities focused on new media are emerging to signal the next evolution in forward-looking, proactive innovations addressing new technological possibilities and changing user needs.

We hope that *Beyond the Information Commons* will suggest some places to look for the information commons (and its next-generation offspring), and help you identify the commons when you see it. Whatever such facilities and programs are called in the future, the information commons has been a rallying point for libraries seeking to reinvent themselves. This trend has had and will continue to have important implications as an evocative new understanding of library services now and in the future.

Part I
The Information Commons

Chapter 1

Origin and Evolution of the Commons in Academic Libraries

Liz Milewicz

This chapter continues the historical study begun in the previous *Field Guide to the Information Commons*, providing a summary of the commons in academic libraries from its conceptual beginnings (1980s to 1990s) through its development and evolution (2000s to 2010s) and the new spaces and approaches that are redefining the role of libraries in higher education. The commons movement has seen the role of academic libraries and librarians transform, from providers of information to facilitators of and then partners in learning and research. By examining the ideas that led to early innovations in library spaces, how they were instantiated, and how these spaces have evolved in recent years, this history documents pivotal shifts in the definition of libraries and librarians and their role in the academic community.

This history will consider:

- predictions about libraries in the digital age, and how the information commons both challenged and embodied these assumptions;
- technological changes and corresponding pedagogical, professional, and legal trends that contributed to the emergence and development of the information commons;
- early instantiations and later evolution of commons environments; and
- recent trends that signal future directions for the spaces and staff of academic libraries.

Understanding what the information commons is and why it emerged is a window into the mindset of librarians at the fin de siècle, as they faced the future of academic libraries and information access in the digital age and attempted to rearticulate their role in teaching, learning, and scholarship. The phenomenon of the information commons is remarkable not simply for its novelty and its widespread adoption, but also for the cachet of the name itself. The appeal of this label, and the decision by so many institutions to adopt the title for their collaborative work spaces, implies shared beliefs about the role of libraries and informational resources in building knowledge. References to "collaboration" and "community" in library articles in the early 1990s (and that continue to color discussions and descriptions of library spaces today) suggest that decisions to renovate and restructure library buildings were predicated in part on egalitarian attitudes toward access to information, shared ownership of the learning process, and the library's position on campus.

In *The Future of Ideas*, legal scholar Lawrence Lessig drew analogies between the physical commons prior to industrialization and the availability and use of electronic information at the end of the twentieth century: just as the physical commons offered shared access to resources that people needed to survive and thrive, the information commons or virtual commons provides shared access to the tools, ideas, and instruction needed to perform one's academic work and create new scholarship.[1] Focused on media ownership, fair use, and other aspects of intellectual property rights, Lessig's use of "commons" followed decades of policy debate in the United States over the merits of common ownership of natural resources and the importance of shared information access to democracy.[2] While the commons in libraries represents very literally a physical space,[3] it operates from the same principles as the notion of commons in legal circles: to encourage free access and collaborative use, which in turn benefits and strengthens the community.

Technology and services available in information commons spaces have expanded and changed over time, and appellations chosen for these spaces have shifted as well, reflecting the emphases and attitudes of different places and times. Originally the concept of a commons simply marked a place of shared access, especially to digitally delivered information. Over time, these spaces and the words used to describe them have evolved to emphasize active, shared production of knowledge. More recently, these spaces are becoming arenas for shared creation and dissemination of knowledge, among and across academic groups. While libraries have long been understood as repositories of knowledge, disseminators of information, and sites for learning and (more recently) instruction, this productive dimension points to a significantly more active and prominent role of libraries as producers of knowledge.

Recent trends suggest that, through these spaces, libraries are not merely expanding the potential for what activities they support but expanding (and altering) the role of academic libraries as well. Through the names they choose for these spaces, they signal not merely their sense of what purposes these spaces serve but also what value the libraries bring to the broader academic enterprise. In the interest of consistency, this chapter will refer to all such spaces generally as "commons" or "information commons," with deliberate attention given toward the end to recent evolutions in these spaces and changes in name.

Contexts of Change, 1980s to 1990s

In the mid-to late 1980s, just a few years before the first information commons developments, predictions abounded on what libraries of the future would be like. Many librarians and educators agreed that the new libraries would be service oriented and computer centered, perhaps merging or collaborating with computer centers.[4] John Budd and David Robinson, attending to predictions of lower college enrollments, proposed that academic libraries could play a more active role in curriculum design and reconfigure traditional patterns of service (including bibliographic instruction) to better accommodate students' needs.[5] In a retrospective article examining the effect of computer technology on library building design, Philip Leighton and David Weber proposed that, as more users accessed resources online, the library space would still retain its value as a learning and work space, offering support services, reference, and other academic assistance, as well as computing space and quiet reading areas for focused study and research.[6]

Others questioned the primacy of the physical building as information became available digitally. Professors Lawrence Murr and James Williams asserted that the "'library,' as a place, will give way to 'library' as a transparent knowledge network providing 'intelligent' services to business and education through both specialized librarians and emerging information technologies."[7] Their exposition on the importance of libraries and librarians for managing flows of electronic information further emphasized the ethereal library over the physical library. Barbara Moran, writing on the fiftieth anniversary of the Association of College and Research Libraries in 1989, predicted that in the near future "users will not have to come to a physical entity, the library, to use its resources."[8]

At the same time, in considering the future of higher education (to which the academic library is obviously and inextricably tied), Moran referenced futurist and philosopher John Naisbitt's observation that the more technology we have, the more we require personal contact with others,[9] and she pondered whether the socializing aspect of these institutions would remain essential. Joan Bechtel's vision of the library as social center struck even closer to the fundamental question of how libraries would meet the demands of a changing information landscape.[10] Calling for a new "conversation" paradigm of library service, she argued that "libraries, if they are true to their original and intrinsic being, seek primarily to collect people and ideas rather than books and to facilitate conversation among people rather than merely to organize, store, and deliver information."[11]

In many respects, all these predictions were accurate. Throughout the 1990s, as the Internet morphed into the World Wide Web, print indexes migrated to CD-ROMs and then online, and OPACs (Online Public Access Catalogs) and databases replaced traditional print resources, libraries witnessed a decline in building usage.[12] Now able to conduct research remotely, many users opted to stay at home or in their offices rather than visit the library. During this time faculty and students increasingly selected electronic resources over print,[13] while circulation statistics and in-house use of materials declined dramatically.[14]

Declines in gate counts, however, plateaued by the end of the century and reversed.[15] Some refer to this as the post-Internet "bounce"—a sign that the initial allure of the Internet had worn off and library users had tempered their irrational exuberance with electronic resources and begun to recognize the enduring value of print.[16] Yet such arguments relegate libraries to a passive role in this process and deeply understate the convenience and appeal of online information.

What changed was the library itself. In the decades spanning the twentieth and twenty-first centuries, libraries actively reinvented themselves—in the types of resources and services they provided and how they provided them, and in the physical space of the library. In line with many predictions, the new library spaces represented collaboration between librarians and IT personnel and other groups as well. Despite tendencies to downplay the power of place in libraries of the future, some forecasters did, in fact, predict these library spaces—distinct from typical pedagogical spaces yet offering unique and complementary learning experiences[17]—that materialized as the information commons.

Through information commons environments, libraries visibly and functionally incorporated networked computing resources and collaborative work environments into their missions. These spaces have served as testing grounds for interdepartmental cooperation and shared resources, provided space for different campus populations to meet and collaborate, supported social learning and intellectual play, and reasserted the value of library spaces for fostering and supporting academic work. New pedagogical approaches to knowledge construction in the classroom and a heightened awareness of the role of social spaces in teaching, learning, and scholarship further contributed to academics' willingness to experiment in and contribute to these spaces. And some (albeit often architects) would argue that the increasing ability to access information electronically, without human intercession, has ironically increased the importance of place as people seek out common spaces for social contact.[18]

Pedagogical Paradigm Shift

In 1995, Robert Barr, a director of institutional research and planning at Palomar College, and his colleague John Tagg, a professor of English, called attention to a shift that was occurring in higher education—a movement away from the goal of merely providing instruction to a passive, receptive audience to a new focus on fostering learning among active student participants.[19]

The Learning Paradigm frames learning holistically, recognizing that the chief agent in the process is the learner. Thus, students must be active discoverers and constructors of their own knowledge. In the Learning Paradigm, learning environments and activities are learner-centered and learner-controlled. They may even be "teacherless." While teachers will have designed the learning experiences and environments students use—often through teamwork with each other and other staff—they need not be present for or participate in every structured learning activity.[20]

This shift could be seen particularly well in educational literature, where for the past two decades researchers had challenged the traditional structures and processes of pedagogical environments. Referencing the works of such early twentieth-century educational theorists as John Dewey and Lev Vygotsky, these scholars argued that knowledge is not something that passes verbally or visually from teacher to student, but something that must be actively constructed through teacher-student and student-student interactions. They eventually proposed that learning may occur anywhere, at any time, not simply in structured learning environments. For example, Kenneth Bruffee, an English professor at City University of New York's Brooklyn College, emerged as an early proponent of collaborative learning outside the classroom, where students could focus on discussing and solving problems without the pressures of competition, performance, and evaluation.[21]

In essence, this shift in educational theory pushed for new conceptions of the roles and relations of teachers and students and of the where, when, and how of learning. Rather than being relegated to recess, play becomes central to learning: tools critical for conceptual development must be accessible to students outside of structured learning situations and students must be allowed to experiment with them. In addition, students' ability to talk about their ideas with peers emerged as essential for learning. Educators rediscovered Vygotsky's notion of social cognition, which views cognitive development as tightly connected to language.[22] It is not enough for students to be able to repeat a professor's lecture on a topic; they must be able to put these ideas into their own words, to explain them to someone else. In this new paradigm, students take greater responsibility for their learning, the instructor moves from "sage on the stage" to "guide on the side," and the notion of the classroom expands. Further, the emphasis shifts from establishing a heuristic model that all students must fit to creating pedagogical practices that are flexible enough to permit a variety of learning styles and levels.

Previous "instruction paradigm" measures of institutional success, which focused predominantly on the deliverer of the service rather than the receiver, also reflected an understanding of education and educational value as quantifiable.[23] Within libraries this paradigm translated into quality measured by volumes of books, and architectural and organizational planning in turn geared toward the storage of print materials. While the user of the books might be considered in collection decisions and in deciding the number of tables and chairs to provide for reference or reading areas, Vygotskian notions of social learning never entered the equation. For much of the twentieth century, the library building served primarily as a storehouse for books. Writing in 1992 on incorporating information technology into academic campuses, Philip Tompkins, then director of library information services at Estrella Mountain Community College, observed that "people's needs, habits, and learning styles [were] rarely considered in library planning… as the ever-growing book stock [was] perceived as the library's contribution to instructional relevancy."[24]

Gradually, this resource-centric approach gave way to a more expansive and inclusive focus. As beliefs shifted about the classroom space and the role of the teacher, so did beliefs about library space and the role of the librarian. Providing computers and other tools and space for academic instruction and student learning became more deeply ingrained in libraries' missions, and new professional organizations emerged to meet this challenge.

Networked Information and Social Learning

The New Learning Communities (NLC) program of the Coalition for Networked Information (CNI) began in the early 1990s as an effort to support student-centered approaches to teaching and learning built upon networked sources of information.[25] Speaking from the perspective of community college libraries, Philip Tompkins argued that libraries must find ways to successfully merge print-based and digital cultures and create spaces and services that support interactive learning.[26] Further, libraries must become more integral parts of the teaching-learning experience, integrating instruction and communication into their traditional service of information storage and delivery.[27] Tompkins observed that "an era of reconceptualization and boundary spanning collaboration is occurring."

This collaboration has implications for telecommunications, microcomputers, the redesign of the classroom and the need for new, sponsored learning environments (spaces) departing radically in design from the theater of the classroom or the traditional library or learning resource center. Above all, a new vision of the role of all campus personnel to accommodate student-centered learning cultures has emerged. It is richly supported by the massing of microcomputer technology and changes in pedagogy. Collaborative and cooperative teaching, and independent, self-paced learning call for new spaces accommodating the massing of newer instructional and information technologies, remote from the theater-style classroom. Multimedia accessibility can usher in changing roles of the instructors who learn to moderate the historic obsession with the "telling" to incorporate skillful coaching and facilitating upon call ("from sage on the stage to guide on the side").[28]

Early on, new technologies were linked to new philosophies of teaching and learning, and both would need new spaces to accommodate them. Most librarians saw a shift in the use and structure of library space as an inevitable consequence of new technology; others saw it as an imperative, with the colocation of resources, tools, and services making the library "the public space for scholarship on campus."[29] The ubiquity of personal computers alongside the remote delivery of formerly print-based resources (e.g., library catalogs, indexes, journals, and books) meant that areas once dedicated solely to shelving current periodicals and reference works or housing card catalogs would need to be repurposed or renovated in order to remain viable.

Community colleges, with their instruction-centered and student-focused missions, were primed to adapt their libraries to this new approach. Writing in 1990, Don Doucette of the League for Innovation in the Community College asserted that community colleges would be "the institutions of higher education in which the widespread integration of computers into instructional practices will first take place."[30] Indeed, they were among the first higher education institutions to develop information commons, with several community colleges adopting the model developed by Philip Tompkins.[31]

Despite predictions that top-tier research libraries would resist this expansion in role from resource center to instruction and service center,[32] many major university libraries figured prominently in the information commons movement, likely because they possessed the resources necessary to develop and maintain these technology-rich spaces. The costs involved in revamping or overhauling infrastructures in order to create an information commons may explain the seemingly lower frequency of information commons development among associate- or baccalaureate-degree-granting institutions.[33]

Connecting People, Places, and Information

The Maricopa County Community College District of Arizona offers one of the earliest-recorded examples of an information commons, with its opening in 1992 of the Estrella Mountain Community College Center—a combined library and technology center "planned as an environment where instructional and information technologies and efforts were to be integrated."[34] From the planning stages, the project sought to leverage new technology for instructional support.

The University of Southern California's Leavey Library, which opened in 1994 but had been in the planning stages for over a decade, arose from the belief that the library could serve as a link between instruction and technology[35] and also as an answer to the information needs of a digital generation of students.[36] Chris Ferguson, then head of the Leavey Library, described it as a place that would provide more than just a convenient and comfortable place to access information: "It will be an intellectual center—a place where students and teachers will come to exchange ideas—and I very much want the Leavey to be a center for campus social life as well."[37]

The same year that the Maricopa County Community College District launched its technology and teaching center, the University of Iowa opened the Information Arcade—"a playground for the mind"—that housed a classroom of 24 computers and an open independent work area of 50 computers and a few clusters of multimedia workstations.[38] The space was intended to support a range of uses; the electronic classroom was designed to accommodate smaller work groups as well as whole-class discussions. For their part, the faculty often had to restructure their curriculum and pedagogical approach to match the type of teaching and learning supported by the electronic classroom: "As a political science faculty member commented, teaching in the Arcade 'changes the focus. Instead of learning by listening, students learn by doing. It puts me, the teacher, into the role of helping, giving advice. It's a different sort of learning'."[39] Besides the novel approach to learning and the diverse array of technology provided within the learning spaces, another significant hallmark of the University of Iowa's Information Arcade was the collaborative effort involved in producing and maintaining it.[40] Members of the faculty, the libraries, and the academic computing center worked together at the outset to procure funding for the space, and this collaborative approach continued throughout its life.[41]

As Joan Lippincott observes, working across professional and organizational boundaries is not merely a developmental aspect of information commons but may be essential to realizing the full potential of these spaces.[42] Varying levels of teamwork are often evident in the creation and support of information commons, from colocation (simply locating different departmental resources and services in close proximity) to cooperation (coordinating efforts to provide resources and services); but true collaboration (interacting at a deeper level, resulting in shared governance, strategic planning, and goals) is rare. Examples she offers of collaboration underscore how such partnerships can help commons spaces meet their goals, especially to support and innovate teaching and learning.

Shifts in Emphasis, 2000s to 2010s

The first decades of the twenty-first century saw the consolidation and wide adoption of commons spaces in libraries, followed (perhaps inevitably) by a splintering, muddying, and, in some quarters, rejection of the term. Efforts to reframe the commons as a space for learning coincided with national rubrics for measuring the quality of library spaces as well as greater attention to the preferences of the Millennials now arriving on college campuses. Attempts to attract more undergraduates and social activities into the library inadvertently downplayed or undermined libraries' commitment to supporting advanced research; later instantiations of the commons would explicitly call attention to their role in supporting scholarly work. Amidst all of this, libraries developed spaces and services to address the growing and complicated needs of digitally driven research, even as the library's relevance in the digital age continued to be questioned by members of the campus community and beyond.

More than Information

By the early twenty-first century, many architects and advocates of the information commons had shifted emphasis: from merely providing networked information sources and services, to creating flexible, collaborative spaces designed to foster learning,[43] with particular focus on the needs and preferences of students who grew up with the Internet.[44] To draw out this difference, many of these spaces were called learning commons.[45]

To be sure, actively promoting learning was not a new development in the information commons movement. Rather, this more pronounced turn toward learning reflected a growing interest in promoting libraries' role in the curricular mission of universities as well as in responding to users' needs when designing library spaces.[46] Where the information commons could be understood generally to provide fluid information access and service delivery, the learning commons underscored the heuristic potential of the space, by enabling students' effortless orchestration of their own learning tasks.[47] Use of "learning" as a qualifier for these spaces demonstrated not just a shift in emphasis but also, in some cases, in operation: the shape and use of the learning commons must be defined and driven by the needs of users and not predominantly by the priorities of librarians or computing personnel. As will be seen, such ceding of control over library spaces and their use was but one marker of how academic libraries were recognizing and responding to community needs, expanding their role in the university, and building new partnerships.

The first and most profound shift in the information commons' evolution occurred with the learning commons movement. Scott Bennett (Yale University Librarian Emeritus) articulated the origins of and motivations for this movement in his 2003 CLIR report Libraries Designed for Learning. Librarians engaged in building projects during the 1990s demonstrated greater responsiveness to the "social dimensions of learning and knowledge," evident in the architecture of these spaces, services added or enhanced, and changes to library policies to accommodate students' needs and preferences.[48] And yet, as Bennett notes, such planning efforts, while successful in attracting greater numbers of students to the library, often lacked an informed and intentional focus on the needs of teaching and learning, "the arenas in which academic library space could have its 'singularly most important outcome' as regards the fundamental mission of colleges and universities."[49]

Bennett defined the key difference between the information commons constructed throughout the 1990s and the learning commons that he hoped would supplant them as a critical shift in emphasis: "The core activity of a learning commons would not be the manipulation and mastery of information, as in an information commons, but the collaborative learning by which students turn information into knowledge and sometimes into wisdom."[50] Pointedly, this subtle but important shift in intention not only placed greater value on responding to and anticipating library users' needs but also on the library's active role in the university's primary mission. In this move from the noun "information" (a static component of knowledge) to the verb "learning" (an action essential in building new knowledge), the library space is located both more centrally and actively in the work of the university, even as the library's focus moves from the information it manages to the person using it.

Bennett's and others' arguments for creating learning commons rather than information commons, while critical in calling attention to and advocating for libraries' significant role in the university, were not ultimately at odds with the original aims of the information commons movement. Rather, the learning commons movement signaled a key milestone in a trajectory of library space development already oriented toward greater integration of academic activities, coordination of services, and responsiveness to the campus community. When Donald Beagle summarized the key features of the physical information commons in 1999, following a decade of development, he pointed to expanded and flexible group and individual study spaces as key to supporting a range of learning styles.[51] Writing several years later, amidst growing emphasis on creating learning commons, Lippincott observed that "a key purpose of an information commons is to leverage the intersection of content, technology, and services in a physical facility to support student learning."[52] Acknowledging that institutions face real challenges in actually facilitating learning, she suggested that information commons may increase their potential for supporting student learning by providing, for example:

- spaces that encourage social interaction and collaboration;
- multiple technologies for accessing and using information, particularly those that students are not likely to own themselves; and
- highly skilled and knowledgeable service personnel who can assist students at point of need.[53]

This last point in particular resonates with the learning commons movement's call for collaboration with other units and individuals who can provide the diverse kinds of support needed in these spaces.[54] Rather than a shift in direction, the learning commons heralded a rededication to the partnerships and philosophies on which the information commons was founded. By expanding the services and resources provided through the information commons, libraries continued the path set by early information commons developers who sought to support multiple facets of the academic experience, including learning. By specifically developing and promoting learning commons, libraries accentuated their growing role in the educational mission of universities, while simultaneously reflecting broad cultural shifts in higher education to prioritize the needs of students.

Making Spaces for Millennials

In the first years of the twenty-first century, with some information commons spaces well into their second decade, some libraries revisited the question of whether information commons were actually meeting users' needs and accomplishing their purported mission. This heightened focus on users reflected in part the reality that the new population of undergraduates (born after

1982 and referred to, among other monikers, as the Net Generation or Millennials) was not only larger and more diverse but also technologically savvy, more likely to work in groups or teams, and less likely to use the physical library to conduct research.[55] Following their 2003 survey of undergraduates at USC's Leavey Library (the site of one of the United States' first information commons), Susan Gardner and Susanna Eng found that these students set high expectations for their academic achievement and similarly high expectations for their study spaces: they desired high-quality, technology-rich, customizable environments in which to work, learn, and socialize with their peers.[56] Technology, particularly computers, was a significant inducement for students; the authors summed up the lesson for libraries with a quote from renowned library architect Geoffrey Freeman:

> Libraries should recognize that, rather than supplanting them, technology "is actually serving to encourage individuals to come into the library where there is activity—where people are coming together to access, use, and turn information into knowledge."[57]

But perhaps most noteworthy was students' preference to have social and academic needs met in one place, and libraries' willingness to comply. The 2000s saw the emergence of the "social commons" and the "academic commons," as academic libraries incorporated services and spaces even more removed from a singular focus on research.[58] The Undergraduate Learning Center at the Georgia Institute of Technology offered a striking example of a commons space intended to support a range of scholarly endeavors, from research to performance to play. Cafés and conversational areas would become both fixtures and draws in many libraries and signal more broadly libraries' evolution from reading rooms to campus crossroads (and all the movement and sound the latter entails). This emphasis on social interactions echoed early hopes that the library would be more than just a place to find information and technology. Commenting on trends in library design, university librarian Peter Graham cited the importance of group study areas at the Syracuse University Libraries: "The library as student center—or 'coffee shop in the library'—encourages social interaction that tends toward learning."[59] Carole Wedge, an architect involved in the design of numerous information commons, underscored this point, noting that "at Dartmouth, they refer to the library as a 'café with books.' It's the hub of activities after classes, as well as the crossroads of all disciplines."[60]

This turn toward meeting students' social and personal needs was consistent with the learning commons movement and its emphasis on student learning, as articulated by Scott Bennett's arguments for less hierarchical, more domestic spaces in libraries: "[S]pace that allows students to manage the social dimensions of learning, that domesticates the foundational character of knowledge...and that celebrates the communal...character of knowledge will indeed foster learning."[61] This now widely accepted link between informal social interactions and learning bolstered the incorporation of structures and services that diverged from traditional expectations of what libraries look and sound like and the role they play in academic life. As part of the continuing evolution of library spaces, calls were already being made for a Commons 2.0 that would provide more flexible, "human-centered" design, both comfortable and inspiring and supportive of a wide array of activities that foster learning.[62]

Losing the Library

Along with a professed interest in promoting libraries' role as academic community centers, designing commons spaces could also reflect a simultaneous desire to increase gate count numbers and daily usage of the main or undergraduate library building. In a 2005 Chronicle of Higher Education article on new library architecture, reporter Scott Carlson pointed to use of library attendance statistics to demonstrate success to administrators, "which means... that librarians are competing more and more with the conveniences and comforts of the dormitory suite and the buzz of the student center."[63] He went on to describe a number of new university libraries constructed specifically with the purpose of creating social and study areas for students, and quotes library directors and architects describing the attractiveness (to students and university administrators alike) of such comfortable, convenient, and multifunctional spaces.

In some ways, the information commons movement was successful precisely because it created new spaces in libraries that differed distinctly (in sound and appearance as well as in name) from the established institution. In the early 1990s, when the first of these high-tech computing spaces emerged, some academic libraries perceived a benefit (perhaps even a necessity) in distancing themselves from their image as book repositories:

> To some, the word library became almost a term of opprobrium, as voices—not uncommonly from among college and university trustees, state legislators, and other laypersons—were heard inveighing against the construction of any more outmoded "book warehouses." To change the popular image from one of miles upon miles of bookshelves, some institutions began designating newly constructed library buildings as their "centers for information service," "gateways," or other euphemism instead of "libraries," and indeed perhaps the new terms were more appropriate.[64]

As an egalitarian and decidedly less formal space marked by conversation, the information commons would often visually and aurally signal a break with the past. Though vaunted by Tompkins and others as a way to bridge the digital-print divide,[65] in practice many of these spaces leaned much further toward the digital end of the spectrum, with numerous high-tech workstations far outnumbering the available print resources. Library technologist Martin Halbert, following construction of the Emory University Information Commons in the late 1990s, shared an anecdote illustrating that, even when print materials were not only still on site but in the same place as before, the renovated area's visual dissonance with what a library was supposed to look like could render these collections invisible:

> [T]he askance confusion of the grizzled faculty member standing in the (still recognizable, surely!) lobby of the new facility, looking out on a sea of computer terminals (the book stacks are still where they have always been though!) and asking over and over, "Can you tell me, where is the library? I'm trying to find the library. It used to be here."[66]

But often, in order to make space for people and new activities, print materials would indeed be consolidated elsewhere in the building or even moved off-site. Commenting on the growing trend among libraries to relocate their collections in order to free up space in the building, architect Joseph Rizzo quipped, "You know the saying, 'Build it and they will come?' Now it's, 'Clear it out and they will come.'"[67]

Reclaiming Research

The removal of print resources raised concerns (and in some cases, open protest) by those who saw such actions as not just undermining research but the very purpose of the university library. One high-profile instance occurred at Syracuse University in 2009, when students and faculty alike forced Bird Library's administration to rethink a plan to move thousands of books to a storage facility 250 miles away. The motivation behind the move, explained library director Suzanne Thorin, was to make more space for the learning commons: "The library has tripled in use since creating the Learning Commons. It is a key place where lots of things happen, but some people see it as a distancing away from the true purpose of a library. I see it as moving closer to that."[68] Two years later, faculty at the University of Denver objected to Penrose Library's plan to keep 80% of its collection in off-site storage following renovations to create an academic commons.[69] Whether or not such moves in the end negatively impacted research and access, they did create public-relations problems: the relocation of libraries' print collections, combined with—and especially in support of—the proliferation of social spaces and activities in libraries, threatened not merely to alienate upper-level academics but also to diminish the library's primacy in intellectual life.

Within this context, the emergence of the research commons,[70] generally understood as "specialized services, spaces, and technologies aimed at supporting graduate students and faculty throughout the research life cycle,"[71] could be seen as a deliberate attempt to re-emphasize the scholarly purpose of the library and rebrand commons spaces for more serious research and scholarly production.[72] For instance, as part of planning in the early 2000s for a research commons, Indiana University library and IT administrators sought explicitly to address the needs of faculty and graduate students:

> To complement the Information Commons, which is focused primarily on undergraduate teaching and learning, we propose to build and test the concept of a research commons devoted to faculty needs. To be located in the Main Library on the east side of the first floor across from the Information Commons in its test phase, this facility will be a joint UITS/Libraries endeavor that will offer integrated research services to faculty and graduate students.[73]

Certainly, the kinds of services offered in research commons tend to support or reflect more advanced research, and websites for a library's research commons often explicitly name graduate students and faculty as among those served, if not as the target or sole audience.[74] In some cases, these spaces are also described as "quiet" spaces for "serious" research and "productivity,"[75] likely in response to users' requests for quieter work areas than a typical commons provides.[76]

But one can also see the research commons as reflecting libraries' attention to and involvement in digital approaches to research and publishing. Indeed, one of the most vocal proponents of the commons has argued for its potential to support digital humanities work. In 2014, as part a series of posts to dh+lib, Donald Beagle cited his early work with a digital humanities project as the impetus behind his own championing of commons environments in libraries:

> I believed then (and now) that faculty researchers and early adopters…faced campus-wide and library-specific challenges in pursuing leading-edge projects, and that my 1990s experience as a library manager developing DH in collaboration with faculty, graduate students, and interagency scholars offered a valuable perspective on how libraries might be repositioned to help incubate and shape DH projects in the future.[77]

Historically, the commons was adopted and evolved contemporaneously with libraries' growing involvement in digital scholarship. The implications and needs of computationally based scholarly work gained particular prominence and momentum in the early 2000s, as granting agencies and professional societies paid greater attention to this area of scholarship and recommended areas for further development and support, particularly among academic institutions. The 2003 NSF report Revolutionizing Science and Engineering through Cyberinfrastructure, which informed and was followed by the 2006 ACLS report Our Cultural Commonwealth (sponsored by the Mellon Foundation), were both the culmination of and catalyst for greater institutional engagement in digital scholarship.[78] In between publication of these reports, the Coalition of Networked Information hosted a 2004 discussion among librarians, technologists, and organizational leaders that emphasized internal collaboration as a critical preparatory step to developing cross-institutional support for e-research.[79] A 2009 Association of Research Libraries survey found that many libraries had begun addressing the needs of e-research communities, primarily through consultations around data management, data discovery, tool development, and training in tool use, and through partnerships with other campus units (mainly central IT) to provide data storage and management systems.[80]

While libraries had not historically been the locus of computational research, the 2000s saw more libraries engaging with these scholarly projects, particularly in the area of digitally inflected humanities research. Much of this was fostered by the National Endowment for the Humanities, which launched a Digital Humanities Initiative in 2006 (later to become the Office of Digital Humanities in 2008).[81] This initiative was itself a response to growth in humanities computing, and particularly to its more expansive redefinition as "digital humanities" in the early 2000s.[82] In 2011 the Association for Research Libraries published SPEC Kit 326: Digital Humanities, which traced libraries' still ad hoc but growing involvement in supporting digital scholarly work.[83] Five years later, when ARL published SPEC Kit 350: Supporting Digital Scholarship, libraries' roles in digital research and publishing had increased, with many libraries offering dedicated services, spaces, and personnel for supporting (and engaging in) this work.[84]

A multitude of new research and publishing methods, questions, data, and issues fostered by digital technologies were captured in the term "digital scholarship," defined by Scholarly Communication Institute director Abby Smith Rumsey as "the use of digital evidence and method, digital authoring, digital publishing, digital curation and preservation, and digital use and reuse of scholarship."[85] In a 2016 analysis of research commons in libraries, digital scholarship librarian Rebecca Dowson draws strong parallels between the values and practices underlying the research commons and those that animate digital scholarship, finding in both "an ethos of openness, interdisciplinarity, collaboration, and focus on knowledge creation and new modes of production."[86] The focus on new forms of knowledge creation and production, in particular, seems to be a key distinction between previous commons spaces and these newer instantiations,[87] in addition to the focus on more specialized research needs and related groups.

Whither the Commons? The Evolving Library

Connecting the research commons to digital scholarly work is an easy fit in many ways, for the reasons that both Dowson and Beagle enumerate: namely, similar underlying values and goals; researchers' need to be able to work and learn together; and the insights and assistance libraries can offer to this work, particularly in areas of assessment and digital curation.[88] One might, by extension, see digital scholarship centers in libraries as yet another instantiation of the commons.

But research commons distinguish themselves from digital scholarship or digital humanities centers most critically in the areas of access and service: where libraries and commons both seek to provide services and resources that can be used by the entire academic community, digital scholarship organizations typically target certain groups and define their work with them in terms of partnerships rather than services[89] (or at least operate under a different notion of "service"[90]). Such fine distinctions get at a growing challenge in the evolution of commons spaces: to what extent can these spaces, and especially the staff supporting them, respond to changing technology and research and maintain relevance if they are not themselves also involved in research and perceived as partners in knowledge production? Given the tension in attempting to be a partner in research while also providing services,[91] can libraries offer both?

Multimedia studios, makerspaces, and physical computing labs present different challenges to the commons model, and to libraries in general, even as they embody and encourage active learning principles, experimentation, and new forms of knowledge production. Unlike digital ideas and information that can be used by many without diminishing value or abundance, labs based in hands-on access to physical materials invite scarcity as well as disarray (and, in the case of makerbots, smell). Though libraries have learned to cede control (and in some cases, expectations of cleanliness) in commons spaces, making areas can reintroduce physical limitations on access to resources and thus may require more active management of their use.[92] Yet these spaces are already making their way into libraries,[93] suggesting that their legitimation as part of libraries is already occurring.

As renowned commons researcher and advocate Donald Beagle observed, "The commons is a moving target that continually incorporates new technologies and pedagogies based on the social construction of knowledge."[94] Some of these newer articulations seem to be quite different beasts than the original, yet they still embody the same aspirations of supporting academic work, drawing together different members of the academic community, and asserting libraries' continued relevance and evolving role in the university. As Joan Lippincott considers in the following chapter, whether these newer articulations qualify as commons spaces, and whether spaces dubbed as commons actually are, is a matter of debate. As entire libraries, and increasingly other areas on campus, adopt the architectural principles once reserved for the information commons—ubiquitous computing, seamless access to resources, flexible support for collaborative work, and the sights, sounds, and conveniences of the student union and the dormitory—one questions whether the commons, as an animating idea, is still relevant.

Librarian and administrator Brian Mathews said as much in a 2011 post to The Ubiquitous Librarian blog, in which he questioned use of the term "commons" to describe new library renovations. He argued that libraries themselves—their value-added services, the activities they support—should be the focal point of these spaces, and that the commons as a space is now so abundant as to be meaningless, often associated merely with its appearance rather than with the concepts and values that (should) animate it. Perhaps this accounts somewhat for the tendency to qualify the type of commons (e.g., learning commons, collaborative commons, knowledge commons, research commons, and so forth); following two decades of varying implementation and development, libraries are compelled to add multiple layers of definition in the title in order to better define their particular commons and its intended audience.

Attempts to find fresher titles reveal not merely the intended audience and purpose of these spaces but also libraries' aspirations. A common thread among these newer developments, and particularly in their nomenclature, is a reemphasis on the resource-rich environments, expert assistance, and room for discovery and experimentation that libraries can provide. Calling spaces "shed" or "sandbox" connotes such explorative play in a low-risk, informal environment. But terms such as "boutique" and "studio" suggest high-touch service and attention for a serious-minded and focused clientele (and also suggest limits on who is served by this space). References to "collaboration" bridge notions of active- and team-based learning with the newer forms of research and cross-cutting partnerships that these spaces are meant to encourage. While libraries have long been understood as supporting the productive play of ideas, the names chosen for some of the newest spaces push the libraries' role further forward as catalyzers and producers of knowledge—from "incubator" to "factory"—at the same time that librarians are positioning themselves more actively and centrally in the university's core work—teaching students, partnering in research, and producing and publishing scholarship.

The commons helped libraries bridge a disruptive moment, when the availability of information digitally threatened to render obsolete library buildings, physical collections, and the librarians who managed them. By embracing these changes—bringing valued technology into the library, partnering with other academic support units, ceding more control over spaces to users, and responding to user preferences and needs—and by actively connecting these changes to the essential role of librarians and libraries in academic work, librarians further anchored their institution in the life of the university and positioned themselves as active participants. The challenge for libraries moving forward, as sites of authority and production in the university become further distributed and decentralized, is building relationships within the academic community that further develop and extend their emerging roles: from collectors and providers of information to partners in the production of knowledge.

Notes

1. Lawrence Lessig, *The Future of Ideas: The Fate of the Commons in a Connected World* (New York: Random House, 2001).
2. Nancy Kranich, *The Information Commons: A Public Policy Report* (New York: Brannan Center for Justice at NYU School of Law, 2004). Kranich cites the following articles as examples of environmental law discussions of the commons: H. Scott Gordon, "The Economic Theory of a Common-Property Resource: The Fishery," *Journal of Political Economy* 62.2 (April 1954): 124-42; Garrett Hardin, "The Tragedy of the Commons," *Science* 162 (December 1968): 1243-48; and Anthony D. Scott, "The Fishery: The Objectives of Sole Ownership," *Journal of Political Economy* 63.2 (April 1955): 116-24.
3. That said, some libraries use the term "research commons" to refer to their open access digital repository rather than a physical space, though the repository obviously serves a similar purpose of encouraging free access to information. More discussion of the term research commons follows in this chapter.
4. Patricia Battin, "The Electronic Library—A Vision of the Future," *EDUCOM Bulletin* 19 (Summer 1984): 13; Richard M. Dougherty, "Libraries and Computer Centers: A Blueprint for Collaboration," *College & Research Libraries* 48 (July 1987): 298-96; C. Lee Jones, "Academic Libraries and Computing: A Time of Change," *EDUCOM Bulletin* 20 (Spring 1985): 9-12; David W. Lewis, "Inventing the Electronic University," *College & Research Libraries* 49 (July 1988): 291-304; Pat Molholt, "On Converging Paths: The Computing Center and the Library," *Journal of Academic Librarianship* 11 (November 1985): 284-88; Barbara Moran, "The Unintended Revolution in Academic Libraries: 1939 to 1989 and Beyond," *College & Research Libraries* 50 (January 1989): 25-41; Lawrence E. Murr and James B. Williams, "The Roles of the Future Library," *Library Hi-Tech* 5 (Fall 1987): 7-23; Raymond K. Neff, "Merging Libraries and Computer Centers: Manifest Destiny or Manifestly Deranged?" *EDUCOM Bulletin* 20 (Winter 1985): 8-12, 16; and Richard L. Van Horn, "How Significant Is Computing for Higher Education?" *EDUCOM Bulletin* 20 (Spring 1985): 8.
5. John M. Budd and David G. Robinson, "Enrollment and the Future of Academic Libraries," *Library Journal* 111 (September 15, 1986): 43-46.
6. Philip D. Leighton and David C. Weber, "The Influence of Computer Technology on Academic Library Buildings," in *Academic Librarianship: Past, Present, and Future: A Festschrift in Honor of David Kaser*, ed. John Richardson, Jr. and Jinnie Y. Davis (Englewood, CO: Libraries Unlimited, 1989), 13-29.
7. Murr and Williams, "The Roles of the Future Library," 7.

8. Moran, "The Unintended Revolution in Academic Libraries: 1939 to 1989 and Beyond," 39.
9. Moran referred to John Naisbitt's book *Megatrends: Ten New Directions Transforming Our Lives* (New York: Warner Books, 1982).
10. Joan Bechtel, "Conversation: A New Paradigm for Librarianship?" *College & Research Libraries* 47 (1986): 219-24.
11. Bechtel, "Conversation," 221.
12. Scott Carlson, "The Deserted Library," *Chronicle of Higher Education* 48 (November 16, 2001): A35-38.
13. Charles Martell, "The Absent User: Physical Use of Academic Library Collections and Services Continues to Decline 1995-2006," *The Journal of Academic Librarianship* 34.5 (2008): 400-407. As evidence, Martell cites collections use assessments from several libraries (including studies at Washington State University, Pennsylvania State University, Fresno State University, and the University of Maryland) that note increases in use of digital information alongside decreases in use of print.
14. ARL statistics show drops in circulation were most pronounced in law, public, and medical universities, which between 1995 and 2006 saw decreases of -7%, -20%, and -58% respectively (Martell, "The Absent User," 401).
15. The lowest gate count total was in 1996 (16,200,000 for all academic institutions); from there the number rose to 19,369,000 in 2006 (Martell, "The Absent User," 401). Martell cites data from the U.S. Department of Education, National Center for Education Statistics, Academic Libraries Survey (ALS), which shows an overall 17% increase in gate counts between 1994 and 2006. NCES Academic Libraries Survey data reports for 1990-2010 are available on the NCES website, www.ala.org/research/librarystats/academic (accessed January 21, 2017).
16. Andrew Richard Albanese, "Deserted No More," *Library Journal* 128 (April 2003): 34-36; and Frieda Weis, "Being There: The Library as Place," *Journal of the Medical Library Association* 92 (January 2004): 6-12.
17. Murr and Williams, "The Roles of the Future Library," 7-23.
18. Craig Hartman, "The Future of Libraries," *Architecture* 84 (October 1995): 43-47.
19. Robert B. Barr and John Tagg, "From Teaching to Learning: A New Paradigm for Undergraduate Education," *Change* 27 (November/December 1995): 12-25.
20. Barr and Tagg, "From Teaching to Learning," 21.
21. Bruffee published a number of articles in *College English* throughout the 1970s and 1980s, arguing for a collaborative learning approach to instruction. See "The Way Out: A Critical Survey of Innovations in College Teaching, with Special Reference to the December, 1971, Issue of *College English*," *College English* 33, no. 4 (January 1972): 457-70; "Collaborative Learning: Some Practical Models," *College English* 34, no. 5 (February 1973): 634-43; "Collaborative Learning," *College English* 43, no. 7 (November 1981): 745-47; and "Social Construction, Language, and the Authority of Knowledge: A Bibliographical Essay," *College English* 48, no. 8 (December 1986): 773-90.
22. Lev Vygotsky, *Mind in Society: The Development of Higher Psychological Processes* (Cambridge, MA: Harvard University Press, 1978).
23. Barr and Tagg, "From Teaching to Learning," 12-25.
24. Philip Tompkins, "Information Technology Planning and Community Colleges: A Variance in a Transitional Era," (Report prepared for the HEIRAlliance Executive Strategies Report #1: What Presidents Need to Know about the Integration of Information Technology on Campus, 1992), https://net.educause.edu/ir/library/text/HEI1040.txt (accessed March 15, 2017).
25. Philip Tompkins, Susan Perry, and Joan K. Lippincott, "New Learning Communities: Collaboration, Networking, and Information Literacy," *Information Technology and Libraries* 17 (June 1998): 100-106.
26. Philip Tompkins, "Quality in Community College Libraries," *Library Trends* 44 (Winter 1996): 506-25.
27. Tompkins, "Quality in Community College Libraries," 506-25; and Philip Tompkins, "New Structures for Teaching Libraries," *Library Administration and Management* (Spring 1990): 77-81.
28. Philip Tompkins, "Information Technology Planning and Community Colleges," https://net.educause.edu/ir/library/text/HEI1040.txt (accessed March 15, 2017).
29. David W. Lewis, "Inventing the Electronic University," *College & Research Libraries* 49 (July 1988): 291-304. Lewis quotes John Sack, who spoke during a panel discussion at the Seminar on Academic Computing Services held in Snowmass, Colorado, 1986.

30. Don Doucette, "The Community College and the Computer: Behind Widespread Integration into Instruction," *Academic Computing* 4 (February 1990): 12.
31. Tompkins also helped develop the Information Commons that opened with the new Leavey Library at the University of Southern California in 1994.
32. Van Horn, "How Significant Is Computing for Higher Education?", 8.
33. See, for example, David Murray's listing of information commons "Sites by Carnegie Classification" as of 2000 (*Information Commons: A Directory of Innovative Resources and Services in Academic Libraries*, Brookdale Community College, https://web.archive.org/web/20070914174325/http://ux.brookdalecc.edu/library/infocommons/icsites/sitestype.htm (accessed March 15, 2017).
34. Philip Tompkins, "Information Planning and Community Colleges," https://net.educause.edu/ir/library/text/HEI1040.txt (accessed March 15, 2017).
35. Doris S. Helfer, "The Leavey Library: A Library in Your Future?" *Searcher* 5 (January 1997): 38-40.
36. Karen Commings, "Inside the University of Southern California's 'Cybrary,'" *Computers in Libraries* 14 (November/December 1994): 18-19.
37. Commings, "Inside the University of Southern California's 'Cybrary'," 19.
38. Sheila D. Creth, "The Information Arcade: Playground for the Mind," *Journal of Academic Librarianship* 20 (March 1994): 22-23.
39. Creth, "The Information Arcade," 23.
40. Creth, "The Information Arcade," 22-23.
41. The Information Arcade is no longer a named space in the University of Iowa Libraries. Its former location on the northwest corner of the Main library first floor (*A Field Guide to the Information Commons*, 2009, 158) is now occupied by the Digital Scholarship and Publishing Studio (The University of Iowa Libraries, "Main Library Directory," www.lib.uiowa.edu/locations/files/2016/09/MainLibrary_Floorplan_Handout.pdf, accessed March 16, 2017). A large portion of the first floor is now given over to a Learning Commons.
42. Joan Lippincott, "Surveying the Landscape," in *Beyond the InfoCommons*, eds. Charles Forrest and Martin Halbert (Lanham, MD: Rowman & Littlefield, forthcoming).
43. Donald Beagle, "From Information Commons to Learning Commons: A White Paper for Presentation at the University of Southern California Leavey Library Conference," (Leavey Library Tenth Anniversary Celebration, University of Southern California, Los Angeles, September 16-17, 2004), www.academia.edu/3910575/From_Information_Commons_to_Learning_Commons (accessed January 19, 2017); and Scott Bennett, "Righting the Balance," in *Library as Place: Rethinking Roles, Rethinking Space* (Washington, DC: Council on Library and Information Resources, 2005), 10-24.
44. Malcom Brown, "Learning Spaces," in *Educating the Net Generation*, ed. Diane G. Oblinger and James L. Oblinger (EDUCAUSE, 2005), www.educause.edu/research-and-publications/books/educating-net-generation/learning-spaces (accessed January 19, 2017); Joan K. Lippincott, "Developing Collaborative Relationships: Librarians, Students, and Faculty Creating Learning Communities," *College and Research Libraries News* 63 (March 2002): 3; Joan K. Lippincott, "New Library Facilities: Opportunities for Collaboration," *Resource Sharing and Information Networks* 17 (2004): 1-2; Joan K. Lippincott, "Net Generation Students and Libraries," in *Educating the Net Generation*, ed. Diane G. Oblinger and James L. Oblinger (EDUCAUSE, 2005), www.educause.edu/research-and-publications/books/educating-net-generation/net-generation-students-and-libraries (accessed January 19, 2017); and Joan K. Lippincott and Malcolm Brown, "Learning Spaces: More Than Meets the Eye," *EDUCAUSE Quarterly* 12 (February 2003): 14-16.
45. As discussed elsewhere in this chapter, the name of a space—whether called a *learning* commons or an *information* commons—is not necessarily indicative of a substantive or even cosmetic difference. As Joan Lippincott has observed, "in practice I have found no direct correlation between what the facility offers and its name" ("Linking the Information Commons to Learning," in *Learning Spaces*, ed. Diana G. Oblinger (EDUCAUSE: 2006), www.educause.edu/research-and-publications/books/learning-spaces/chapter-7-linking-information-commons-learning (accessed January 19, 2017)). Rather, these appellations reflect trends in thinking about the kinds of spaces that libraries should develop and, by extension, about libraries' role in the academic mission of the university.
46. Scott Bennett, "Libraries and Learning: A History of Paradigm Change," *Portal: Libraries and the Academy; Baltimore* 9.2 (2009 April): 181-97.

47. Scott Bennett, *Libraries Designed for Learning* (Washington, DC: Council on Library and Information Resources, 2003).
48. Bennett, *Libraries Designed for Learning*, 19.
49. Bennett, *Libraries Designed for Learning*, 37.
50. Bennett, *Libraries Designed for Learning*, 38.
51. Donald Beagle, "Conceptualizing and Information Commons," *The Journal of Academic Librarianship* 25 (March 1999): 82-89.
52. Joan K. Lippincott, "Linking the Information Commons to Learning," in *Learning Spaces*, ed. Diana G. Oblinger (EDUCAUSE, 2006), www.educause.edu/research-and-publications/books/learning-spaces/chapter-7-linking-information-commons-learning (accessed January 19, 2017).
53. Lippincott, "Linking the Information Commons to Learning."
54. The 2006 Canadian Learning Commons Conference defined the learning commons as both supporting "numerous aspects of undergraduate and graduate student learning" and, through campus collaborations, providing "a rich array of learning supports." At this conference, University of Guelph CIO and Chief Librarian Michael Ridley focused his remarks specifically on the importance of working across different units and areas of expertise ("The Importance of Forging Strong Partnerships," in "Towards a Learning Ecology: Canadian Learning Commons Conference Proceedings, June 19-20, 2006," University of Guelph, http://lcconference.awesomeindustries.ca/resources/presentations/StrongPartnerships.pdf (accessed January 20, 2017). In his keynote address at this conference, Scott Bennett likewise underlined the pivotal role of collaboration in creating spaces that attend to diverse learning needs ("Communication Technology Improvements: Designing in Spite of Uncertainties," in "Towards a Learning Ecology: Canadian Learning Commons Conference Proceedings, June 19-20, 2006," University of Guelph, http://lcconference.awesomeindustries.ca/resources/presentations/proceedings.pdf (accessed January 20, 2017)).
55. Neil Howe and William Strauss, *Millennials Rising: The Next Great Generation* (New York: Vintage Books, 2000); and Stephen R. Merritt and Shelley Neville, ed., "Generation Y: A Perspective on America's Next Generation and Their Impact on Higher Education," *The Serials Librarian* 42 (2002): 1-2, 41-50.
56. Susan Gardner and Susanna Eng, "What Students Want: Generation Y and the Changing Function of the Academic Library," *Portal: Libraries and the Academy* 5.3 (2005 July): 405-20.
57. Geoffrey Freeman's quote comes from p. 169 of his chapter "The Academic Library in the 21st Century: Partner in Education," in *Building Libraries for the 21st Century: The Shape of Information*, ed. T. D. Webb (Jefferson, NC: McFarland, 2000), 168-75.
58. Architects Carole Wedge and Janette Blackburn noted this further expansion of the commons space with their discussion of the academic commons—a space that goes beyond teaching and learning to provide a staging area for social interactions that connect the campus community ("Breaking Down Barriers to Working and Learning," in *A Field Guide to the Information Commons*, ed. C. Forrest and M. Halbert (Lanham, MD: Scarecrow Press, 2009): 39).
59. Jeff Morris, "The College Library in the New Age," *University Business* 5 (October 2002): 28.
60. Morris, "The College Library in the New Age," 29.
61. Scott Bennett, "Righting the Balance," in *Library as Place: Rethinking Roles, Rethinking Space*, ed. Kathlin Smith (Washington, DC: CLIR, 2005), 10-24, www.clir.org/pubs/reports/pub129/bennett.html (accessed April 14, 2017).
62. Bryan Sinclair, "Commons 2.0: Library Spaces Designed for Collaborative Learning," *EDUCAUSE Quarterly* 30 (November 4, 2007): 4-6. Sinclair cites the concept of "human-centered" design offered by Malcolm Brown and Phillip D. Long in their chapter "Trends in Learning Space Design," in *Learning Spaces*, ed. Diane G. Oblinger (EDUCAUSE, 2006), www.educause.edu/research-and-publications/books/learning-spaces/chapter-9-trends-learning-space-design (accessed April 14, 2017).
63. Scott Carlson, "Thoughtful Design Keeps New Libraries Relevant: Not Everything Students Want and Need is Online," *The Chronicle of Higher Education* 52 (September 30, 2005), B1, www.chronicle.com/article/Thoughtful-Design-Keeps-New/16326 (accessed April 14, 2017).
64. David Kaser, *The Evolution of the American Academic Library Building* (Lanham, MD: Scarecrow Press, 1997), 163.
65. Tompkins, "Quality in Community College Libraries," 506-25.
66. Martin Halbert, "Lessons from the Information Commons Frontier," *The Journal of Academic Librarianship* 25 (March 1999): 90-91. In the same issue of *The Journal of Academic Librarianship*, Philip Tramdack

cautioned of potential conflict between the design of the information commons and users' expectations for library spaces: "Traditional library users may be sympathetic in acknowledging a complex function addressed by the idea of the IC. However, when the design is seen as an alternative to the familiar book-centered and print-bound reference center, anxiety may be the result." Philip Tramdack, "Reaction to Beagle," *The Journal of Academic Librarianship* 25 (March 1999): 93.
67. Christopher Conkey, "Libraries beckon, but stacks of books aren't part of pitch; Valparaiso's new building has PCs, a café, a Steinway; 'Quiet's not the thing'," *Wall Street Journal* 248 (October 21, 2006): A1.
68. Jennifer Epstein, "A Win for the Stacks: Facing faculty uproar, Syracuse library pulls back—at least for now—from plans to move thousands of books off campus," *Inside Higher Ed* (November 13, 2009), www.insidehighered.com/news/2009/11/13/syracuse (accessed April 14, 2017). The twenty-four online reader comments for this article were robust and ranging, with many addressing libraries' role in the mission of the university.
69. Kevin Kiley, "No Room for Books: U. of Denver's Plan to Remove 80% of Volumes from its Library Upsets Some Professors and Renews Debate over How Best to Store and Share Information," *Inside Higher Ed* (April 27, 2011), www.insidehighered.com/news/2011/04/27/university_of_denver_removing_most_books_from_its_library (accessed April 14, 2017). In the 44 online comments to this article, readers expressed sharp division over this issue, particularly over providing researchers with ease of access to information.
70. Similar monikers are scholars commons or graduate commons, but studies of these kinds of spaces often include places dubbed "hubs," "centers," and "labs," often with an explicit focus on supporting digital scholarship or digital humanities work. See, for example, the Digital Scholarship Lab within the Helmerich Collaborative Learning Center at the University of Oklahoma Libraries (https://libraries.ou.edu/node/4023/); the Emory Center for Digital Scholarship at Emory University Libraries (http://digitalscholarship.emory.edu/); the Research Hub at the University of North Carolina at Chapel Hill Libraries (http://library.unc.edu/hub/); and the Scholars Lab at the University of Virginia Libraries (http://scholarslab.org/).
71. Rebecca Dowson, "Research Commons: Site of Innovation, Experimentation, and Collaboration in Academic Libraries," *Scholarly and Research Communication* 7.2 (2016), http://src-online.ca/index.php/src/article/view/259/504 (accessed April 14, 2017).
72. Others have characterized the "research commons" as "a physical space offering a differentiated service, i.e. a service that is offered only to a subset of users, seeking to achieve specific purposes through library use, by staff who have been specially trained and who have no other duties," which tends to align these spaces more with digital scholarship centers, digital media centers, and other more specialized units (William Daniels, Colin Darch, and Karin de Jager, "The Research Commons: A New Creature in the Library?" *Performance Measurement and Metrics* 11.2 (2010): 116-30, http://dx.doi.org/10.1108/14678041011064043 (accessed April 16, 2017)).
73. Library/UITS Research Commons Committee, "Research Commons—Report by Joint Library/UITS Committee," (March 15, 2004), www.library.illinois.edu/committee/integrative/documents/ResearchCommonsReportFINAL.doc (accessed April 15, 2017).
74. See, for example, the services descriptions web pages for the following research commons, which name graduate students and/or faculty specifically in descriptions of their services:

- The University of Washington Libraries Research Commons, www.lib.washington.edu/commons/services, which offers graduate students writing and funding assistance and provides digital scholarship project assistance;
- The University of Maryland Libraries Research Commons, www.lib.umd.edu/rc/services, which offers data and text mining services, data management support, and publishing and archiving services and advice for authors;
- UCLA Library Research Commons, www.library.ucla.edu/destination/research-commons, which contains the Scholarly Innovation Lab (SIL), providing project meeting space for cross-professional digital project teams; and
- Port: digital research commons at Virginia Tech University Libraries, www.lib.vt.edu/port/index.html, which offers "above-average technology" for its "primary audience" of graduate students and faculty.

Similarly, research "hubs" or "scholars" commons also designate upper-level researchers as their clientele: see, for instance, the University of North Carolina at Chapel Hill Research Hubs, http://library.unc.edu/hub/about/; Florida State University Libraries Scholars Commons, www.lib.fsu.edu/department/scholars-commons; and Indiana University Scholars Commons, https://libraries.indiana.edu/scholars-commons.

75. The Bobst Library Research Commons at New York University is described as "quiet and collaborative spaces on Floors 4, 5, and 6 of Bobst Library [where] the staff, technology, equipment, and furnishings…ensure that users can work with maximum productivity" (http://library.nyu.edu/spaces/research-commons-bobst-library/).
76. While the Scholars' Commons that was eventually constructed at Indiana University Libraries is not promoted as being a quiet space, the IC2 that preceded it, and that followed the first Information Commons, was specifically designed to provide all the same conveniences as the first IC, with the added value of "quiet" (Indiana U's IC2, *Library Journal*, 2005 May 1, 15).
77. Donald Beagle, "Digital Humanities in the Research Commons: Precedents and Prospects. [Introduction]," *dh+lib* (January 30, 2014), http://acrl.ala.org/dh/2014/01/30/digital-humanities-in-the-research-commons-precedents-prospects-3/ (accessed April 16, 2017).
78. NSF Blue Ribbon Advisory Panel on Cyberinfrastructure, *Revolutionizing Science and Engineering through Cyberinfrastructure*, (National Science Foundation, 2003), www.nsf.gov/cise/sci/reports/atkins.pdf (accessed April 15, 2017); ACLS Commission on Cyberinfrastructure for the Humanities and Social Sciences, *Our Cultural Commonwealth*, (American Council of Learned Societies, 2006), www.acls.org/cyberinfrastructure/ourculturalcommonwealth.pdf (accessed April 15, 2017).
79. Diane Goldenberg-Hart, "Libraries and Changing Research Practices: A Report of the ARL/CNI Forum on E-Research and Cyberinfrastructure," *ARL: A Bimonthly Report on Research Library Issues and Actions* 237 (December 2004): 1-5, www.cni.org/wp-content/uploads/2010/11/arl-br-237.pdf (accessed April 15, 2017).
80. Catherine Soehner, Catherine Steeves, and Jennifer Ward, *E-Science and Data Support Services: A Study of ARL Member Institutions* (Washington, DC: Association of Research Libraries, 2010), http://old.arl.org/bm~doc/escience_report2010.pdf (accessed April 15, 2017).
81. Matthew G. Kirschenbaum, "What Is Digital Humanities and What's It Doing in English Departments?" *ADE Bulletin* 150 (2010): 1-7, https://mkirschenbaum.files.wordpress.com/2011/01/kirschenbaum_ade150.pdf (accessed April 15, 2017).
82. The field of humanities computing had moved beyond textual analysis to include aspects common to social scientific study such as geospatial and quantitative data, and digital humanities expanded this further to include rhetoric and public engagement in humanistic work.
83. Tim Bryson, Alain St. Pierre, Miriam Posner, and Stewart Varner, *SPEC Kit 326: Digital Humanities* (Washington, DC: Association of Research Libraries, 2011).
84. Rikk Mulligan, *SPEC Kit 350: Supporting Digital Scholarship* (Washington, DC: Association of Research Libraries, 2016), http://publications.arl.org/Supporting-Digital-Scholarship-SPEC-Kit-350/~FreeAttachments/Supporting-Digital-Scholarship-SPEC-Kit-350.pdf (accessed April 15, 2017).
85. Abby Smith Rumsey, *Scholarly Communication Institute 9: New-Model Scholarly Communication: Road Map for Change* (Charlottesville, VA: Scholarly Communication Institute and University of Virginia Library, 2011), 2, www.uvasci.org/institutes-2003-2011/SCI-9-Road-Map-for-Change.pdf (accessed April 15, 2017).
86. Dowson, "Research Commons: Site of Innovation, Experimentation, and Collaboration in Academic Libraries." See also Michael Perini & Beth Roszkowski, "The Scholars' Commons: Redefining Services and Spaces for Graduate Student Success," *Current Issues in Libraries, Information Science and Related Fields* 39 (December 5, 2015): 215-40, www.emeraldinsight.com/doi/abs/10.1108/S0065-283020150000039015 (accessed April 14, 2017).
87. Daniels, Darch, and de Jager, "The Research Commons: A New Creature in the Library?", 119.
88. Dowson, "Research Commons: Site of Innovation, Experimentation, and Collaboration in Academic Libraries"; and Donald Beagle, "The Research Commons in 2014 and Beyond," Part III in "Digital Humanities in the Research Commons: Precedents & Prospects," *dh+lib* (January 30, 2014), http://acrl.ala.org/dh/2014/01/30/the-research-commons-in-2014-and-beyond/ (accessed April 16, 2017).

89. Dowson highlights the fact that digital scholarship centers typically do not define themselves as service units, even if their outputs do benefit the broader community, since their project work is not intended to provide a service to users but rather to answer a research question ("Research Commons: Site of Innovation, Experimentation, and Collaboration in Academic Libraries," *Scholarly Research and Communication* 7.2 (2016), http://src-online.ca/index.php/src/article/view/259/504 (accessed April 16, 2017). A number of digital scholarship librarians and researchers have been particularly vocal about the obstacles to and arguments against offering libraries-based digital scholarship work as a service. For more on this discussion, see especially the following articles and authors: Trevor Muñoz, "Digital Humanities in the Libraries Isn't a Service," (August 19, 2012), http://trevormunoz.com/notebook/2012/08/19/doing-dh-in-the-library.html (accessed April 16, 2017); Miriam Posner, "What Are Some Challenges to Doing DH in the Library?" (August 10, 2012), http://miriamposner.com/blog/what-are-some-challenges-to-doing-dh-in-the-library/(accessed April 16, 2017); and Bethany Nowviskie, "Skunks In the Library: A Path to Production for Scholarly R&D," *Journal of Library Administration* 53.1 (January 25, 2013): 53–66, http://libraprod.lib.virginia.edu/file_assets/libra-oa:2746, (accessed April 16, 2017).

90. Muñoz, in particular, points out the instability in notions of "traditional library service" and calls attention to the business management principles underlying and still animating information commons services ("In Service? A Further Provocation on Digital Humanities Research in Libraries," *dh+lib*, June 19, 2013, http://acrl.ala.org/dh/2013/06/19/in-service-a-further-provocation-on-digital-humanities-research-in-libraries/ (accessed April 16, 2017)).

91. This tension has been referenced earlier, in discussions of "service" by Nowviskie, Muñoz, and others. Another useful reference is the 2015 CLIR report on digital scholarship organizations worldwide, which calls attention to equity, compensation, and service issues that can undermine this work (Vivian Lewis, Lisa Spiro, Xuemo Wang, and Jon E. Cawthorne, *CLIR Report 168: Building Expertise to Support Digital Scholarship: A Global Perspective* (Washington, DC: Council on Library and Information Resources, 2015), www.clir.org/pubs/reports/pub168 (accessed April 16, 2017).

92. John Burke, "Making Sense: Can Makerspaces Work in Academic Libraries?" Association of College and Research Libraries Conference, Portland Oregon (March 25–28, 2015), www.ala.org/acrl/sites/ala.org.acrl/files/content/conferences/confsandpreconfs/2015/Burke.pdf (accessed April 16, 2017).

93. Librarian Sharona Ginsberg at SUNY Oswego maintains a list of makerspaces in libraries, http://library-maker-culture.weebly.com/makerspaces-in-libraries.html. Notably, these tend to be located in art, architectural, or engineering libraries, rather than the main library.

94. Donald Beagle, "From Learning Commons to Learning Outcomes: Assessing Collaborative Services and Spaces," *EDUCAUSE Center for Applied Research* (September 27, 2011), https://library.educause.edu/-/media/files/library/2011/9/erb1114-pdf.pdf (accessed February 17, 2020).

Chapter 2

Surveying the Landscape

Joan Lippincott

Over the past twenty years or so, information commons have become ubiquitous, although use of the designation learning commons seems to have surpassed the earlier terminology. Even though they are more prevalent in academic libraries than they were two decades ago, there is no one clear definition or model of an information or learning commons. This chapter describes the characteristics and variations of information commons, examines the forces that drive the development of new types of learning spaces in academic libraries, provides examples of existing information commons around the United States and outlines their features, reviews the kinds of services offered and the staff needed to support the commons, and presents a number of opportunities and challenges for commons today.

Information Commons—A New Normal for Academic Libraries

In 2017, some academic libraries were implementing information or learning commons for the first time, and others, like Georgia Tech, were on at least their third iteration of the concept in their library. It seems fair to say that lack of funding has been the primary reason that some libraries have not implemented the concept until now. While there have been many definitions suggested for information/learning commons and debates as to whether the terms information commons, learning commons, and commons can be used interchangeably, for the purposes of this chapter, information commons bring together content, technology, and services in a physical library space in order to support the educational mission of the institution. The profiles included in this volume provide a sense of the range of commons and both the similarities and the variations that can be found among them. In addition, a web resource kept up-to-date until 2014 included links to 234 information commons in the United States, Canada, and a few other countries.[1]

In the past, academic libraries were viewed as the place on campus for quiet, solo study and as a place to access and interact with print materials. Changes in the use of technology and changes in styles of pedagogy in universities and colleges have led to adaptations of library spaces and services. A primary characteristic of information commons counteracts the traditional notion of libraries as entirely quiet spaces by offering spaces for collaborative learning, which by definition involves interaction among learners. Collaborative spaces in information commons may take the form of enclosed group study rooms; tables in open seating areas where conversation is not only permitted but encouraged; or partitioned spaces, which provide some degree of separation without enclosure. Many commons have a set of large whiteboards on wheels, and students often move them around the floor to create temporary walls that give them a writing surface as well as a degree of privacy. Generally commons provide access to technology and include some comfortable lounge seating, and many offer food and beverages in a café. Vending areas for food or office supplies, and printing and scanning stations are features in many commons. Some libraries have an information commons on one floor, often the main floor; others have expanded the concept to an additional floor of the library; and others consider the entire library as the information commons. In addition, there are some information commons in specialized libraries that are housed in classroom buildings that serve specific colleges within a university. Some libraries that have space and service configurations that are typical of information commons do not use the terminology to identify their space at all.

The technology available in the information commons promotes seamless access to information. For example, high-speed network connections permit users to view streaming video; wireless Internet connections encourage students to use their own laptops to access the Web; and a range of software enables students to write papers, prepare presentations, or create multimedia products, such as short videos. The variety of software installed on workstations in the information commons typically covers more applications than were available in traditional library reference areas. Rather than focusing on software applications that only facilitate access to information, the software also supports analysis and management of information and the creation of new information products. Much, although not all, of the content that students use today is available online and students have less need to access library resources onsite. However, their work can now move iteratively from accessing content to creating new content, whether in the form of a text paper, a website, a video, or a data visualization. This aggregation of technology availability and information enables users to do their academic work in a way that enhances access to information in different formats. For example, students using books from the library's collection can scan images to use in their papers or presentations, while they simultaneously download articles from library-licensed journals and access web sites of nonlicensed materials. This emphasis on connection to content in all formats distinguishes information commons from computer labs.

In addition, information commons intentionally provide user services for technology support, as well as services related to content. In traditional library areas, staff members are not trained to support a wide array of software applications or to diagnose many technical problems. In contrast, at least a portion of information commons staff is recruited because of their technology skills, and they provide technology support as part of their primary service mission.

As librarian D. Russell Bailey notes in his survey of the information commons literature, information commons are "library-centric." At their core, they have traditional library content and services, but they also incorporate other elements, such as technology and software, that had formerly been characteristic of computer labs run by campus information technology departments.[2]

Rationale for Information Commons

The development of information commons was a response to the increased need for the campus community to have access to information technology (networks, hardware, software, and digital content) to accomplish their work. When the first information commons opened in the early 1990s, high-speed Internet access was not generally available campuswide, wireless access was not available in libraries, only a small percentage of students owned their own computers, and the amount of scholarly digital content—often licensed by the library and sometimes available only within its walls—was on the rise. Turning some prime library space into an area where students, faculty, and other users could have access to high-speed network connections, large numbers of computers, and digital content seemed to be a winning strategy. Information commons also provided a mechanism for offering library users the kinds of services they increasingly required, such as assistance with computer hardware and software problems.

The information commons movement is also a response to some trends in the higher education environment. As the technology skills of incoming students advanced and their facility with using multiple devices to perform a wide range of activities increased, campuses needed spaces that accommodated the high level of technology use of those students. Providing computer labs was not sufficient for a number of reasons. Students did not necessarily need hardware—they increasingly brought their own laptops to campus—but they needed spaces where they could work and have wireless connections. Students increasingly wanted to work in groups, and the library information commons space was generally reconfigured to offer more group space than had been the case in traditional libraries or computer labs. Students also wanted access to a wider range of software in the library so that they could create their projects as well as access information.

During the late 1990s, many campuses expected a widespread change from traditional teaching methods to technology-enabled methods, but that has generally not happened. Factors such as faculty reluctance to change, inconsistency and unpredictability of technology in classrooms, lack of understanding of the relationship of technology to pedagogical goals, and insufficient staff support of faculty, both in preparation of new types of teaching materials and in assistance with equipment and software in the classroom, have slowed this transition from traditional methods. Even though many faculty members do not use technology to a great degree in their classrooms, students use technology in a variety of ways in support of their learning. For example, students use course websites and course management systems; access electronic reserves; search for information via the web or library catalogs and databases; employ software (such as spreadsheet programs or GIS) that is relevant to their major disciplines; embed visuals and audio in their papers; and create presentations, websites, and short videos as class projects. Much of student learning occurs outside the classroom, and libraries have traditionally been a venue where students (and faculty) could broaden their learning outside the classroom's confines. To support today's students' learning styles, libraries can provide technology-rich environments, such as information commons, which offer physical spaces for collaborative work, expert assistance, technology, and content.

Collaborative Learning, Technology, Plus Access to Campus Services

A characteristic of many information commons is that they provide a "one stop" model for a variety of student services. In recent years, such a model is often linked to student success initiatives on campus, whereby students are encouraged to take advantage of advising and tutoring services in order to persist at the institution and graduate in a reasonable number of years. As stated on the website of the University of Iowa Libraries, "The Learning Commons is a tech-infused, comfortable, flexible learning space with a one-stop academic help center in the UI Main Library. There is a café, Food for Thought, and many reservable rooms and areas for learning and teaching." (www.lib.uiowa.edu/commons/).

While some information commons do not have tenants from other campus services, others have had units such as the campus writing center or student advising in the library for a couple of decades. Many commons have the model of Penn State Libraries, described in these terms on their webpage: "The Knowledge Commons offers collaborative spaces for students to study and work with their peers and friends on the University Park's campus. Students working in the Knowledge Commons are close to many great resources, including reference, research, and writing support, technology assistance, and our Media Commons" (https://libraries.psu.edu/knowledgecommons). While these services may be inside the footprint of the commons or adjacent to the commons, they may operate entirely independently of the library.

Colocation, Cooperation, Collaboration

The term collaboration is often used very loosely to describe any type of working together of various parties, but in the management literature, it has a much more precise meaning. Bringing various units that are administratively separate from the library into the physical location of the information commons is frequently referred to as an example of collaboration. However, the presence of these other units may merely be one of convenience or of superficial interaction with the library. If one thinks of a continuum of colocation, cooperation, and collaboration, it may assist planners to think through the type of working relationships and partnerships they might want to establish within information commons.

In the planning phase, the notion of bringing together a number of campus services is generally one of colocating services to provide convenience to the user population, especially undergraduate students. Students who need help writing papers or preparing presentations may require assistance from writing center staff who can assist them with the mechanics of writing, from library staff who can aid them in locating information resources, or from information technology staff who can assist them with any hardware or software problems they encounter. Colocation provides convenience to users, but it does not imply the creation of new services that leverage the joint expertise of more than one type of professional group. Colocation of services also provides opportunities for informal staff contact across sectors, especially to encourage easy referral to appropriate service points. When services are colocated, each unit generally has a physically separate service point (a desk or designated area) within the information commons.

In some information commons, the staff of various separate units move beyond colocation to genuinely cooperate in some ways. Cooperative activities can include joint planning for service hours, establishing the scope of each other's work in order to minimize overlap in services, sharing publicity or marketing efforts, and developing centralized workshop schedules. This type of cooperation can lead to increased understanding among units that results in developing an overall plan for services and filling gaps in service offerings. In addition, cooperative efforts can lead to the personnel in the units learning about each other's expertise and being able to make better referrals and plan new types of services.

Few information commons have realized the potential of developing fully collaborative services among unit partners. In collaborative efforts, the units involved would demonstrate that they

- develop shared goals;
- engage in joint planning;
- share governance or administration;
- pool expertise to develop new services;
- contribute resources, such as space, staff, or equipment.

For example, if the library had a collaborative relationship with a center for teaching and learning in the information commons, library staff and the center staff would establish goals and create programs to help faculty develop new curricular materials that involve technology and digital content.

Librarians at the University of Tennessee, which has had several successful library/information technology collaborations, suggest that there are readiness criteria by which institutions can judge their capacity to engage in a genuinely collaborative project. These criteria include:

"Culture" (encouraged to innovate)
History of Collaboration
Executive Support
Willingness to Reallocate Funds—"Bootstrap"
Ability to Leverage Existing Expertise (Library and IT)[3]

> Information Commons campus partners include:
> Library (usually lead partner)
> Information Technology
> Faculty Academic Computing Center (Research Computing)
> Center for Teaching and Learning
> Writing Center
> Career Center
> Academic Advising
> Student Success Initiative

One example of collaboration is the newly renovated main floor of the Odegaard Library at University of Washington, where the Writing and Research Center (https://depts.washington.edu/owrc/staff), which offers tutoring and consultation, includes librarians, professionals from the university writing center, and undergraduate and graduate student tutors. In addition, the library offers a combined computer help desk and library reference service (http://itconnect.uw.edu/learn/technology-spaces/odegaard-learning-commons/). The Brigham Young University Library also offers a writing center service in the learning commons, staffed by individuals from both the library and the university writing center (https://lib.byu.edu/services/research-and-writing-center/). Grand Valley State University Library's Knowledge Market provides centralized peer consultation on research strategies, writing skills, and presentation techniques (www.gvsu.edu/library/mary-idema-pew-library-21.htm). One of the most long-standing programs integrating services from several campus units via jointly trained peer tutors is the RWIT program at Dartmouth College, a collaboration between the Institute of Writing and Rhetoric, the Library, and Academic Computing (http://writing-speech.dartmouth.edu/learning/support-writing-research-and-composing-technology/rwit).

Features of the Information Commons

There are so many variations of information commons that it is difficult to devise distinctive categories that describe identifiable types. However, some of the features that may distinguish information commons from other areas of the library are spaces configured for special purposes, technologies, and services. Flexibility and change are essential to the success of any information commons, so these features are a snapshot of the current scene.

As mentioned earlier, most commons have a variety of collaborative seating areas, both in enclosed group study rooms and in open areas. Many libraries have instituted an online capability for students to reserve group study rooms for segments of time. Group study rooms usually include a seminar table surrounded by chairs, but some libraries have a portion of their group study rooms with soft, upholstered seating arranged in a conversational grouping. In open areas, it is generally first-come, first-served. Seating configured in a diner booth style seems especially popular. Many information commons still include rows of workstations with one chair per workstation, thus not genuinely supporting collaborative learning. In open areas, areas for sofas and comfortable chairs are available for students to get together or may be lined up facing a soothing outdoor view for relaxation and contemplation.

Presentation practice rooms, which have a podium and chairs for an audience and a built-in camera for recording, have become less popular in an age where students can record themselves practicing a presentation in any group room available. However, for more formal recordings, some information commons include media production in open areas or in studio spaces. Some include audio recording rooms and videoconferencing rooms. Most academic libraries have a dedicated room for accessibility equipment (for example, to assist individuals with visual disabilities), and this type of room may be located in the commons. Frequently the commons area offers printers, may offer a scanner, and may house the library's plotter, or large format printer.

Services are one of the aspects of information commons that distinguish these areas from similar informal learning spaces elsewhere on campus; for example, group seating areas in a student union. In a commons, there is generally some type of service desk, which may be staffed solely by the library, jointly by the library and the campus IT unit, or may provide a range of services for different campus units. Another model is to have staff (professional staff, support staff, or students or a combination) from each of these units at separate service desks in the commons. Often the library will have an area for one-on-one reference consultations with users, and other units such as the writing center may have a designated area for their consultations. The service desk, in addition to providing answers to questions, may be the location of the library's reserve collection and/or the venue for equipment lending, which could include such items as laptops, tablets, cameras, cables, projectors, and calculators (the equipment available for loan at the North Carolina State University Libraries is a good example, www.lib.ncsu.edu/techlending). Some staff offices or cubicles may be located in the commons.

On occasion, classrooms may be part of the commons, either a room for information literacy instruction by librarians or a general-purpose classroom assigned through the registrar's office. A small number of libraries have developed classrooms configured in a problem-based learning style, again sometimes for use by the libraries and in other cases by the campus (one example is at University of Washington, www.lib.washington.edu/ougl/learning-spaces/active-learning-classrooms).

While many library spaces have bare, bland walls, some libraries have brightened their information commons spaces using digital signage, artwork, and exhibits, both virtual and physical. These may include posters that students present as part of their capstone project or a conference presentation, visualizations of data of all types, photographs, paintings, sculpture, artworks representing aspects of libraries (incorporating reading or books, for example), and displays of faculty work. All of these engage students and other library users and assist in maintaining the library as a cultural center for the campus. Some libraries also have an area in the commons where readings can take place or events can be held, such as a poster session. Cafés are popular in information commons areas since they are already meant for conversation and as places where various parts of the campus community can get together. Since libraries are open longer hours than most buildings on campus, cafés also provide a way for students to take a break when they are spending much of the night working on their assignments in the library. Vending areas may supplement or replace a café and may include machines that vend supplies such as pens, notebooks, and earphones.

Features of an Information Commons
Individual workstations
Workstations that accommodate small groups, often with a large, shared screen
Group study rooms equipped with computers or space for laptops; ceiling-mounted projector
Informal, comfortable seating areas
Presentation practice room, equipped with video recording capabilities
Multimedia production areas or studios
Rooms equipped for videoconferencing
Rooms equipped with adaptive technologies
Scanning stations, printer stations
Consultation areas (where students or faculty can consult with librarians, tutors, technical assistants)
Service desk(s) for reference, technology consultation, writing assistance, and other functions
Staff office(s)
Classrooms for information literacy instruction
General-purpose classrooms for campus use (traditional seating or problem-based learning configuration)
Art or library materials exhibit areas
Event space
Large screen display(s)
Café
Vending area

Extending the Information Commons Concept

In addition to collaborative learning spaces that have basic technologies or even just access to power and Internet, some commons incorporate specialized functionalities. There is a great deal of variation among libraries in this regard. For example, in some libraries, the primary multimedia production area is physically part of the commons although it may be staffed separately or even by another unit (such as the campus Information Technology unit). Other libraries may have a media production unit, but it is physically separate, perhaps on another floor of the library. Can this also be called an information commons or part of a commons? Some libraries are developing advanced technology-enabled spaces such as visualization labs or gaming labs. Are these part of a commons or something separate? In terms of the staff offering expertise in such areas, generally these specialized facilities are not part of a commons, although exceptions can be found such as the Vitale Digital Media Lab that is part of the University of Pennsylvania's Weigle Information Commons (http://commons.library.upenn.edu/).

Another development is the creation of scholars' commons, graduate student commons, or spaces reserved for faculty and graduate students, often accessed via key card such as the one at the Hunt Library at North Carolina State University (www.lib.ncsu.edu/spaces/graduate-student-commons-hunt). In some cases, these areas are refurbished rooms with a combination of solo and collaborative seating; in others, such as at Ohio State University, the commons resembles what many refer to as a digital scholarship lab or center, where high-end technologies and expertise are available to work with individuals or teams involved in new forms of scholarship such as data visualization, text mining, or 3-D modeling. Innovation @ the Edge (https://libraries.ou.edu/edge) at the University of Oklahoma Library is another example of this type, and it is part of their Learning Commons and open to any member of the university community. These kinds of specialized facilities may have common administration, staffing, and service delivery as the learning commons but are more often developed on a separate track.

Informal Learning Spaces in Other Campus Buildings

Interestingly, renovations of campus buildings such as student unions and classroom buildings are now including the types of collaborative learning spaces associated with information commons, such as group study rooms, technology-enabled seating clusters, informal lounge spaces, and cafés. A small number of institutions have embedded library commons into new or newly renovated classroom buildings such as at the Miller Learning Center of the University of Georgia (www.libs.uga.edu/locations/mlc) and the Wilmeth Active Learning Center at Purdue University (www.lib.purdue.edu/walc/). Classroom buildings may also have media production facilities, makerspaces, and visualization walls, which may also be found in libraries. Often these specialized facilities in classroom (or departmental or college) buildings are available only to students taking courses or majoring in a particular field, and often no regularly scheduled staff is available to provide assistance with the high-end technologies. This is in contrast to libraries, which generally provide facilities, equipment, and expertise to all members of the community.

Conclusion

As technology becomes more ubiquitous and also more essential to the core functions of universities and colleges—research, teaching, and learning—library information commons have the potential to play an essential role in the university, or they may become just one alternative, comfortable environment among many on campus in which students can study. Information commons are one component of learning spaces on campus. Libraries continue to play a very important part in the lives of students, providing long hours for study, quiet places for deep reading and contemplation, areas for collaborative learning, ubiquitous access to wireless technology, and collections spanning the academic interests of the institution. In addition, libraries are places of community, where students and faculty can gather, where exhibits, workshops, and events can enrich the campus environment, and where people can get together over a cup of coffee.

Information commons play an important role in the learning and community aspects of libraries, and they will continue to do so for the foreseeable future.

Notes

1. David Murray, "Infocommons and Beyond: A Directory of the Evolution of the Commons Model in Academic Libraries." http://infocommonsandbeyond.blogspot.com/.
2. D. Russell Bailey, "Information Commons Services for Learners and Researchers: Evolution in Patron Needs, Digital Resources and Scholarly Publishing" (paper presented at INFORUM 2005: 11th Conference on Professional Information Resources, Prague, May 24-26, 2005), www.inforum.cz/inforum2005/prispevek.php?prispevek=32.
3. Barbara Dewey and Brice Bible, "Relationships and Campus Politics in Building the Information Commons" (paper presented at Academic Libraries 2005: The Information Commons. NY3Rs Association and the Academic and Special Libraries Section of NYLA. Saratoga Springs, NY, November 11, 2005), www.ny3rs.org/al2005.html.

Chapter 3

Twenty-First-Century Library Service Design

Elliot Felix and Matthew Swift

Libraries are places not only to access information but to create it—in all its forms, whether a paper, a video, a presentation, an app, a device, or a performance. Libraries are also not only places to work individually; they are places to connect with people—collaborators, experts, and colleagues. As the types, quantity, access, and use of information have changed, so too must the purpose of the library.

To fulfill a new purpose focused not just on access but on creating and connecting, libraries must enable new experiences and offer new services. In doing so, this fundamentally challenges their organizational design. While in the past defining the library's role, services, and departmental structures based on the lifecycle of the book from selection to acquisition to cataloging to shelving to circulating to reshelving to preserving might have sufficed, it must change. Now, libraries must not only be designed for the lifecycle of information but also organized around and continuously adapting to the teaching, learning, and research needs of students and faculty.

The growth of the information commons seemed to represent an opportunity to support these needs. However, they rarely deliver on the full promise of their name. They succeed in providing an open, accessible place for people to come together, but often do not hit the mark when it comes to supporting the kinds of activities that are taking place. As Joan mentioned in Chapter 2, they are "library-centric" not "user-centric."

How can libraries fulfill this new role by offering new services and rethinking their organization to do so? To answer this question, this chapter will draw from our experience working with over 45 academic libraries, our review of relevant articles and statistics, and our own research. We will first identify the emerging user needs reshaping library services. Second, we will identify the steps to rethink library services, walking through the why, what, where, when, and how of service design, using a case study to illustrate each step. Third, we will outline strategies for how libraries can redesign their organizations—their roles, structures, and processes—to better design, deliver, and assess their services, including embracing the user focus and the iterative prototyping of design thinking as well as building cultures of collaboration and assessment. Finally, we will provide some tactics on how to get started.

Part I: How the Purpose and Role of Libraries Are Changing

Libraries offer so much to so many—information, technology, expertise, inspiration, community, and spaces for all these—and the usage of libraries is increasing: up 16% among academic libraries from 2004 to 2012.[1] Offering information that you cannot find or access anywhere else was and still remains fundamental to the role of libraries. However, the format of that information is rapidly changing. Library collections are becoming increasingly digital. Whether they need digitized original source materials, large data sets, or online journals, researchers can access library collections in a variety of ways.

Creating things with that information—such as writing a book, illustrating an article, or charting and analyzing data—has also always been part of why people come to libraries. But now creating is a larger part than ever before.[2] So, libraries have to move beyond providing access to supporting creating and doing so in even more diverse physical and digital forms. Every day library users are still creating books and articles, images, and data, but they are also writing code, developing apps, filming and editing videos, printing 3-D objectives, and performing—to name a few.

Just as a shift has taken place from access to creating, a similar shift has taken place from catering to the individual to catering to the group.[3] Research has become more collaborative; for instance, the number of authors per article has increased 17% from 2003 to 2013.[4] Pedagogy has become more collaborative; for instance, in a 2015 Cengage Survey 63% of students cited collaboration out of class.[5] The workplace has become more collaborative, with knowledge workers spending 65% of their day collaborating or communicating.[6] So, the library must shift from seeing its primary customer as individuals who want access to information and a quiet place to study it. Now, it's more about the library as a place that facilitates connection and collaboration—among users, among staff, and between users and staff. Students may come to the library to work on a group view project and need support on anything ranging from brainstorming an idea, to writing a script, to checking out and learning equipment, to shooting on a green screen, to editing. Likewise researchers may come to share their work, get inspired by others, or find collaborators. Rather than work in siloed departments separated by discipline or function, library staff also need to work together to uncover needs, solve problems, and showcase results.

To support new forms of information, creation, and collaboration libraries must offer new spaces and new services.

Emerging User Needs Driving Service Changes

Increased adoption of digital technologies has resulted in library users having more self-service options available to them. This is a positive development for both the user (e.g., increased autonomy, convenience) and the library (e.g., increased efficiency). Because users are accomplishing the simple tasks on their own, when they do need help from a service provider their requests tend to be more complex. This results in more in-depth consultations and side-by-side work between staff and users. Many libraries have recognized this shift and are redesigning service points to accommodate these new modes of services.

As collections have become increasingly digital the behavior of people accessing those collections has changed significantly. Researchers no longer need to hunker down in the library for hours at a time, pulling materials from the stacks. They can access a large majority of the collection from anywhere. As a result, some of the heaviest users of the library are no longer visiting the library on a regular basis. Faculty members, in particular, are content to access collections from the comfort of their office. Libraries are responding to this in multiple ways. The first is going out to their users. Librarians are embedding themselves in various academic departments to ensure strong relationships with faculty and to stay up-to-date on changes in research and curriculum. The second response is providing services and programs in the library that cannot be experienced or accessed remotely. This could take the form of professional development services or enabling faculty to host seminars or symposia with their colleagues.

As libraries have increased their focus on creating, they have also expanded their capabilities and offerings to provide training and support for the various technologies that users are leveraging to create. Whether creating film, an app, a visualization, or a 3-D object, library users rely on specialized tools that they may or may not be familiar with. Take, for example, a student looking to create a 3-D model. This student must not only understand how to operate the 3-D printer, but also be able to create the 3-D file for the object they want to print. For libraries' investment in 3-D printing technology to pay off, they must also provide training and support for each of those activities.

Similarly, the increased focus on collaboration has influenced the mix of library service offerings. Teaching, learning, and research are becoming more collaborative. Subsequently, it is critical for students and faculty to have not only a place to come together with collaborators but also a platform to build their network of like-minded peers. As a result, many libraries are providing more robust services for event planning so that faculty and students can convene peers and colleagues around shared topics of interest. They are also creating platforms for researchers on campus to showcase their work and in turn increase collective awareness of the research taking place on campus and the role that the library can play in supporting that research.

As libraries continue to do more things for more people, they are getting creative about how they meet that demand. In many cases they are partnering with other academic or administrative service providers on campus to provide complementary offerings in a single location. This results in a more convenient experience for library users as well as providing interesting opportunities for collaboration between libraries and these partner groups. Another approach to meet the demand is increasing the ratio of student staff to full-time staff. This enables experts to spend more time focusing on complex challenges and less experienced, less expensive staff to focus on more straightforward challenges and transactional tasks. However, increasing the number of student staff presents some new challenges. Because that population of workers has high turnover (they graduate!), libraries must come up with effective and efficient training programs to ensure that the quality of service they are providing is not negatively impacted by the high turnover.

Finally, as more services, more resources, and more experts are becoming available, the task of navigating those services is becoming more complex. Libraries are looking for a variety of ways to support the navigation of those resources. One simple way is rethinking how services are communicated. Traditional service categories (i.e., access services, IT, reference) do not align with how target users think about their work. As libraries become increasingly complex organizations, it is critical for them to clearly and simply communicate what services they offer and how those services create value for their users.

Part II: Steps to Rethink Library Services

To respond to these changes, libraries need the right process to design their services. Is there one "right" process? No. Designing new services is a complex task. Services encompass a wide range of interactions between a service provider and a user (i.e., touchpoints) and include both the

Six Questions About Service Offerings

QUESTION	TOOL	PURPOSE
Why	Service Philosophy	A concise expression of the values and principles at the heart of why you do what you do
What	Service Portfolio	An organized way of describing—without jargon—what you offer in easy-to-navigate categories
Where	Service Points	An understanding of where services will be delivered and how users and providers will interact
When	Service Hours	An approach for making services accessible for users at their convenience, within your budget
Who	Service Providers	A description of necessary roles and the types of individuals best suited to fill them
How	Service Delivery	A blueprint for how services will be delivered and everything necessary to ensure seamless interactions

"front-of-house" and the "back-of-house" activities. In other words, they include all of the people, tools, interactions, and spaces that users see when they engage in services, as well as all of those that they don't see (i.e., everything that must be done behind the scenes).

To keep things simple, we often ask our partners six questions regarding their service offerings. Below is a summary of those questions and some tools that can help them answer those questions.

Why: The Service Philosophy

At the onset of any service design initiative it is important to establish the overall vision for your services. In other words, what kind of service experience do you want to create for your users? The answer to this question will serve as a north star for the many decisions you'll have to make when designing and implementing new service offerings. During our collaboration with Emory University, we asked this very question. After engaging a team of service providers from the library in a series of participatory activities and working sessions to articulate and unpack their goals associated with service delivery we created the following service philosophy: "Every interaction is a unique opportunity to strengthen our community." This statement, while brief, speaks not only to the role of the library on campus but also to the mindset of service providers and the diversity of the people they serve.

What: Creating a Portfolio of Service Offerings

Libraries often struggle to describe the services they offer in a way that is both memorable to their users and useful to organize library staff and spaces. This is typically because of three divides: users often use different words to describe what they need than those the library uses (i.e., "research" versus "reference"); descriptions of services online may differ from how they are communicated within spaces; and library department names are often conflated with service names, but departments are often a legacy from when libraries were solely organized around the selection, acquisition, cataloging, circulation, use, and preservation of the physical book rather than the broader mission of today's libraries. This is further complicated in that many libraries do not have an accurate catalog of their services. As part of an extensive library renewal project, we worked with Georgia Tech to audit the current service portfolio and propose new services to address the needs our user research uncovered, such as greater administrative support for researchers. To do this, we used a tool from the Learning Space Toolkit called the Service Location Planner to list current services as rows in the table and group like items, and to map to physical points of service in the columns. This resulted in a sorted list of services we could describe in plain English, thus paving the way to identify the people and spaces associated with a service for future planning.

Where: Bringing Together Services to Support the Twenty-First-Century Student

As libraries broaden their mission to enable student success, they naturally work in closer partnership with other academic service providers on campus, particularly regarding written and verbal communication, math and statistics, and supplemental instruction through tutoring. However, these program offices are often spread across the campus. The University of Miami sought to bring these and other services together so that students could learn to conduct research, write and communicate, collaborate and discuss, work with data, and publish and present. With this vision in mind, we determined what services would be offered and forecasted how much space would be needed based on the "partner style" of the group—that is, whether the space within the library would be their headquarters, a satellite, a place for them to visit, or a place for them to provide behind-the-scenes support. With the services and partner types established, we then honed in on the service points. We determined there would be a general central service zone for check-in, triage, and basic support that is complemented by a shared consultation zone for specialized expert help by appointment and on-demand. To do so, we grappled with questions of the identity and visibility of services, whether access to specialists was direct or by referral or both, and flexibility to accommodate different volumes of traffic and new modes of delivery.

When: Using Programming Styles to Forecast Staffing and Space Needs

Shared service hubs have many benefits: they bring services together so they are more convenient to use and more efficient to staff, they reduce the amount of space needed, they enable collaboration across different groups, and they can provide more programming over a greater number of hours. However, it can be challenging to reap these benefits, and coordinating schedules—who's going to offer what programs when—is chief among these challenges. The University of Virginia sought to holistically improve student advising by creating a "Total Advising Center" within a library that brought together academic, career, and personal support provided by over two dozen entities on campus. As part of the service design, we solved the "when" problem by identifying the "programming styles" of each group according to their anticipated program offerings, which could include anything from a one-on-one consultation, to an info session on studying abroad, to a workshop on designing your own major, to exhibits on career opportunities. We were then able to focus staffing and space needs by determining how many people might staff and attend a program, when the programs would fall, and whether they were continuous or episodic.

Who: Leveraging Students in a New Service Model

Rethinking who provides your services can also be a path to innovation. At many institutions, students are playing larger roles in providing library services, and for good reason. At the James B. Hunt Jr. Library at North Carolina State University, we worked with the library to develop new service and staffing models that would make students a key face of help—and generally the first one a user would see. We did this as part of a process to forecast staffing levels for each service, first determining whether the staffing for each was fixed or varied by demand and then secondly projecting the FTE needed for each service by level, including library staff and student staff. Leveraging students in a peer-to-peer model made the help more accessible, since people don't always ask for the help they need. It also created work experience with development opportunities for students and enabled the library to access experience (e.g., with specific technologies or navigating specific coursework) that full-time staff may not have. In a time of diminishing resources, students can be an affordable option for libraries. Student work hours also enable a closer match between staffing and need, as students can work later in the evenings whereas most libraries have the most staff in the building at the times of the least use.

How: Storytelling as a Planning Tool

As libraries are becoming more networked organizations, their day-to-day operations are becoming more complex. At Harvard Libraries, which consists of 70-plus libraries, navigating that complexity is particularly challenging. Recently, Harvard asked us to help them identify new services that would not only address emerging user needs but also increase coordination and collaboration across locations within their Science and Engineering Libraries. We started by understanding user needs as they relate to teaching, learning, and research and then used those identified needs as a frame of reference for generating new service concepts. Once we developed concepts, we created storyboards for each. These storyboards were a series of drawings that depicted various "moments" in the service experience from the user's perspective. The storyboards not only helped us socialize some of our early service concepts but also allowed us to think systematically about how the services would be delivered and how each library would play a part in that service delivery.

Part III: Redesigning the Organization for New Service Offerings

Once you've determined the why, what, where, when, who, and how for your library's services, there is a critical step to implementing twenty-first-century library service design: changing your organization to deliver new service offerings or deliver existing services differently. To make these shifts and address common challenges, we recommend thinking about library organizational design in three parts: roles, process, and structure. Define the roles staff need to play in the future in terms of their responsibilities, skills, and performance measures. Then, define the key processes people need to lead or participate in to fulfill these roles. Finally, think about the structures needed to connect the roles and facilitate these processes. Of course, these three areas are related and need to be considered iteratively; describing a role (e.g., "user experience") often sparks thoughts about processes (e.g., "assessment"), which leads to new structures (e.g., "user research taskforce"), which in turn beget new organizational development activities (e.g., "user research training").

Common Organizational Challenges

As libraries think about how to reorganize to better deliver services and fulfill their missions, we've observed three major challenges. First, many libraries are stifled by legacy names, structures, and mindsets that pertain to traditional libraries but not contemporary ones; for instance, organizing staff in departments that correspond directly to the selection, acquisition, cataloging, circulation, use, and preservation of the physical book. Second, there is often a mismatch between the skills and dispositions of library personnel on the one hand and the roles needed on the other; for example, many introverts go into librarianship for their love of books and then find themselves in roles whose success is dependent on their ability to network with researchers, connect them to other people and projects, and facilitate discussions among them. Third, we see general resistance to change and fear of uncertainty—which is understandable but also unavoidable.

Defining New Roles

As libraries seek to implement a new service model, inevitably library staff/faculty will need to play new roles within the organization, particularly in the areas of making, connecting, data, marketing, and user experience. The diversity of scholarly "products" and the ways of making them continue to increase—students and faculty are now creating things like videos, apps, performances, devices, and websites in addition to the more familiar papers. So, this leads to new roles that facilitate making these things. As search becomes an increasingly collaborative and interdisciplinary endeavor and libraries become conveners and connectors, new roles emerge in order to facilitate connections among researchers, connecting them to each other and project opportunities in addition to information resources. As data has become more available, more expected, and more complex, new roles to acquire it, curate it, analyze it, visualize it, and manage it also have emerged. As libraries seek to make their services more visible and valued—particularly as things become more digital—there's also a real need to better market services, programs, and spaces. Finally, with the recognition that libraries must constantly evolve with their user needs, library positions are being created to understand, assess, and improve the user experience.

Creating New Work Processes

As we reflect on the work processes that we see exemplary libraries embracing so that library staff/faculty can fulfill both new and traditional roles, it's clear that much has changed. First, there is a new attitude toward planning: rather than making long-term and unrealistically detailed plans despite rapid change and high uncertainty, libraries are adopting a more agile approach where they set the overall vision and then more opportunistically pursue projects to realize their vision depending on conditions like funding, workload, and partner availability. Big projects are the new normal. The cadence of work also has changed in that, rather than working steadily on the same series of tasks week to week and semester to semester, more library staff/faculty are involved in some major project as all or part of their role, such as planning a new space, analyzing a collection to move parts off-site, launching a new service, or incorporating a new technology. We've also seen libraries approach these projects with a "design thinking" mindset so they are prototyping and piloting ideas to get feedback, build momentum, and scale up. Finally, library staff/faculty must now embrace more mobility within their work and a greater reliance on technology; they are embedding within classes and research teams around the campus, roving within the library spaces, and traveling to work with partners, so a smaller and smaller percentage of work can happen in the quiet of a fixed desk or office, and more happens on the go and on the road.

Establishing New Structures (and Then Changing Them)

New services, new roles, and new processes all beget new organizational structures, including both how people and roles are grouped into categories as well as the reporting lines within and between groups. The University of Kansas has a particularly interesting structure (https://lib.ku.edu/sites/lib.ku.edu/files/images/general/KULibraries-Structure-June2019.pdf). Changes in structure include reorganizing departments so as to better align with services offered, as noted earlier, or just simplifying structures to provide greater clarity and flexibility; for instance, UVA Libraries reorganized into just five departments. To complete the kind of ongoing and sporadic projects noted earlier, there are also more short-term taskforces or working groups created within libraries that are specific to a project and not necessarily aligned with functional departments. Libraries are also creating departments that include multiple functions, with some like "learning commons" groups often serving as a microcosm of the library as a whole with their own circulation, reference, and technology functions. These sorts of departments serve as good examples of what author Dave Gray refers to in *The Connected Company* as a "podular" organization. Finally, perhaps the biggest shift in structure within libraries is the embrace of nonlibrary partners; whether driven by resource scarcity, project complexity, or the need for a holistic approach, libraries are partnering to get things done, including work they might have done internally in previous eras.

Getting Started

While service design is challenging, especially in complex organizations like libraries, don't let that stop you from getting started. We have highlighted a few activities that can jump-start your service design efforts.

1) Understanding the current service experience

When is the last time you put yourself in the user's shoes? When is the last time that you talked to your users about their service experience? With very little preparation, library service designers can develop empathy for their users and identify opportunities to improve their service offerings by simply talking to users and participating in their experiences.

2) Audit Existing Services

Documenting the current state of service offerings can be every illuminating. What services do you offer? What about by department? What needs do those services address? Write down the answers to those questions. The format does not matter (i.e., a graph, a list, a table, a diagram). What matters is that you give form to the current state in some way such that you can look at it and think about it in a different way. Similarly to understanding the current service experience, auditing existing services will undoubtedly highlight new opportunities for service design.

3) Prototyping New Services

Have an idea for a new service? Great! Now all you need to do is communicate that idea in such a way that you can get feedback from your colleagues and from users. Simple, right? Prototyping new services can be as complex as a live pilot or as simple as a sketch. As long as you are forcing yourself to define the service and give it form in some way, you are making progress.

Conclusion

Answering "why, what, where, when, who, and how" for your service offerings and creating new roles, processes, and structure that will enable your organization to adapt to the evolving needs of your users will lay the foundation for a truly "user-centric" library.

Understandably, these shifts will not happen overnight. Significant organizational change is complicated. And truly understanding your users is an ongoing exercise. However, your intention can change overnight. Any path forward starts with commitment to a clear vision. Once you've committed, there are a variety of things you can do to build momentum and buy-in quickly (see "Getting Started").

Notes

1. IPEDS Data (https://nces.ed.gov/ipeds/) from 2004 https://nces.ed.gov/pubs2007/2007301.pdf (19,368,745) to 2012 https://nces.ed.gov/pubs2014/2014038.pdf (22,404,805).
2. For instance, in the Pew Research Center 2015 Public Libraries Study, "Libraries at a Crossroads," 80% of respondents said libraries should either definitely (45%) or maybe (35%) provide "3-D printers and other digital tools to ... make different kinds of objects."
3. For instance, in three recent brightspot surveys across a range of institution types, 82% of students cited collaboration with peers as their primary reason for visiting the library.
4. Publish or Perish? The Rise of the Fractional Author. www.researchtrends.com/issue-38-september-2014/publish-or-perish-the-rise-of-the-fractional-author/.
5. In a 2015 Cengage Learning Survey of student collaboration, 88% of faculty thought students collaborated well in the classroom and 66% outside the classroom. Meanwhile, 87% of students thought they collaborated well in the classroom, and 63% said they collaborated outside class. https://blog.cengage.com/college-student-collaboration-in-and-out-of-the-classroom/.
6. McKinsey Global Institute: "The Social Economy: Unlocking Value and Productivity through Social Technologies," July 2012. www.mckinsey.com/industries/high-tech/our-insights/the-social-economy.

Chapter 4

Integrating Technology into the Information Commons

Parke Rhoads

The Context for Technology in the Information Commons

The role of technology in our society has evolved at a staggering rate; the phone in your pocket is more advanced than the computers that sent Apollo rockets to the moon, and the information one can access through it has grown tenfold every seven years. However, the more things change, the more they stay the same—the concept of a modern library (by any name) in the technology era can and should be as it always was: a welcoming area that supports its community with resources that they would not easily be able to access otherwise.

This chapter offers a conceptual overview of the role technology can play in the modern information commons, with the goal of deconstructing the goals and factors that go into planning for and integrating of technology into it. Where possible we have provided some recommendations, examples, or case studies to illustrate more clearly how the key concepts have been incorporated into a wide array of programs. Inevitably the literal technology specifications will become dated at some point after publication. Planning, especially with the rapid change of technology, is a forward-looking exercise and is by its nature at odds with examples that look into the past (no matter how recent or successful). With that in mind I intend to put the focus on the "first principles" that start this chapter and are woven into the fabric of the entire book:

- What is the mission of your information commons (and how is technology relevant)?
- What are the needs and uses of the information commons community (and how technology in any era supports and enhances that vision)?
- What are the general trends that have emerged, are emerging, and that the book authors feel are coming over the distant horizon? How might they inform and broaden the horizons of the information commons planner?

Integrating Technology into Place and Purpose

As the information commons concept first evolved in the library community[1] there existed a tension: most librarians and library planners agreed that the future was intimately associated with technology but were concerned that the traditional library (with its print collection and library staff serving as the friendly, supportive "search engine") was increasingly irrelevant to its community. Proponents of technology saw the opportunity, often referred to as a Blue Ocean Strategy (Mauborgne, 2004), to integrate emerging applications into the core of the library to serve the same mission with new and exciting tools of the digital era. The information commons enhances the institution by consolidating technology functions, facilities, and systems aimed squarely at information access, information exchange, and expanding horizons.

Seek a True Path to Innovation

In our experience, spreading out computers or hanging any technology like wall decoration is not true technology integration. Technology is not a silo nor is it wallpaper; technology is a systematic treatment,[2] a tool that is interwoven into the fabric of the building and the functions of the institution.

In technology conversations, often a high priority is placed on "being innovative" or taking the "best-in-class" innovations from peer institutions. True innovations, ones that gain attention and that are lauded within the industry, are rarely accidents or incremental improvements on the work of others. They most frequently germinate first as thoughts about what is unique about the vision of the people and institution at the heart of the commons, an application of the spaces and technologies to serve those thoughts, and then an ongoing process of exploration and improvement with the institutional vision for guidance. In short, the best and most innovative approach is your own.

Know Thyself: Recommendations on Where to Start

Understanding the goals of an institution's information commons is key to understanding what purpose technology might serve within it. Often these concepts are captured broadly within a strategic plan (and are discussed in greater detail in other chapters of this book). Following are some key examples:

> Mission: The goals and services of your learning commons—This information will provide the goal, the work needed to achieve that goal, and the use cases for technology needed to accomplish that work.
>
> What is the mission of the institution/community in broad context, and the role of the information commons within it? Some examples:
>
> To improve learning outcomes
>
> To enrich research and projects
>
> To make the modern (and future) tools of collaboration available to all
>
> To orient and prepare students (and/or others) for the environments and technologies they will encounter after graduation
>
> To provide a learning lab where the institution can experiment and accelerate their capabilities; where they can synthesize the familiar and the new
>
> To serve as a nexus for knowledge and idea sharing from around the campus

> To provide a space that is highly curated/high touch with staff and services abundantly available
>
> To provide a space that is open and self-guided, with little or no staff assistance in the user experience

Risk tolerance:[3] The threshold and culture for testing (technological) boundaries at your institution. This information helps inform where to look (inwardly, at emerging trends, at peer institutions, etc.) for inspiration and technological solutions.

> Where do the learning commons stakeholders fit in the spectrum of interest in, and ability to embrace, change or innovation (Rogers, 2003; Moore, 1991)?
>
> > Early Innovators who are never satisfied, often developing new initiatives or engineering new solutions in-house whether or not they fit a trend
> >
> > Early Adopters who are always at the forefront of trends
> >
> > Early Majority who are open to the adoption of new ideas over time
> >
> > Late Majority who adopt ideas once they have been more established in the peer community
> >
> > Laggards who prefer to hold on to tried-and-true methods until obsolescence

Champions and Stakeholders: The thought leaders for, enthusiasts of, and people most impacted by the information commons. This information helps to map partners and skills to leverage in the planning and management of the learning commons.

> What is the right team to set and sustain the vision of the information commons?[4]
>
> > Administration
> >
> > Library and Archival Groups
> >
> > IT and Academic Technology
> >
> > Faculty and Research Users
> >
> > Computer Science, Engineering, Arts & Humanities, etc.
> >
> > Student Users
> >
> > Institutional and Information Commons Staff

Understanding Planning, Designing, and the Tension of Building versus Technology Lifecycles

Even with identity and mission in clear focus, planning and developing technology can be challenging. I often encounter people who are paralyzed in their planning process, certain that technology designs made today will be rendered obsolete by the next wave of innovation; technology decisions seem to include a high risk of future failure. Questions are frequently asked around a few common themes such as "Why can't technology last?" or (more constructively) "How do we design the space with enough flexibility to accommodate whatever the future may bring?"

Working around this barrier often requires an examination of why it exists.

Many of the underlying reasons for these frustrations stem from the different event horizons of buildings and the technology within them. The life span of our spaces (especially buildings and renovations to them) are relatively linear and long-term, while technology after the industrial age follows a constant cycle of change inherent in a rapidly innovating industry. After years of

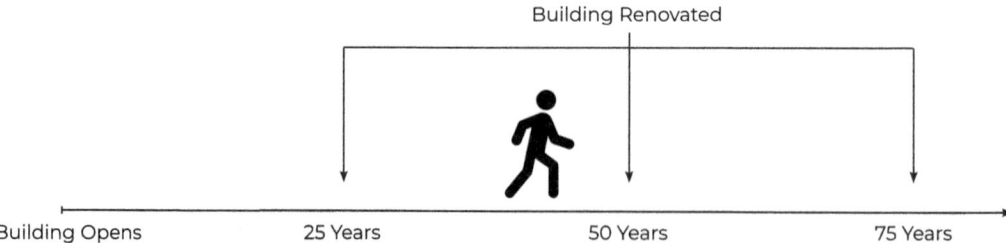

Facilities Life Span
Source: Parke Rhoads

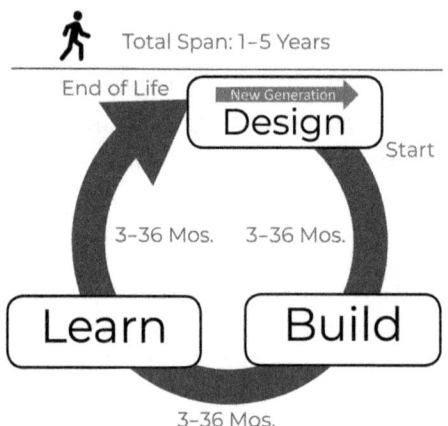

Technology Life Span
Source: Parke Rhoads

skilled design, the archetypical building can stand for over 100 years with renovations (small and large) every 15 to 30 years. By contrast, most technologies are part of an industry that rapidly prototypes and innovates; very little of the technology installed in a classroom will be considered "new" in seven years.

Because there are two superimposed time spans at play, good technology planning often requires two separate levels of thinking and problem-solving to address each:[5]

> Planning the Building for Generations of Technology—This includes any measures to add resiliency to the physical building and long-term vision (for staff and programs):
>
>> Building infrastructure, such as mounting points and cable pathways (conduit, electrical boxes), that is beyond the immediate needs of the opening day, including:
>>> Extra power in equipment locations, possible future locations (such as places where a camera or display may go), and at regular intervals throughout the building
>>> Cable pathways that are universal and accommodate more than one configuration, such as
>>> A "perimeter and cross" pattern of cable tray above the ceiling for AV and IT
>>> Access flooring, with cable traveling under floor panels that can be removed for access and adjustment

- Investment in IT and AV cabling architectures that are more flexible, such as fiber-optic or late-standard twisted-pair cabling (particularly in lieu of more AV industry-specific cabling like "HDMI")
- Mounting points (e.g., steel struts, pipe grids, and/or "blocking") on/in the ceilings and walls to encourage more rapid demounting/remounting of equipment, lowering the barrier to user-led reconfiguration
- An initial complement of technology designed to satisfy the current vision of the space, but with added capacity to be modified over the life span of the equipment or system
- Preparing the Organization for Technology Innovation (Catmull, 2014)—This includes an ongoing cycle of innovation (and organizational learning) that allows for frequent adjustments to the technology solutions used serve the institutional mission, such as:
- Collaboration and pooling of resources with other institutional departments (such as campus IT, instructional technology, facilities, and other faculty programs)
- Establishing goals and regular review and learning process events
- Regular funding designated for technology support and improvements in a timely manner

Budgeting for Technology: Capital Expenditure versus Operations

Most information commons projects evolve from (or are funded in some part by) a construction project. Frequently this anchors the technology to the traditional "Capital Expenditure" budgeting model: a relatively large fund is raised to procure raw materials and building labor when a renovation or a new building is needed. This process works well for the long life span of a building project, but it can actually be a disservice to technology unless careful planning mitigates the following risks:

- The large technology component of the building project quickly overwhelms the existing staff, whose resources have not been adjusted to address the change.
- Over time, systems fall into disrepair or obsolescence because renovation of technology systems is anchored to the funding and timing of the next building renovation.
- Users are hesitant to innovate in the planning phase, and spaces identified for experimentation are abandoned once built, because stakeholders are not invested, have no champion who "owns" the vision for the space, or are not funded to reengage in a process of constant improvement.

Software Licenses	Every Year
Computers	2-4 Years
Computer Peripherals	3-5 years
IT Wireless	3-5 Years
AV Systems & Equipment	< 7 Years
IT Closet Equipment	4-8 Years
IT Cabling	6-12 Years

NOTE: These values are approximated from the CoreData (Educause, 2016) database and are in many cases higher than industry recommendations for future best practices.

We recommend institutions project the impact to future annual operational costs, in addition to the up-front technology installation costs, when considering a high-technology renovation of an information commons. In particular, there may be systems (such as data storage centers or spaces for experimentation with new technologies) where the resources required to satisfy the mission (such as regularly testing new instructional technologies) is equal to or greater than the initial build-out of the renovated space. At the very least, planning should accommodate regular maintenance replacement cycle of technology on a period of 2-5 years for equipment (e.g., computers, printers) and every 5-10 years for integrated systems (e.g., audiovisual systems, data network).

The concept behind this funding model often helps to free information commons planners and stakeholders from the burden of "getting it right, right now." It is also the basis of several trends (such as Rapid Prototyping/Perpetual Beta/Technology Sandboxes), which will be discussed in additional depth in later sections of this chapter.

Applications for Technology in the Learning Commons

The following sections investigate common trends in the information commons and other places where a similar mission has been integral in the planning and application of technology. These scenarios vary from the commonplace to the unconventional. Though futuristic in focus, these scenarios could be enacted today using existing technologies to support the institutional needs of research, teaching, and learning. Where possible we have included case studies or sample applications to capture specific ways in which a mission or idea developed into a real space with a technological solution.

Everyday Technology: Core Technologies to Support the Commons

Modern technology planning, like any other aspect of planning for the information commons, is as much about how the whole puzzle fits together as it is about the individual pieces. A well-thought-out space includes the right mix of spaces, uses, and technologies to support the diverse range of activities within. In addition to the individual applications (technologies and spaces that serve a focused need, such as a group study room or makerspace) there are technological concepts that can connect the entire building and aid in unifying the entire commons ecosystem. Following are some examples.

Activating the Building: Power and Data Access

How do you make sure your information commons will be active—that people will want to come and stay and engage with each other and the space? Common logic suggests that lots of power outlets and good wireless connectivity are important; but our own research indicates they are the most important place to start.

Activating a space is often as simple (or as challenging) as satisfying the basic needs of the users. While information commons spaces often offer a variety of spaces to accommodate a wide range of activities, there are a few basic core provisions, such as bathrooms, that are required to ensure the space is hospitable. With the increased reliance on mobile computing and mobile devices, reliable access to the following is now considered a necessary utility (NextGov, 2015):

AC Power Outlets—Users need a place to keep their laptop running or charge up a mobile device. Providing a large complement of accessible outlets is key to ensuring users visit and stay without cables strewn across the floor (or similar scenes from the airport terminal). Ample power also improves future flexibility in the integration of technology in the space. Some recommendations:

- Table boxes, power strips, etc. integrated into furniture, particularly tables and carrels
- A regular pattern of floor boxes with power in "lounge" areas where seating can be moved—this may lead to access flooring that can be reconfigured to continuously refine the layout of floor power as building use patterns develop
- Power strips along low-traffic walls or where furniture abuts walls (e.g., benches, café tables)
- Designated charging stations inside and outside the building in places where people will naturally congregate (e.g., lounge furniture, park benches, café servery tables)

Wireless Data (Wireless Access Points, or "WAPs")—By now there is little disagreement that users depend on a robust wireless network throughout an information commons. However, the planning and design of wireless networks often underestimates the demand for bandwidth and future growth needs (especially with emerging trends in media consumption and software/virtualization, discussed later in this chapter). As a planning tool, we frequently recommend providing a grid of wireless access points to accommodate between three and five connected devices per user.

Phone Data and Communications; the Distributed RF Antennae System ("DAS")—Many of the materials developed for new ecologically friendly buildings/renovations, such as high-insulation glass windows, also reduce the sort of signals used for mobile phone data service and two-way security radios. A DAS system repeats or "leaks" these signals back into the building to restore key services. Identifying and planning ahead for this need avoids many surprises and complaints that send users away shortly after a building opens.

Wayfinding and Scheduling

One of the greatest successes of any information commons is that the people using it feel comfortable navigating through and finding the resources they need. The application to library media, a card catalog search, is clear. But what if technology empowered space users (e.g., students, staff, and faculty) to find rooms (and librarians or commons staff) and manage room schedules (e.g., reserve rooms, find their meeting) on their own? There are several established or emerging technologies that apply, including:

Room Signage and Scheduling Displays—These systems typically include small screens at the entrance for each room or area that are capable of displaying the day's schedule for the space and indicate if/when a space is open and available for use. These screens frequently connect to a larger buildingwide scheduling system that allows staff to manage access and calendars. More advanced systems integrate with the building environment to shut down and start up lights and heating/cooling as needed, saving power. These systems may also or alternatively interface with user mobile devices, offering additional scheduling and building navigation from a smartphone or tablet.

Augmented reality uses the camera and screen of a user's mobile device to provide a navigational map overlay, and additional interactive information, of the spaces in a fashion similar to the "Pokemon Go" game.

Integrating Technology into the Information Commons

These types of technological solutions enhance the sense of community and help users orient to and distribute through the commons space.

Security and Physical Asset Management

The rapid pace of innovation in security technology is an often overlooked but major contributor to the conversion of libraries into commons spaces. Specifically, technology has made security more sophisticated, allowing commons spaces to control access (and limit risk) without having to rely on the traditional narrow mazes of corridors and desks and cumbersome rings of keys. Cameras, keypads, and swipe cards are able to more closely follow special assets (such as expensive technology equipment or rare collections), and RFID tags can turn an entire building into its own guardian, preventing a rare book from ever leaving.

More importantly, better security has the paradoxical effect of physically opening up space and giving planners more confidence to provide assets, such as rare books once locked out of sight behind closed doors, a more visible presence in front of the commons community. At the Brody Learning Commons in Johns Hopkins, this allowed the archivists to create an entire restoration lab that is visible to the public and includes digital displays that offer a museum-like interpretation of the day-to-day activities of the staff inside. Security cameras (and cameras embedded into fume hoods and other apparatus) can be transmitted to screens outside the space for more visibility, and visitors frequently comment on a newfound appreciation.

Building-as-Sensor

Occupancy sensors, smart thermostats, any of the technologies above, and myriad other appliances within a building can be used to test ideas and learn more about the space of the learning commons.[6] For instance, research at NIH was able to program a building to study its own patterns of occupancy and heating/cooling to learn (and proactively adjust the system for) busy and quiet moments, improving productivity and saving energy (Yun, 2012). At Montclair University, the library and academic computing departments collaborated to create a dashboard that shows all computer labs/computer work areas, each represented with a pie chart showing how many computers are in use at that moment. This system was initially launched around 2012 as an experiment to see which areas were the most used (and needed expansion), but students quickly began to access the system and use it to find less crowded locations, thus self-correcting and balancing use.

The same concept may be used to integrate across multiple systems in new and innovative ways—linking the exterior lighting system to the campus news feed, for instance, to illuminate the building in school colors during special events or important sports victories.

Technology for Exchange: The Commons as Social and Idea Nexus

The information commons is emerging as an important player in the collaborative nexus where ideas and disciplines can be intermingled to find new opportunities. In the past two decades, academia has begun to acknowledge that in addition to exploring deeper, new frontiers can be forged when people from different disciplines collaborate on a common topic (Gazni, Ali, and Dedgah, 2011).

The information commons is often the ideal location to host cross-pollination, and providing high-technology platforms for collaboration enhances this purpose—a mix of curated spaces, where collaboration is facilitated by knowledgeable commons staff,[7] and open-use spaces.

Open Experiences: Rapid Prototyping, Perpetual Beta, and Technology Sandboxes.

There are some functions that are best left open-ended or available for all, as places where users can engage with each other and the commons environment to expand institutional horizons. Some example applications include:

- The Technology "Sandbox"—Designated spaces where new technological explorations can be tested with little sense of risk. New ideas can be rapidly prototyped and bolted onto a skeleton system and evaluated. If successful, an initial concept can be further refined and deployed to other spaces as a new standard. If unsuccessful, the process can be a useful tool in defining future successes.
- Commons "Perpetual Beta" Initiatives—Similarly, the staff and facility can be organized around a concept of constant adaptation. Students can be empowered to reconfigure furniture and partitions into a constantly evolving environment that adjusts to the context of the moment. Screens and research platforms can incorporate "high-velocity" information from social media or other sources into new exhibits and test environments.

Curated Experiences: The Concierge/Hosted Space

There are some functions where the careful attention and commitment of information commons staff can enhance the user experience. Some examples include:

- The "Service Front" where users are confident someone will have an answer to their quest or concern, such as:
    - An IT campus-technology and user device help-desk, similar to the "Genius Bar" in an Apple retail store, staffed by IT or student workers cross-trained to resolve a wide array of user technology issues on-site.
    - Hands-on competency-based learning spaces, including student "technology sandboxes" or "train-the-trainers" spaces for faculty. These environments often include trained information commons staff who can assist users in orienting themselves to and gaining competency in new, rare, or esoteric technologies.
    - The incubator space, where a diverse range of the information commons community (local entrepreneurs, faculty, students, information commons staff) can work together to quickly refine and expand ideas in serendipitous or curated moments, such as "hackathons."
- Makerspaces and Media/Technology Labs, where equipment and supplies are available to produce or fabricate using new methods, including:
- Green screens, motion capture, and video editing software
- Flatbed printers, letter presses, paint hoods, sewing machines, and silk screen or sublimation machines
- Modeling software and virtual reality visualization hardware
- Forensic tools and data visualization systems
- 3D printers and/or light—or heavy fabrication machinery

The Digital Era: Convergence, Digital Asset Management, and Software/Virtualization

Technology Convergence

As technology is maturing, various "silos of knowledge" are beginning to converge into one unified technology frontier. For instance, consider the evolution of the computer cable:

- VGA cables transmitted analog signals (a bit like a modem) from computer to projector;
- DVI and HDMI cables introduced more precise digital video but still used cables and connectors unique to the AV industry.
- New standards, such as AVB and HDBaseT, migrate audiovisual signals over to IT Data cabling (such as Cat6 cables with Ethernet data jacks) and, in some cases, use IT or "IP-like" Ethernet data packets to transmit signals.

In addition, the BYOD (bring your own device) movement has enhanced convenience with connectivity through the wireless data network, in many cases obviating the need for Audio/Video cabling at all.

Essentially, AV and IT technologies are migrating together into one unified digital platform. Within a building IT and AV systems will use the same infrastructure and core equipment, allowing AV equipment to be reconfigured anywhere there is access to the building's data network.

These advancements open up the possibility for multimodal collaboration: content from a student screen can be ported to an instructor's tablet wirelessly, where the instructor annotates additional feedback in real time. While the instructor walks around, his or her screen display is shown on a wall-mounted screen and on the nearby table surfaces. Other students' screens are filled with support information (closed captioning, enhanced content from the textbook) until the instructor completes the demonstration, saves the new file, and instantly transmits an updated version to all devices. Within the hour a recording and transcript of the session is available from the learning management system.

After the session the tables, screens, cameras, and speakers are disconnected from data jacks in the floors and walls and reconfigured for the next use: a meeting with the provost.

Digital Asset Management

In the last edition, we explored the possibility of integrating physical and digital text into a unified searchable database. Today these portals are largely well established, and new levels are being built upon this foundation. First is the expansion and consolidation of all databases into one institutionwide system, incorporating text, photo, video, music, and other contextual information into one rich research and discovery platform. This provides different users (or the same user who may have a wide array of needs) access to the full spectrum of services and materials from one searchable platform.

These systems can also be expanded to supply data on context and use—how many different ways has an historic photo of the first campus hall been searched for and reused in other archived assets—that can inform and refine administration of the system. This context can also be used to link up and streamline similar research efforts or resources.

The Continued Rise of Software and Virtualization

Increasingly, collaborative software platforms are providing alternate solutions for hardware-based AV and IT systems. For instance, web conference collaboration tools like Skype, Zoom, or WebEx provide a similar service to hardware "videoconference codec" appliances such as Cisco/Tanberg or Polycom.

When compared to hardware-based systems, these software solutions are often available for a lower initial "build cost" but require regular (usually annual) renewal fees. They can be fully upgraded as new versions of software/firmware are made available (but also increase the administrative overhead to monitor and deploy updates and "roll back" or reverse them should bugs appear).

In addition, a large blade server on campus can simulate hundreds or thousands of individual computers, accessible over the network, within the space of a broom closet. The experience of using these virtual machines is indistinct from having one on the desk next to you (other than less clutter) but allows the commons to give its users access to a wide range of special and unique resources from any location in the commons (or even from their own kitchen tables). Examples include:

- Special terminals and research platforms, such Bloomberg or CANARIE
- Licensed software such as GIS or CAD
- Research databases and other subscription research portals

The future promise is of a technology environment where every device is enabled with software smarts that, once on the network, can be interconnected and used in flexible and ever-current ways. When users experiment with a new teaching environment and determine a feature is missing, they can work with the information commons staff to upload new apps and reconfigure the system within minutes. Every space can be "in perpetual beta" to the extent that each room recognizes the identity of its user and uploads his or her preferred room type. Based on the personal or room schedule, the room automatically connects the user, through their tablet, to a session with a virtual computer loaded with the correct software and then opens up the correct media files from the Digital Asset Management System. The room has already been cooled to everyone's liking and adjacent spaces are cooling in advance of breakout sessions that will happen in approximately 35 minutes (this instructor frequently runs long).

Conclusion

Today's information commons represents a snapshot in the evolution, from libraries of the past to a wide range of cutting-edge collaboration and experimentation opportunities in the future. While these spaces will continue to evolve and shift, the importance of technology as an integral part of their mission will not. Information commons will always provide access to tools and resources that are out of reach to the average user, and will serve as a central hub to bring all those users together as a market for idea exchange.

The information commons is an abstract ideal and can be difficult to define. The "commons" isn't delivered through any one technology, facility, or service but rather in the thoughtful convergence and application of many supporting parts into a place that is unified by a modern mission. The next year's information commons will have evolved to incorporate new functions and opportunities, but its vision to serve as the central facilitator to its communities is less of a moving target.

Notes

1. While the information commons concept has historically evolved from libraries, we, the authors of this book, believe the future of the information commons and its variants doesn't need to be anchored to library renovations. The concept of a modern technology and information resource can be applied to many other communities and locations. This includes makerspaces, collaboration platforms, conferencing and event spaces, and incubators.
2. Literally: teknologia is interpreted as "systematic treatment" from a Greek portmanteau of the words for "art" and "craft" (OED, 1997). Scholars in many fields often link "technology" with the concept of "tool use," which is also a helpful planning framework to take a step back and think of technology as simply a tool to accomplish the work needed (Seeley, 2006).
3. Risk profile can often be shaped by limited resources, including knowledge and funding (discussed later). Addressing these resources may be an important part of the planning process and opening up to technology innovation.
4. See also later discussions in this chapter about the evolution of the information commons as the nexus for ideas. Are there opportunities for interdepartmental/intramural collaborations at the early planning stages for technology that might expand the horizons of the core information commons stakeholders?
5. A third factor, the emerging trend of software replacing hardware, may help hedge some planning risk but also has implications for budgeting. This trend is discussed in greater detail later in this chapter.
6. We acknowledge this is not a concept to be taken lightly. Conversations about civil liberties are beyond the scope of this book, but care should be taken to ensure and reassure no individual's personal information is captured. None of the technologies discussed are, at present, capable of tracking and acquiring unauthorized personal information. We also recommend consulting the IT administration responsible for information security.
7. This is the role of the librarian, rephrased and repurposed for the learning commons context.

Chapter 5

Designing Flexible Spaces

Summer Cook and Betsy Maddox

The collaborative and bright information commons prevalent today exists in contrast to the traditional learning areas found in many established higher education facilities. In avoiding interior updates, these university libraries lack the infrastructure to support what is now essential everyday technology. Their valuable real estate is still supporting immense reference volumes and older information processes. With the digital storage available today for reference materials, that space could be working better for the school as an attraction and support system for faculty, staff, and students.

For information commons to be effective, they must balance human needs. They should provide space for expressing ideas through writing, drawing, listening, and speaking along with the technological tools students and staff require to be successful in the twenty-first century. Of course, being in the twenty-first century means facing constantly changing factors like rapid advancements in technology, evolving learning methods, tighter construction budgets, restricted space, green building requirements, and requests from incoming leadership, to name just a few.

What if spaces were originally designed and built to support ongoing change, both large and small? What if we shift our mindset to fully embrace and celebrate the ignorance of not knowing what the future holds while being perfectly poised to adapt to it?

The relationship between our built environment and how we interact with it is a complex one, particularly in education spaces. Now, more than ever, faculty, staff, and students seek environments to support their unique goals through a combination of aesthetics, function, and multiuse adaptability. Architects and designers are tasked with creating spaces that simultaneously support multiple group sizes, various levels of collaboration, emerging technologies, and future flexibility, all on time and on budget. Decision makers, meanwhile, understand that every decision could ultimately impact the lives of generations to come. On top of all this, the information commons in particular is meant to be a place of innovation, plentiful information, and a physical demonstration of the school's approach to advancements in technology.

It's a tall order for all involved.

Flexibility Is Crucial

Simply stated, a flexible interior is a permanent solution to ongoing change. It is vital to the creation and/or maintenance of a successful information commons because the biggest obstacle to updating a space, whether it is a relatively small change like changing out technology or a large one like repurposing rooms, is the pain, cost, and time of demolition and construction. However, if the information commons is built with adaptive building materials, it remains an effective learning zone no matter the changes that come. Interiors that embrace flexibility protect the initial investment, support changing goals, meet diverse needs, and embrace technology.

Adaptive prefab has been present in commercial office environments for decades and has been variously called modular, demountable, or movable. And while technically adaptable to changing needs, this "movable" idea of prefab was rife with restrictions and came only in standard sizes, aesthetics, performance capabilities, and with limited configurations.

Recent advancements in technology alter the whole idea of prefab by removing dimensional restrictions, improving the overall quality, and integrating high performance into the built environment. Surprisingly, we can attribute these improvements in prefab capabilities to video game technology. That industry's graphical, real-time interactive, 3-D experience is added to engineering and design technology. This new form of communication informs and empowers all the stakeholders on the school's team. Everyone gets instant feedback on the aesthetics, performance, and price during design iterations, which are shown and interacted with in 3-D. Once the design is approved, it goes directly to the prefab production facility floor, where the 3-D experience becomes physical components used to build the information commons. The products are designed, engineered, and built to allow for fast, clean construction and downstream renovations where there is no down time, noise, or labor costs

This video game platform, when applied to computer aided design (CAD) software for the construction and manufacturing industries, supports ultimate customization. The result? Interiors that precisely align with the school's goals.

In the planning of a new information commons or renovations to an existing space within an old building, the effects are felt at every stage of construction. In the planning stage, visual communication ensures relevant parties understand a potential design and can make modifications as necessary without translating 2-D drawings. Confident decisions are made quickly and expectations are managed from the start.

With this technology, complexity isn't punished. Pricing is based on the amount and quality of materials used, not according to deviations from a standard offering. With design freedom, flexible interiors are prefabricated to meet the exact needs of the space, new or old, and built with long-term adaptability and function in mind. Modifications in the design phase are instantly reflected in updated pricing, scheduling, and all other specification data, so impacts are known immediately.

When tight schedules require a project to be completed during an academic break, for example, if a university library is being updated into an innovative information commons before students start their year, this method is the most logical option.

Off-site manufacturing means other construction trades work on a clean, open, and safer job site. The simplification of their portion of the project should lead to lower labor requirements and therefore more competitive bids. This ensures the budget for the project remains the same or is less in spite of the higher level of fit and finish and performance of the information commons.

Prefab components such as quick-connect power and data, wall frames, glazing, millwork, and doors arrive on the job site in the sizes specified, ready to quickly tilt up and click together. Due to the precision of the software and its ability to feed the approved design directly to the production machines, the manufacturing time is 2–4 weeks and total construction time is one-third faster. On the job site there are no off-cuts, drywall dust, or indoor air quality issues to contend with. Several information commons projects have been accomplished during the school calendar. That same factory precision, paired with advanced design and specification software, means flexible solutions can fit unique base buildings and can be created to smoothly integrate with the existing aesthetic or brand.

Adapting to Advancements in Technology

Wall-embedded technologies that support the information commons need to protect the equipment while keeping it accessible to the facilities and IT departments. Prefab walls designed with removable skins and universal mounting brackets mean that technologies such as TV monitors, acoustics management technology, tablets, and more can be maintained or updated during a commons' opening hours, with minimal concerns about noise or reduced air quality.

This flexible prefab approach puts user-focused design considerations front and center from the get-go. Technologies and design elements that support diverse needs can be

Writable surfaces
Source: Summer Cook/Betsy Maddox

Designing Flexible Spaces

integrated during the planning phase and then updated to meet changing needs throughout the duration of that information commons' life cycle. The school has the freedom to build an environment that elevates performance now and into the future with details such as wheelchair-accessible wall technologies, acoustics management, writable surfaces, and custom graphics.

Teams that have experienced the impact flexible building interiors have in the information commons setting report improved learning outcomes and experiences for the people using those spaces. Staff and faculty can be better supported with up-to-date environments that support evolving curriculums and technologies found in everyday business, while students may access spaces that support unique learning goals and embrace constant state-of-the-art technologies.

Education teams prove through experience that flexibility built into information commons has a realized and long-term positive impact by creating a space that supports ongoing change and remains relevant in the long term.

Case Study 1: Northern Arizona University Cline Library Learning Studio, Completed 2014

Location
Flagstaff, Arizona

Project Abstract
With its largest freshman class ever about to start the academic year, Northern Arizona University's space was at a premium. The university's library, Cline Library, had an infrequently used space. The university chose to remodel their existing microform storage room into a next-generation learning space for students and faculty.

The new Cline Library's Learning Studio is now a highly configurable, advanced technology classroom space in an environment that's seamless and intuitive to use. It's about 2,500 square feet and has seating and laptops for up to 70 students and writable glass surfaces throughout, among many other features.

The goals of the project were as follows:
- Create a student-centered, active learning, technology-enriched, high-engagement classroom.
- Increase faculty options for designing, using, and evaluating a learning environment in a highly flexible space.
- Incorporate universal design furnishings and concepts into a collaborative student space.
- Expand and deepen faculty collaboration with college librarians.
- Increase integration of the library's digital content into courses.
- Provide a learning environment with technology support provided by library staff.

The project team achieved these goals through many initiatives. First, it pulled design components from similar SCALE-UP models. For instance, there is no "front of the classroom" where a faculty member delivers a lesson to students. Rather, the classroom itself becomes the third teacher, in conjunction with the teacher and the students themselves. All walls serve the universal purpose of engaging students more deeply through high- and low-tech

Northern Arizona University Cline Library Learning Studio
Source: Summer Cook/Betsy Maddox

means. LCD screens live in the walls behind writable glass, and the walls flanking the technology are writable as well.

Second, the planning team identified 30 staff members who were interested in teaching in the new studio and had technology expertise to offer. They collaborated as a team through meetings, surveys, and conversations, and the learning studio began to take shape. These staff members served as ambassadors for the new space, ensuring that the rollout went as smoothly as possible.

And third, technology has become the "new normal," and the space had to support their needs today and well into the future. According to NAU, a successful technology classroom breaks down the barriers to success by creating a simple, elegant interface that provides the tools students and faculty need, with an underlying infrastructure that can be changed and expanded upon as the demands on the library evolve over time.

Jill Koelling-Friedman, the library project manager and Assistant Dean of Cline Library, contends that the biggest factor in their choice to go with DIRTT-manufactured construction was its versatility. This meant that not only could the wall solution serve two different purposes on either side, but they could move it around if they wanted to. They haven't had to ... yet.

Sources:
https://library.nau.edu/services/learningstudio/
https://library.nau.edu/services/learningstudio/proposal.html

Case Study 2: University of Iowa Library Commons

Location
Iowa City, Iowa

Project Abstract
This university was faced with finding ways to support students while still dealing with the residual real estate losses due to the local river flooding through the campus. The school decided to turn a 37,000-square-foot administration area in the library building into a flexible and interactive learning commons. Collaborative study rooms, informal study nooks, writable walls, bright graphics, integrated millwork, and technology are among the features of this bright, airy learning area. Feedback from students within the space is excellent. Somewhat surprisingly, they were universally drawn to using the dry-erase walls to write on, but took a little longer to take advantage of the large screens and computers integrated behind the writable glass walls. In fact, some of the film in the space was not writable, yet it enticed students to carry their thoughts onto it. The school has since replaced that film with a writable version.

For the A/V equipment that is continually experiencing updates, the university's director of learning spaces technology is pleased his team can easily access the A/V equipment and quick-connect electrical and data housed inside the walls without subcontractors to cut into and repair drywall. Brittney Thomas is the Coordinator of the University of Iowa's Learning Commons. For her the technology integration is vital to stay ahead of the curve. "This technology is new and emerging right now," said Thomas. "But in five years it might not be. When we're flexible like that we can really give the students what they need."

The architect on this project was surprised a system that included prefab walls could be produced to match both the design and the difficult base-building conditions. He was also appreciative of the short manufacturing lead time that allowed the team to choose the best technology at the last possible, responsible minute. "We didn't know what technology was going inside this wall system until about six months before move-in," said Kent Lutz (Smith Metzger). "To have a prefab system that can be designed to suit whatever is chosen and then work with a six-week lead time to manufacture, deliver, and build is invaluable."

Case Study 3: University of Texas, Perry-Castaneda Library

Location
Austin, Texas

Project Abstract
This university felt a need to update its library's circulation desk and admin area. These areas were original from 1977. The main goals identified from the outset were to improve the overall flow of student and faculty traffic, to complete all construction over just two academic holiday breaks, and to have a space that met current technology processes while remaining adaptable to future needs. Construction had to be fast, and there needed to be a smooth transition time between the two phases of the project. A modular and premanufactured construction approach best met these critical goals.

Outcome: The university chose various elements that worked to meet their goal of improved traffic, while logistically the construction met necessary goals such as timelines and transition needs. Base-building characteristics included 3-D ceiling tile shapes and existing air distribution system. Flexible construction solution worked with these existing traits with minimum other requirements. Precision manufacturing and fast installation of the modular components met the university's tight timelines.

Case Study 4: Avila University, Learning Commons

Location
Kansas City, Missouri

Project Abstract
Avila University is a private Catholic university with a student body of about 2,000 graduate, undergraduate, and continuing education students. They are committed to small classroom sizes that top out at 40, and 47% of their students attend thanks to Avila's robust scholarship program. The mission of the university is to give students a life they never thought possible; however, the old library did not reflect this ambitious mission. Renovating it was a priority with many challenges. The construction had to be completed over the summer break, and donors needed to be assured that their monies would support a long-term solution. As most learning commons do, it had to accommodate many different types of spaces for individual or group work, a place for commuting students to touch down between classes, and technology-infused interior architecture to connect students beyond the walls of the school.

They chose to use manufactured interior construction to achieve their goals. The building components included access floor, modular power and data, solid and glass walls, doors, millwork, and A/V support. By using the interactive 3-D software that comes with the manufactured construction solution, the stakeholders were able to visually explore and make changes to the design. Everyone was informed and empowered to make decisions, whether they could read an architect's plan or not. The outcome looked and performed as expected, while meeting the

Avila University, Learning Commons
Source: Summer Cook/Betsy Maddox

Designing Flexible Spaces

Avila University, Learning Commons
Source: Summer Cook/Betsy Maddox

budget and the accelerated schedule. "I think it's a tremendous asset to this university," said Ronald Slepitza, Avila's president. "It says, 'This is an environment dedicated to your learning and dedicated to your success as a student by providing optimal technology and space for interaction and collaborative learning.'"

For the donors, this method of construction ensured a long life cycle for their investment, as the space is futureproof and allows ongoing accessibility for the facilities team to make changes to power, data, or technology equipment. "What I would say about the modular power and data," explained Ronald Slepitza, "is it really enables us to, on the fly, swap out new screens, new modes of communication, new ways to connect students to their own devices to whatever is the future of technology."

Conclusion

Until now the speed and certainty of prefab construction could not overcome the compromises when it came to aesthetics, standard sizes, and integration with the rest of the building and its furniture, fixtures, and equipment. Due to advancements in object-oriented software combined with CAD, engineering, and even video game software, prefab is now appropriate for all educational environments.

In parallel, the prefab components referred to in these case studies bring adaptability to the information commons they were used to build. Each space is permanent and durable while simultaneously remaining accessible and flexible for the facilities and IT departments.

Avila University, Learning Commons
Source: Summer Cook/Betsy Maddox

Education environments carry a heavy responsibility to stay inspiring and provide appropriate tools for learners and educators. The physical space housing them is now able to pull its weight.

Chapter 6

Tying It All Together

Kelly Brubaker

Colleges and universities continue to focus on the design of physical spaces that support their institution's mission by creating unique research-focused environments that will advance them into the twenty-first century. When designing these spaces, it is important to consider the end-users—what their needs and expectations for these environments are, and what they might be in the future.

As generational patterns shift and Generation Y makes room for today's post-millennial Generation Z, institutions must understand that the needs and expectations of their students also are shifting. Where the Gen Y student typically seeks out a physical piece of equipment or space, such as a collaboration room, for a specific purpose, the Gen Z student is looking for an overall experience based on available devices, inspiring physical spaces, virtual connections, and a host of ancillary services not typically associated with libraries of the past.[1] They are used to being "connected" at all times, often using their smartphone, iPad, and laptop simultaneously, and are looking for cutting-edge, innovative spaces that align with all facets of their lives.

The information commons needs to adapt to these changing demands and incorporate flexibility and additional services to create a space that integrates collaboration, interdisciplinary learning, technology, and the creation of content. Evaluating existing spaces on campus and creating a vision for the future of the information commons is the first step in planning and designing a successful commons.

Evolution of the Information Commons

The original concept of the information commons was driven by the transition of campuses to a technology-rich learning environment. A number of commons were designed to reenergize the library, and many made improvements by consolidating circulation, reference, and technology support and by providing greater access to technology and collaborative environments. The design challenge today is to create a commons where research, discovery, ideation, and creation can occur in an interdisciplinary setting that provides support and services for students and faculty. Today's students are educated consumers who expect their university to adapt and refine spaces to meet their changing needs. Through a variety of surveys, students have indicated that they will not come to the commons if what they have at home is of higher quality—in terms of both technology and physical space.

Commons Planning Themes

There are many challenges and opportunities that both architects and institutions face when designing a new information commons or transforming an existing one. The following are themes that will help establish goals and set the vision for a revitalized commons:

- The Experience—Designing to create both an emotional and physical connection to the activities of the commons
- Partnerships and Services—Understanding what balance of partnerships and services will advance the commons and align with the university's mission
- Creation and Dissemination—Providing tools to encourage experimentation
- Technology—Planning for the intersection of physical and virtual aspects of technology
- Identity—Developing an identity that resonates with the campus community and reinforces signature programs and services

The Experience

All-Inclusive

Students and faculty seek out spaces that yield an all-inclusive experience. Commons planners should ask themselves what today's library patrons really want to see and experience, from first impressions to available services. The information commons is not one size fits all: Each commons should be customized to fit within the institution's mission and goals for program, space, and aesthetics.

Technology Presence

Access to cutting-edge technology is crucial to the experience of the commons, and patrons need to know the extent of what is available to them. Since some forms of immersive technology necessitate controlled environments located behind closed doors, interactive displays can be used to help showcase the full range of resources and programs available in the commons. Many institutions also employ these interactive displays to highlight content created by students, faculty, and staff as a way of broadcasting the type of leading-edge work being done across campus, thereby creating a greater sense of connection and pride.

Visibility and Connection

The ability of the space to provide visibility into its activities and to enhance students' sense of belonging and connection has a strong impact on the experience of the information commons. Visibility into collaboration rooms engages students in new ideas and exposes them to the innovation potential of active problem solving and research. In open spaces, students may utilize moveable white boards and furniture components, marker boards, or writeable glass walls to create their own personalized work zones for group problem solving. Glass walls allow visual connections into spaces that feature available tools and services, and also provide sightlines for supervision of the overall space.

Tying It All Together

Zoning

One key area of focus will be on the location of the information commons within the confines of the physical building. An information commons can be located front and center in the building, making the key services very visible, or it can be a destination, inviting patrons to engage with the building on their way to the commons. Commons hours of operation that vary from those of the larger building may play a role in its location.

Partnerships and Services

Information commons are civic spaces that are an extension of the campus community. Bringing patrons together for social exchanges and cross-disciplinary work involving a blend of cultures and programs should be a priority. A successful commons is one in which students, faculty, and community serendipitously interact with one another on a daily basis and are connected with tools and resources to advance their work.

Library, technology, and academic programs are developing partnerships to provide a cohesive academic support network for students. The commons may provide a home base for these services, or act as a central touch point for services dispersed across campus. Each institution needs to identify who the right partners are and how they will advance the purpose of the commons. It is important to understand that the partnerships that an institution brings in on day one will likely change over time and that the space design needs to allow for that flexibility.

At Salem State University, for example, the information commons is located on two floors of the library. Operationally it is not part of the library proper, and many of the services are funded through grants, which increase and decrease depending on funding cycles. The designers deliberately built flexibility into the layout of the space so that these services can expand or contract within the defined space of the commons. The layout located offices around the perimeter of shared open spaces to allow for the different departments to flex. A number of collaboration rooms were intermixed to allow for either future office or small group consultation space, creating multiuse zones

It is becoming increasingly common for libraries to partner with other services on campus and even with outside businesses to provide commons patrons with a wide range of options to meet their needs. Partnering with local businesses provides students and faculty with research and learning opportunities beyond the classroom. As partnerships evolve, business incubators and entrepreneurship commons will become key spaces that support academic scholarship. How these new partnerships manifest within the learning commons will vary among institutions. If space is limited and the commons is unable to provide dedicated space for its partners, a flexible "touch-down" or "hoteling" space that can be repurposed when not in use could be incorporated into the design. The commons space can host seminars or workshops led by their partners to highlight tools and resources located elsewhere on campus. Understanding how patrons will use the space and access the services provided will guide the planning of the commons so that it works for the institution in the context of its overall network of learning environments.

Creation and Dissemination

Physical spaces that support innovation and experimentation, and allow patrons to conduct research, experiment, prototype, and disseminate content, are increasingly being provided by the information commons.

For contemporary scholars pushing creative and intellectual boundaries, the revamped commons provides a one-stop shop with equal access to resources for all of its users, regardless of level or discipline. The expertise of the commons staff supports students and faculty in learning how to use its tools and resources. Providing the right mix of spaces that allows for maximum creativity is important and should include both individual and collaborative spaces that encourage experimentation.

The David B. Weigle Information Commons at the University of Pennsylvania serves as a central hub that brings together teaching, research, and learning partnerships across campus. It provides a central point of access to tools and resources that allow students and faculty to discover, create, and imagine what is next.

At Ringling College of Art and Design, a creation space provides students with the tools to take their ideas to the next level of development. The Project Work Room is outfitted with a sink, magnetic whiteboard, tools such as large paper cutters, and flexible furniture to allow for variable layouts. This space encourages physical and digital hands-on experimentation with art projects that are inspired by the library's collections and resources.

The Workshop, located on the lower level of Cabell Library at Virginia Commonwealth University, houses the Innovative Media department. This space encourages interdisciplinary work between faculty and students by providing support and guidance to advance coursework through technology. It is a central place on campus that encourages exploration of both physical and digital prototyping and is accessible to all students, regardless of their major. The Workshop provides many resources, services, and workspaces in a creative environment that blends the use of both physical and virtual tools through specialized software, a makerspace, and audio/visual studios. The service desk located at the entrance of The Workshop, as well as the staff workspaces directly adjacent to the open computer stations, create a sense of readily accessible support. The transparent glass walls reveal the activities that are taking place within, while the versatile layout and furnishings of the immediately adjacent spaces will allow The Workshop to easily expand hours and resources in the future.

Technology

Technology-rich spaces should provide access to equipment and resources that exceed student and faculty expectations. Power, power, and more power, along with high-speed, high-capacity wireless networks, are the most frequently requested assets. Looking beyond initial infrastructure investments, space design needs to prioritize the accommodation of continually changing technology.

There is a distinct shift in how younger generations use technology. Vision Critical, a leading customer intelligence platform, conducted an extensive study that looked at the most-used devices on an "average of hours/week" basis and found that Gen Z uses smartphones, TV, and then laptops the most. They are also more apt to use sound- and video-rich social media platforms such as YouTube, Periscope, and Houseparty for their everyday communication.[1] As designers, educators, and librarians, we need to understand how the preferred content sharing methods of postmillennials are becoming new platforms for learning.

The commons can double as both instructional space and experimental space for students and faculty. It can also serve as a place where faculty can engage with the latest technology and seek

Cabell Library at Virginia Commonwealth University
Source: Kelly Brubaker

support on how to incorporate it into their instruction. Virtual reality is now being integrated into instruction and research, and the commons should be able to support not only the full range of technology available today but also future technology platforms.

The Smith Learning Theater in the Gottesman Libraries at Teachers College, Columbia University, for example, provides a transformable learning space that can be used for scenario planning, immersive learning, and education research. To meet the varying research needs of the faculty and students, the space includes a rich and versatile audio/visual tool kit that provides capabilities for broadcasting, recording, and playback, as well as large-scale visual display through screens and the use of walls, ceiling, and floors as projection surfaces.

Supporting Technology

As technology becomes ever more prevalent, additional staff and space are needed to support it. In determining the level and type of staff support, it is important to consider technology assistance as closely integrated with other teaching, learning, and research services that may also have roles in the commons. While it may be ideal to have support staff adjacent to technology-rich zones, role descriptions and space pressures may make this difficult to achieve. Does the staff need to have a permanent presence, or can they rotate through a service point or "hotel" in the space during peak hours? Imagine a self-service model where staff is paged when support is needed for a more personal experience, thereby meeting demand as it arises and creating time to focus on other critical tasks.

Versatility

In any given 24-hour period commons spaces and technologies will need to accommodate many different activities. Design of an acoustically controlled room with a flexible lighting system and reconfigurable furniture will allow a presentation practice room to double as a Skype interview room or transform into a group collaboration space. A room that meets needs for both privacy and visibility, depending on use, may be created through the use of smart, electrochromic glass that can transition from clear to opaque when the room is "in session."

Content Showcase

Digital display screens prominently positioned throughout the commons can be used to highlight services and tools available. When staff time is available for content creation, screens can be used to promote commons projects and to highlight student and faculty work that the greater campus community might not be aware of.

Technology continues to evolve at a lightning pace, with new models, devices, and upgrades coming on the market daily. The commons will need to keep pace in order to meet patrons' expectations but also need to work within the institution's budget. Alternative funding, such as grants available through tech companies, should be explored to ensure institutions offer modern technology that is at the forefront of design. Consumers have the option to upgrade a smartphone to the latest and greatest version by "renting" the device. Imagine if technology within the information commons could be treated the same way!

Identity

"Information Commons," "Learning Commons," "Innovation Commons," "Research Commons," and "Academic Commons" are just a few examples of how institutions name their information commons. Programmatic elements vary among institutions, and each needs to take into account the variety of spaces and services it wishes to include. The name "Learning Commons" or "Information Commons" sometimes has a negative connotation even though these spaces have already transitioned by bringing in additional partnerships and services to support student and faculty development.

As a result, many universities have pulled away from these traditional labels and have created names that better resonate with their clientele and mission. For example, Duke University has created The Link, which is their teaching and learning space, and The Edge, which is their research commons, to create a more site- and institution-specific brand identity. The SMART commons at The University of Minnesota has a variety of locations throughout campus to provide support for research, technology, and writings. SMART has created a brand identity that students and faculty recognize and associate with a consistent level of service and resources, no matter where it is located across campus.

Organizational Models

Our role as planners, librarians, and designers is to create spaces that address the challenges and opportunities that institutions encounter. The notion of the library has transformed from a model of information repository to one that offers a more focused space for acquiring knowledge of all types, making the concept of a commons more relevant than ever before. Where physical collections once occupied half or more of a library's footprint, now user services and learning environments constitute the majority of library space. Students expect innovative spaces that will both support and challenge them.

The five themes of Experience, Technology, Partnerships and Services, Creation and Dissemination, and Identity are the foundation of a leading-edge information commons. The goal of a commons is to create a space that is intentionally planned to foster research and innovation and to locate it at the heart of where campus teaching and learning activity takes place. The information commons is the nexus for advancing research, learning, and technology in an immersive environment. It is the crossroads of intellectual and social activity on campus.

A variety of factors play into the design of the information commons, including the size of the institution and whether the commons will be located in a renovated space or in new construction. Each has design implications in terms of what services and programs can be provided. The following are three organizational models into which information commons tend to fall:

> The Destination Commons
> The Distributed Commons
> The Library Is the Commons

The Destination Commons

The information commons was initially developed to create a technology-rich environment that moved the library into the digital age. It was often the center of activity, providing resources and services for students to collaborate, discover, and create content in a single location. The destination commons is a space within the walls of the library or is immediately adjacent to the library, creating a synergy between library resources and the services provided by the commons.

The Conaton Learning Commons at Xavier University, for example, is directly adjacent and connected via a large portal to the University's main library. By locating it outside the library proper,

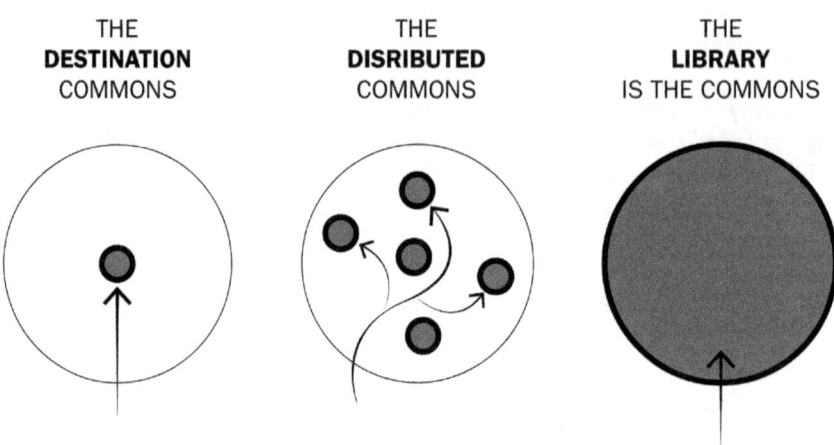

Three Organizational Models for the Information Commons
Source: Kelly Brubaker

the learning commons serves as the connector between social and academic services on campus. The Center for Teaching Excellence and a variety of teaching spaces are incorporated into the technology-enhanced space, which also houses community assets such as the digital media lab, classrooms, and an auditorium that double as experimental spaces for teaching and learning. Academic partners, such as the Math Lab, Reading Lab, and Language Lab, are all housed within the commons to provide additional resources to students in a central location.

The research commons of the Fenwick Library at George Mason University is a focal point of the library and encourages interdisciplinary work across all fields of study to advance student scholarship. The integrated combination of resources provides students and faculty with spaces that allow them to progress from discovery to content creation within a single hub. Subject specialists, the Writing Center, the Digital Scholarship Center, University Dissertation and Thesis Services, and the Special Collections Research Center are all within immediate adjacencies to one another in a flexible space that can accommodate additional tools and services as needs evolve. Patrons are connected with technology tools, collaboration spaces, and access to any necessary support to facilitate their work.

The Distributed Commons

As information commons evolved to provide a wide variety of services, some have shifted from a single destination to a distributed model. The distribution of services provides optimal adjacencies between library-focused programmatic functions and the other services provided in the learning commons. The activities in the commons become destinations within the library and often create their own sense of identity.

As part of the Perkins and Bostock Libraries at Duke University, there are several information common spaces distributed throughout the complex, each with its own identity, providing students with a clear understanding of the type of services being offered. These include, but are not limited to, the Link Teaching and Learning Center, The Edge: The Ruppert Commons for Research, Technology, and Collaboration, and the TWP (Thompson Writing Program) Writing Studio.

The Link Teaching and Learning Center at Duke is located in the lower level of Perkins Library and provides an innovative, technology-rich academic environment that is used for teaching during the day and transforms into patron space after hours. It is a flexible, collaborative setting that integrates technology into the spaces. The university's full-service technology help desk is located at the entry to the space. The media wall adjacent to the desk promotes large-scale content and data visualization as a valuable tool to foster the exploration of innovative teaching and learning methods.

The Edge, which encompasses the main floor of Bostock Library, provides access to research materials and technologies in an interdisciplinary environment that fosters collaboration to further student and faculty research. The variety of workspaces engages users to explore both individually and collaboratively with peers, highlighting a shared exploration of research. The mix of spaces allows students the freedom to formulate their own work environment by using flexible furniture and moveable whiteboards and provides access to different types of research in both the physical and virtual sense. A workshop room and a zone for social interaction complement a mix of project rooms, study nooks, and open research labs. Data-driven research is conducted in the Data Visualization lab with access to specialized software. The variety of resources and expertise offered by The Edge facilitates experimentation and provides the tools to collaborate, discover, and create.

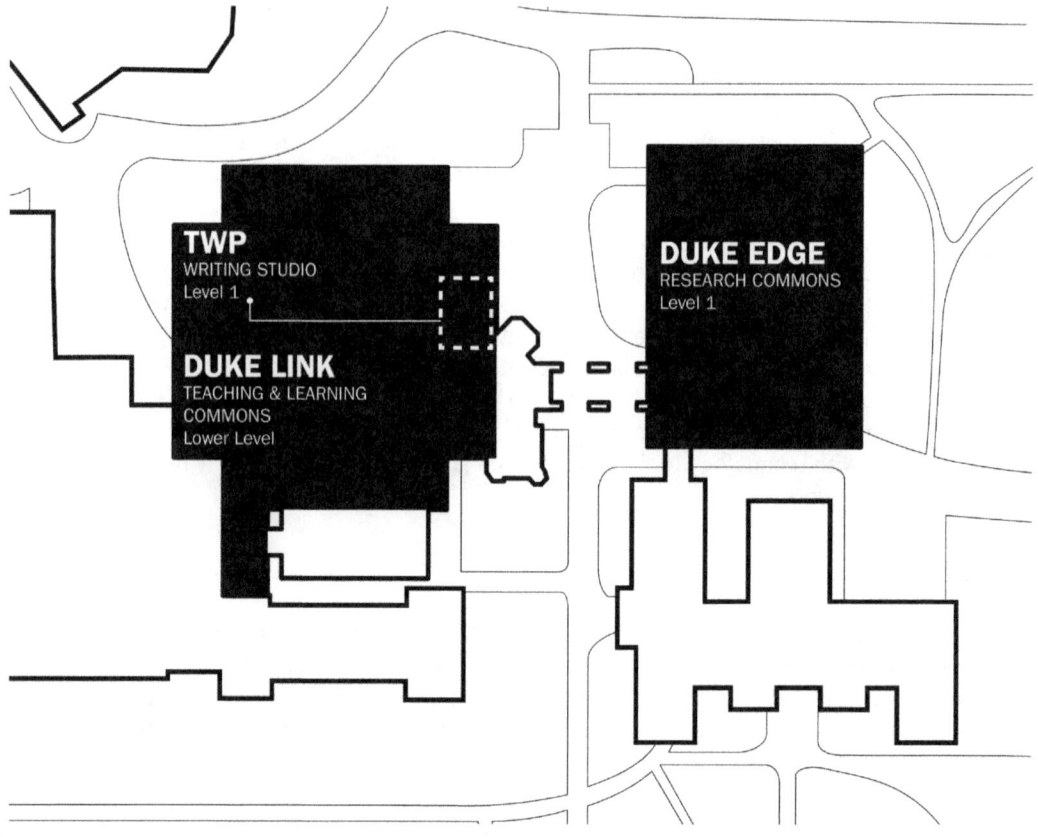

Perkins and Bostock Libraries at Duke University
Source: Kelly Brubaker

The TWP Writing Studio on the first floor of Perkins Library is a prime example of a library working with a partner to enhance the student's education. The studio offers the services of the Thompson Writing Program in a space outside the TWP's primary location on campus. The Studio's goal is to enhance students' critical and creative thought and help them improve their skills as writers through consultations, seminars, and a variety of workshops.

The Library Is the Commons

As services, resources, and technologies evolve, programs are becoming fully integrated such that all components of the library contribute to the information commons and vice versa. The commons is no longer a distinct space, but has transitioned to accommodate all the resources and services that support the academic mission of research, ideation, collaboration, and creation. In this model, the entire library is used for research from the discovery stage through creation and dissemination of content.

The commons is intended to stimulate both social and intellectual growth. Hesburgh Libraries at the University of Notre Dame, for example, created neighborhoods of services to support all areas of research. The first two floors of the library include active, public spaces that create a cohesive commons with sightlines and visibility to the variety of available services. Each of the neighborhoods has spatial, functional, and aesthetic commonalities that tie the library together.

The Teaching and Collaboration Hub is testing new technologies and positions a number of collaboration rooms adjacent to instructional spaces. This suite of flexible spaces can be used by campus partners during specified hours and is otherwise made available to students.

Technology Row is a technology-enhanced space that supports research through experimentation and creation. Several media presentation rooms allow for audio/video capture and creation. A visualization lab and high-tech classroom have been designed as flexible spaces to allow students and faculty to configure them to best meet their needs. A variety of workstations with integrated charging bars are located outside the specialty rooms and provide access to advanced computer programs. Students have enough room to work with multiple materials and devices. Digital displays will be located in the Tech Commons to highlight student and faculty work as well as available program and support services.

The Woodruff Library of the Atlanta University Center Inc. expanded its original learning commons from a contained area of computer work stations adjacent to the reference desk into a dynamic destination that encompasses the entire entry level of the library. Today, the commons integrates all programs located on the main entrance level, including media creation and presentation spaces, research support, multiuse teaching and learning studios, as well as a 24-hour study zone.

The Future of the Commons

As the information commons continues to evolve, it will reach beyond the walls of the library and weave its way through the entire campus, fully integrating resources for innovation and cross-disciplinary work. The emerging form for the library/commons is that of a central hub augmented by pop-up venues that create a campuswide network of support services for research and learning that break down disciplinary silos.

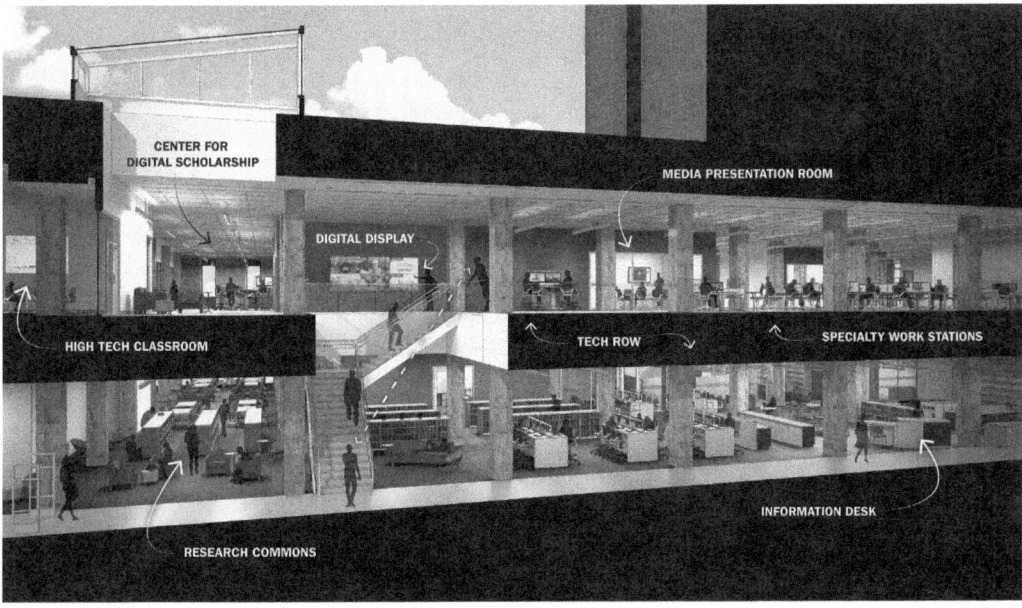

Hesburgh Libraries at the University of Notre Dame
Source: Kelly Brubaker

The library can be the impetus for innovation across campus. As a nondepartmental building, it can push the boundaries and be a resource for discovery and creativity. Since library space is often limited, it may not be possible to bring all of the desired services and partnerships into the commons: instead, the commons can act as the hub that seamlessly connects users to the wide array of resources and services available throughout campus.

Today's Gen Z students have higher expectations of what resources are available to them and are more focused on entrepreneurship opportunities than previous generations. They want to know that their university is pushing the envelope in terms of research and will give them access to the latest technologies. The possibilities are endless with innovation and interdisciplinary work. The question is, how will students navigate this quickly evolving array of options, and what support services will they need to succeed in the midcentury innovation environment? Today's carefully planned commons can provide a model. Analysis of usage patterns and spatial systems will illuminate how best to plan expanded networks of commons spaces that are designed to foster productive collaboration, promote interdisciplinary learning, and support groundbreaking research across campus.

Notes

1. Matt Kleinschmit, "Generation Z Characteristics: 5 Infographics on the Gen Z Lifestyle," *Vision Critical*, December 4, 2015. www.visioncritical.com/generation-z-infographics.

Part II
The Field Guide

Kristi Burns

Field Guide

The editors of *Beyond the Information Commons* created and distributed a Qualtrics survey to all of the institutions believed to have library integrated service programs or facilities called "Information Commons" or other related terms such as "Technology Commons," "Knowledge Commons," "Learning Commons," or "Makerspace." Part II of this book consists of the descriptive entries submitted by these institutions, as well as visual illustrations of what their commons look like, and floor plans that illustrate how they structured their space. The entries are divided into two parts: a quantitative section with summary data and a qualitative section with narrative response descriptions. Most questions were formatted as fill-in-the-blank with the exception of location and photo submission. In the event of a lack of specific information, the institution was encouraged to provide an informed estimate. If no answer was given for a question, the answer is represented as "n/a." Please refer to Appendix A for the complete survey form and instructions.

Claremont Colleges Library: Collaborative Commons
Claremont, California, USA

Carnegie Classification	
Basic:	Baccalaureate Colleges: Arts & Sciences Focus
Undergraduate Instructional Program:	Arts & sciences focus, no graduate coexistence
Graduate Instructional Program:	Postbaccalaureate: Single program-Business
Enrollment Profile:	Very high undergraduate
Undergraduate Profile:	Four-year, full-time, more selective, lower transfer-in
Size and Setting:	Four-year, small, highly residential

Total Student Enrollment: 30,484
Year established: 2016
Year of expansion/renovation: 2015-2016
Name: Collaborative Commons
Square footage of publicly available space associated with your facility: 5,000
Location: Main Library
Typical access hours per week: 106
Typical service hours per week: 106
Number of service points: 2
Number of desktop computers available for use: 1
Number of laptop computers available for use: 20
Other types of devices provided: Program is designed to encourage BYOD (Bring Your Own Device)
Average monthly door count: 54,000
Average monthly service transactions: 48,000

Workstation sessions/logins: 1,000
Library website: http://libraries.claremont.edu/

Purpose

The Claremont Colleges Library (CCL) proposes transforming the main open seating area in the Honnold Mudd building (H/M), adjacent to the North Entrance Lobby on the second floor, into a dynamic technology-enabled research, teaching, and learning space. This bright, new Collaborative Commons will enable teams from individual colleges or intercollegiate programs to engage in problem-based learning by utilizing Steelcase media:scape technology. The space will reflect students' desire for collaborative learning and combining social interaction with academic work. The area will also include other furnishings to facilitate individual study. Librarians, staff, and peer-to-peer student workers will populate this space, providing users with expertise, instruction, research consultation, information resources, and digital tools.

Services

General research technology and help services, all of which will be new in this tech-enabled space. Existing service unit will extend into the new space.

Software

The collaborative commons offers media:scape technology, laptops for checkout that include standard Microsoft Office software and Acrobat Pro for use with the mediascapes. Future enhancements will include all major webinar software clients as well. Support includes student staff at our Service Point to assist with basic troubleshooting, etc.

Print Resources

The Collaborative Commons is in proximity to our Special Collections reading room and other Main Service Points. This space will integrate print resources through breakout workshops with librarians and faculty as well as nearby print collections shelved throughout the building.

Collaborative Commons
Source: Claremont Colleges Library

Staff

Staffing in the Collaborative Commons is integrated into our Student Worker Program. Student staff are recruited across all seven Claremont Colleges and trained appropriately for basic technology troubleshooting as well as traditional service desk customer service, reference triage, etc. Student staff are present all hours the library is open and Research Assistance is scheduled regularly during most busy hours.

Funding/Budget

The source of our funding comes from Strategic Library Reserve and our parent organization's strategic reserve with ongoing management from parent organization. Staffing and programming is supported by the library's User Services division, expansion of staff and student presence to service points throughout the library.

Publicity/Promotion

Our communication plan consists of multiple levels and channels. Working with our parent organization's Director of Communications—marketing is targeted at higher-level administration and faculty. Outreach to students includes advertisements via locally posted signs and posters, social media, student worker program word of mouth, etc.

Collaborative Commons
Source: Claremont Colleges Library

Evaluation

Evaluation of the collaborative commons includes faculty and student focus groups and surveys, pre-and postassessment of the space itself, integration of informal feedback gathering via software such as TextnTell, etc. Outcomes and metrics are outlined in our strategic plan, which all assessment aligns with supporting.

Evolution of Facility

N/A—We're brand new!

Future Steps

Future plans include aligning and collaborating with other enhanced spaces within our library including our Digital Toolshed, Teaching and Learning Spaces, Digital Research Studio, etc. Future programming could also include enhanced campus tours, spillover reception and exhibit space, etc.

Dartmouth College: Jones Media Center
Hanover, New Hampshire, USA

Carnegie Classification	
Basic:	Doctoral Universities: Higher Research Activity
Undergraduate Instructional Program:	Arts & sciences focus, some graduate coexistence
Graduate Instructional Program:	Research Doctoral: STEM-dominant
Enrollment Profile:	Majority undergraduate
Undergraduate Profile:	Four-year, full-time, more selective, lower transfer-in
Size and Setting:	Four-year, medium, highly residential

Total Student Enrollment: 6,298
Year established: 2001
Year of expansion/renovation: 2015
Name: Jones Media Center
Square footage of publicly available space associated with your facility: 10,000
Location: Main Library
Typical access hours per week: 82
Typical service hours per week: 82
Number of service points: 2
Number of desktop computers available for use: 30
Number of laptop computers available for use: 30
Other types of devices provided: We have a large pool of circulating multimedia production equipment: digital cameras, video cameras, audio recorders, microphones, flatbed scanners, game consoles, projectors, lighting kits, graphics tablets, MIDI keyboards, hard drives, etc.
Average monthly door count: 5,500
Average monthly service transactions: 1,500
Workstation sessions/logins: 1,700
Library website: www.dartmouth.edu/~library/mediactr/

Purpose

The Jones Media Center was renovated to respond to changing patterns of usage, including: less reliance on microformat and analog materials, more collaborative work, increasing numbers of multimedia and multimodal course assignments, and more students engaged in creative production academically and personally. In addition, more students were seeking out the library as a destination, so we also sought to increase overall seating capacity. Finally, we wanted to offer different types of study and work spaces that may not readily exist on campus currently, such as a studio space, gaming space, and an audio recording facility.

Services

The Jones Media Center continues to be the primary location to access physical audio and video recordings, with over 30,000 DVDs, videotapes, CDs, CD-ROMs, and cassette tapes. The collection now includes video games, PC games, and tabletop games. In addition, the JMC offers a wide range of multimedia production hardware, including video cameras, digital still cameras, audio recorders, microphones, and light kits, which we regularly replace to remain current. While we do not offer traditional reference services, we do offer advice and assistance on multimedia production, both hardware and software, and run a limited number of workshops each term. With the new facility, we now offer more support for light-duty studio production techniques, such as green screen videography, and are hosting more events on-site.

Jones Media Center
Source: Dartmouth College

Software

The majority of our computers are Apple iMacs running multimedia software, including: Final Cut Pro, iMovie, the Adobe Creative Cloud suite (Photoshop, Illustrator, Premier, InDesign, etc.), Logic Pro, GarageBand, Motion, and After Effects. We also offer free and/or open-source software such as Gimp, Inkscape, and Audacity. We facilitate the academic use of media via the MediaHuman Audio Converter and the iSkySoft Media Converter applications. We offer and support the Microsoft Office 2016 applications as well as the Apple iWorks suite. For math and data visualization, we offer Mathematica, Maple, SPSS, State, R, Stella, and Cn3D. Additional software includes Final Draft, Github Desktop, jEdit, SourceTree, and iBooks Author. Our comfort and ability to support all the software varies, and many specialized packages are installed to support academic programs, though JMC staff may provide little to no direct support for those applications.

Print Resources

The Jones Media Center is located in the main campus library and is, therefore, in close proximity to the primary print collections and we are adjacent to the Evans Map Room, which houses an extensive collection of maps. The gains that we made as part of our renovation could only be realized by our decision to remove our microfilm and microfiche collections to off-site storage. A few titles with more frequent request rates were kept on-site in the main Baker Library, but are no longer in the Jones Media Center. Subject specialists still actively collect new DVD content, but we are gradually weeding and deaccessioning more of our older VHS collections, especially as DVD versions of titles become available.

Staff

The Jones Media Center is staffed by a head, three additional exempt positions, and four nonexempt positions, including a fellowship position who is a recent graduate. The majority of staff work a standard day, covering hours between 7:45 a.m. and 6:00 p.m. One staff member works the closing shift from 2:00 p.m. to 10:00 p.m., Sunday through Thursday. The remaining staff are on a rotating schedule to individually cover the 10:00 a.m. to 6:00 p.m. open hours on Saturday. All staff members are expected to share a basic understanding of the operations of the facility and of the majority of our equipment. Becoming familiar with circulation procedures, department and library policies, and learning to use our circulating equipment is a somewhat informal process that all new staff members undertake, through instruction provided by all staff. Furthermore, all JMC staff members usually are members of at least one librarywide committee. Though each staff member is expected to be a generalist, it is only natural that each person is hired into a position seeking specific skills as well. Current staff have expertise in instructional design, analog audio preservation, computer lab management, music production, film preservation, animation, and television production.

Funding/Budget

Staff and general operations are paid via subvention funding, but the majority of the Jones Media Center's services, facilities, and equipment are made possible through a single endowment fund. In addition, the previously mentioned fellowship is also funded by the endowment. Planning and management is largely the responsibility of the Head of Digital Media and Library Technologies, who reports to the Associate Librarian for User Engagement & Technologies.

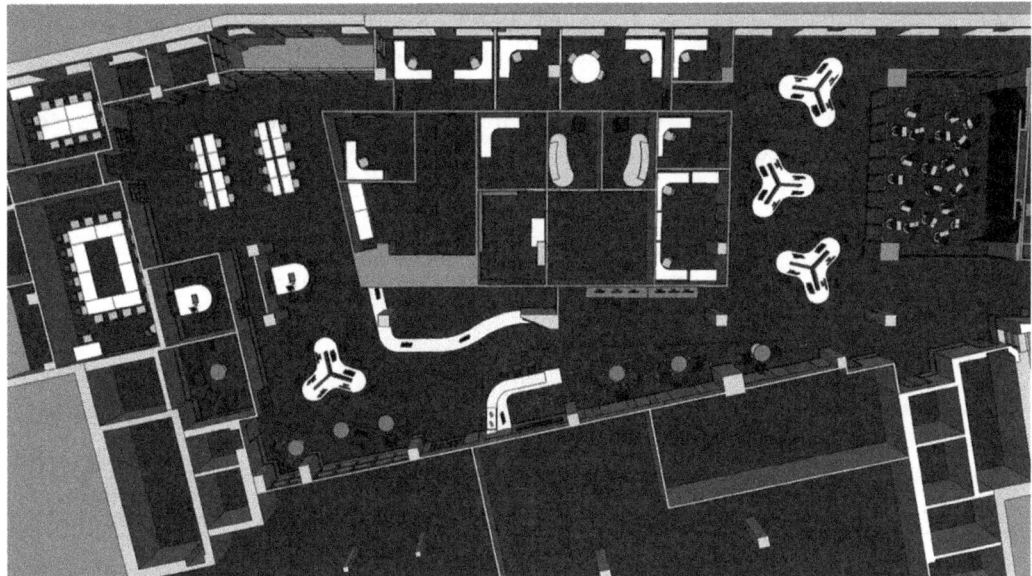
Jones Media Center
Source: Dartmouth College

Publicity/Promotion

Following the renovation, there was a grand-reopening event. Every fall, the library hosts an Open House event for new first-year students, and the Jones Media Center is a destination for that event. During the event we try to offer different types of activities in the facility, such as hands-on time with the equipment. Workshop offerings throughout the year are advertised campuswide, and with the Innovation Studio, a new space within the facility, we are hosting more class presentation sessions, miniconferences, and even hosted our first student dramatic production. We collaborate closely with instructional designers and faculty on course media projects and with recent efforts to produce content for EdX online courses. On our nine screens we promote content and services within the JMC and make use of other library signage. We also maintain a social media presence.

Evaluation

As with many institutions, though we want more feedback and data, we are also keenly aware of institutional survey fatigue. As part of the library, the Jones Media Center does gather some feedback as part of a triennial survey process, and we also collect feedback following workshop offerings. Since the renovation, we track most of the usage of the facility using the Suma mobile web-based assessment toolkit developed by the North Carolina State University Libraries. Periodically, we may collect targeted data at our service desks, such as with 1-5 short answer surveys regarding service.

Evolution of Facility

The Jones Media Center originally opened in 2001. The 2015 renovation was the first significant renovation process since the opening. The renovation doubled the seating capacity, offered more flexible and collaborative seating arrangement, and created specialized study and work areas, including a collaboration room, a "living room" with comfortable soft seating and enhanced video viewing and video gaming capabilities, a WhisperRoom for audio recording, and the flexible, multipurpose "Innovation Studio," which converts from classroom to presentation/event space to light-duty studio space depending on need.

Future Steps

We are continuing to monitor and evaluate the postrenovation facility. At this time, no significant new initiatives are being considered.

Duke University: The Ruppert Commons for Research, Technology and Collaboration ("The Edge")
Durham, North Carolina, USA

Carnegie Classification	
Basic:	Doctoral Universities: Highest Research Activity
Undergraduate Instructional Program:	Arts & sciences plus professions, high graduate coexistence
Graduate Instructional Program:	Research Doctoral: Comprehensive programs, with medical/veterinary school
Enrollment Profile:	Majority graduate
Undergraduate Profile:	Four-year, full-time, more selective, lower transfer-in
Size and Setting:	Four-year, large, highly residential

Total Student Enrollment: 15,856
Year established: 2015
Year of expansion/renovation: 2016
Name: The Ruppert Commons for Research, Technology and Collaboration ("The Edge")
Square footage of publicly available space associated with your facility: 17,000
Location: Main Library
Typical access hours per week: 149
Typical service hours per week: 40
Number of service points: 1
Number of desktop computers available for use: 15
Number of laptop computers available for use: 0
Other types of devices provided: Users may utilize one of the nine large flat-screen monitors by connecting their laptop and displaying their work to their group. We also check out projectors to users seeking to take advantage of our whiteboard walls for note-taking or viewing displays.
Average monthly door count: n/a
Average monthly service transactions: 350
Workstation sessions/logins: n/a
Library website: https://library.duke.edu/

Purpose

Duke University Libraries created The Edge (formally known as The Ruppert Commons for Research, Technology and Collaboration) in 2014 to meet the growing needs of interdisciplinary, team-based, and data-driven research at Duke. Plans for this space came about through a multi-year planning process in which faculty, students, and library staff explored how Duke researchers are increasingly conducting their work in the context of interdisciplinary collaborations and digital production. The first floor of Bostock Library was transformed into an academic service hub equipped with tools and workspaces for digital scholarship, reservable rooms for project teams, and expanded technology and training facilities—the kind of space that, in the words of University Librarian Deborah Jakubs, "invites discovery, experimentation, and collaboration." In creating The Edge, the Libraries were responding to the highly interdisciplinary and innovative research environment at Duke, where academically diverse teams undertake socially and digitally engaged research projects as part of the curriculum. At the same time, the Edge provided an opportunity for showcasing this work, including the Libraries' technology-focused services and partnerships to create new scholarship.

Services

The key service The Edge provides is a common, flexible space that encourages collaborative work and research sharing through our program and space policies. Our reservation system (available online, through a kiosk at the service desk, and room-based iPad kiosks), as well as our scheduling policy for rooms, help ensure that rooms are available and also regularly used by teams of collaborative researchers. We also promote and host programs, including brown bags, research talks, discussion groups, and workshops that help develop skills in digital research. In addition, users may take advantage of services and office hours in the Data & Visualization Lab and the Digital Studio. Staff members in these areas offer expertise on data sources, data management, data visualization, geographic information systems, financial data, statistical software, project planning, qualitative research methods, and text analysis.

Software

The Edge features two digital labs that offer hardware and software for conducting digital research projects. The Data and Visualization (DVS) Lab has twelve windows workstations with the latest data visualization (Tableau, R, Adobe Suite), digital mapping (ArcGIS, QGIS, Google Earth), and statistical software (R, Stata, SAS, Matlab). The Digital Scholarship Lab has three iMacs featuring a range of software for performing qualitative research (Nvivo), organizing digital materials (DevonThink), and testing new software. Additionally, the DVS Lab also offers three Bloomberg Professional Terminals for the latest financial data and news. In both labs, lab staff provide consultations on using the software as part of both class-based and project-based research. Additionally, each of the labs provides a range of training opportunities and research events designed to both train researchers on the software and showcase research projects and their associated methods and tools. As researchers increasingly desire to build online platforms for digital projects, The Edge increasingly employs a wide range of cloud-based tools in providing services in the Edge. Many of the digital projects in the Edge rely on central Duke IT services providing storage/collaboration (Box.com, Office 365), online blogging (Wordpress), and server hosting (Duke OIT Virtual Machines).

"The Edge"
Source: Duke University

Print Resources

The Edge collects some print materials in addition to the software and hardware in the space that are intended to interact with texts and other collection materials. The Edge Reference collection currently consists of a small, core collection of titles of interest to users of the space. These topics range from software manuals supporting work in the Data & Visualization Lab and Digital Studio to project management guides and textbooks on the digital humanities and quantitative analysis. The Data Visualization Lab also houses a small collection of data manuals and software guides. In addition to the print materials it houses, the high-definition scanners and the software housed in The Edge are primarily intended to provide text analysis capabilities of items from the library collection as well as outside materials.

Staff

The day-to-day operations are managed by the Coordinator of The Edge who manages the general service desk, communicates with numerous users of the spaces (e.g., teams using project rooms), manages the physical space as well as The Edge's website and events calendar, oversees the print book collection, and more. For most of the academic year The Edge is open 24 hours per day with more limited hours on Fridays and Saturdays. The Edge has a general service desk that is staffed from noon–6 p.m., Monday–Thursday, noon–5 p.m. on Friday, and 3–8 p.m. on Sunday by six student assistants who are trained and managed by the Coordinator of The Edge. They come from a wide range of academic backgrounds. The Data and Visualization Lab is staffed by a mix of full-time and part-time library staff and by two graduate students with statistical software and data analysis expertise. These graduate students are hired in partnership with the Economics Department and are managed by the Data and Visualization Services. The Data and Visualization Lab is staffed approximately 34–36 hours per week with staffing focusing on peak research hours in the afternoons and early evenings. Digital Scholarship Services averages two graduate student assistants per year, with as many as five direct reports, whose primary responsibilities are contributing to digital project development and/or development of training tools and guidelines for conducting digital projects. Digital Scholarship Services staff regularly consult with researchers and with faculty-led project teams in the Digital Studio, which also provides an informal space for individuals and teams to present and discuss digital project work.

Funding/Budget

The Edge is comanaged by leadership from Data and Visualization Services, Digital Scholarship Services, Research and Instructional Services, and Information Technology Services. An Edge Management Team is made up of heads from these departments as well as the Coordinator of The Edge, who is a member of Research and Instructional Services. This group collaborates to maintain the vision for the space, set policies, and identify user needs and opportunities to support The Edge's mission. The majority of operational expenses, including student staffing, supplies, and marketing materials, are managed through the separate budgets for these departments. Hardware and software needs are budgeted through the Libraries' IT budget channels.

Publicity/Promotion

Duke University Libraries' Office of Communication and Development provided early leadership in developing a marketing plan for The Edge, and continues to support publicity of events through the Libraries' website news carousel and blog. Two display monitors just inside the entrance promote a range of events and services both within the Edge and the Libraries generally. Signposts are used to signal the location of specific events and to alert patrons when areas will be closed for event-related activities. Also, an interactive kiosk just inside the entrance provides access to a list of upcoming Edge-sponsored events as well as a floor map. Much of the promotional work for events in the Edge is achieved through email announcements to listservs and through postings to the Libraries' and individual library departments' websites. The event registration system used by the Libraries features an automatic email reminder to event registrants. For events in the Workshop Room, the Panopto system allows for posting recorded events later, which also helps in promoting Edge activities beyond the event itself.

Evaluation

During the first year of the Edge's operation, and especially during its first semester, assessment was fairly intensive. With guidance and assistance from the Libraries' Assessment and User Experience department, we evaluated the volume and nature of use of the different spaces, gathered demographic data and feedback from event participants, surveyed teams' satisfaction with project rooms, and conducted smaller and more specific studies to address usability issues. For instance, we used SUMA, an open-source mobile web-based assessment toolkit for collecting and analyzing observational data, to conduct regular headcounts of who was in the space at different times of day, which we used to inform and adjust our desk staffing hours. A standardized evaluation form was used following all events, to help us gain a sense of who was attending Edge programming. Following the first semester of project room use, we distributed Qualtrics surveys to teams who regularly used these rooms, to gain

THE/EDGE

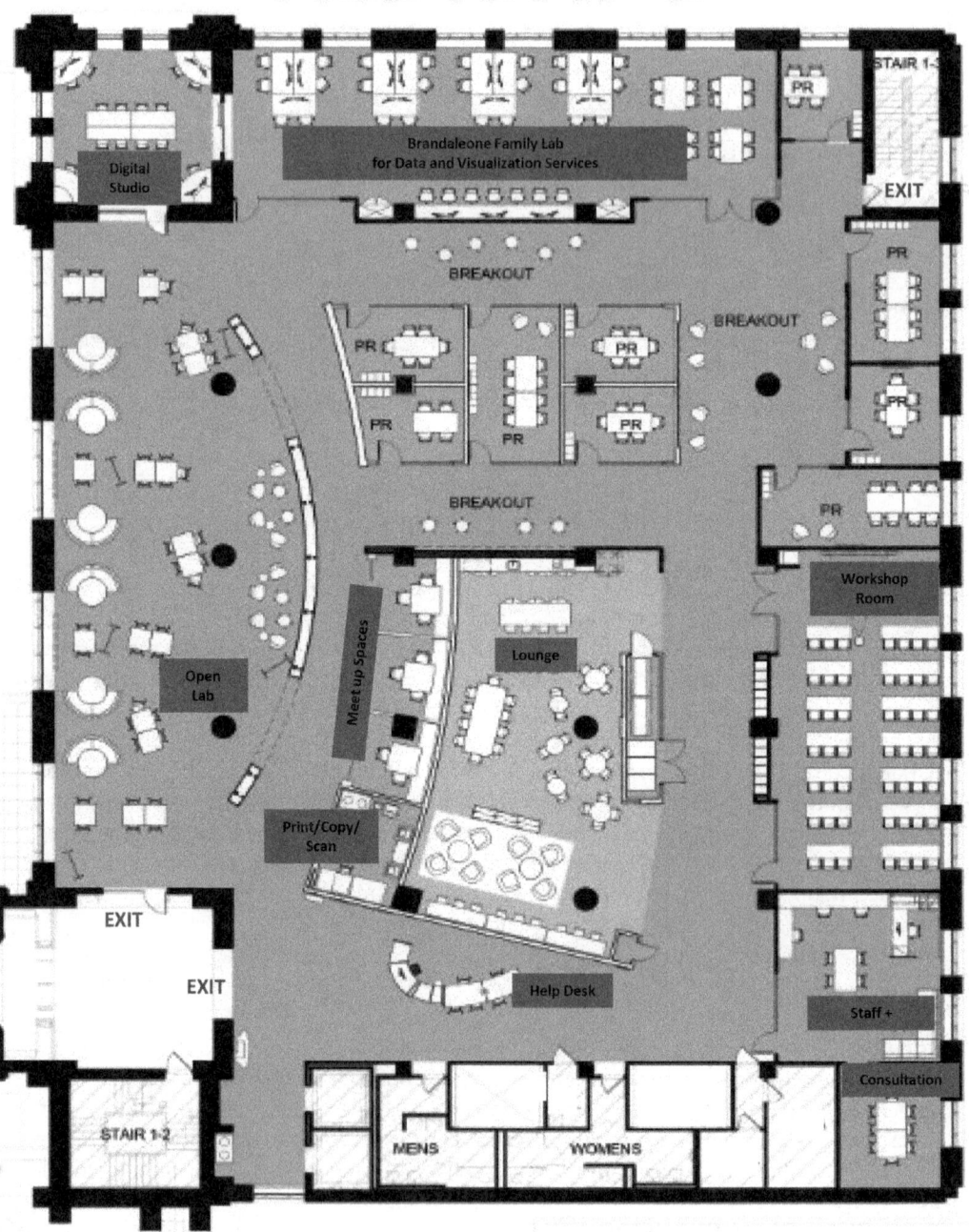

"The Edge"
Source: Duke University

a better sense of how to improve the user experience; these responses, in particular, led to changes in the room locking mechanisms, technology available in the room, and policies for room reservation.

Evolution of Facility

While our facility has only been open for a year, we are continually reexamining our policies in light of the new and emerging needs of Duke researchers. The only major change has been a formalization of a policy to increase access to our shared, and limited, computer resources by automatically logging out unattended workstations. We've modified our student worker job duties to include daily "basic maintenance" rounds to check on cables, monitors, etc. We've seen a very high demand for The Edge Workshop Room, and adjacent Lounge area, for use in conferences and workshops. This was a planned use for the space, but we underestimated the time and effort needed for coordination of the events. In particular, the need for preplanning meetings, contact with caterers, and arranging for housekeeping during and after the event has led us to be more explicit on what we can and cannot do for "day-of" event support, and we now require campus fund codes in cases for which we need to charge housekeeping expenses. As might be expected from a facility that has writable and nonwritable surfaces, we have run into issues with people drawing on the wrong walls, requiring several repainting and touch-up requests. We are looking to add more writable/whiteboard surfaces where appropriate.

Future Steps

The reaction from the research community has been impressive. Our rooms are heavily used, and events and conferences are held in The Edge on a regular basis. In the first year of service, the Edge hosted a range of digital events ranging from the American Statistical Associations' Datafest Contest, a virtual reality art exhibition, and a series of research talks by a range of scholars working in the Edge and visiting Duke. We are now looking to increase the amount of library-sponsored programming in the space as a way to bring more contact between librarians and researchers, increasing the role of the library in the research process. Our hope is that Edge will serve as platform to facilitate research collaboration both inside the library, across campus, and with the wide research community. Looking ahead, it is clear that we will need to grow staff positions and campus partnerships so that The Edge can continue to explore innovating programming and meeting researcher needs. Given the time and effort we're seeing for event support, we have asked for a new staff position to be created to assist with event planning, coordination, and "day of" support. A number of partnerships have already sprung up—Research Computing and the central Office of Information Technology (OIT) do regular seminars and workshops in the space—and we are looking to expand those to other campus groups. Since The Edge is a technology-heavy space, we are also looking for ways to expand our technology offerings, directly or with other university partners. Research Computing has been active in our space and we will continue to refer patrons to them for large-scale computing needs. We are working with a student-based 3-D printing club, as well as staff in OIT's 3-D scanning facilities to collaborate on ways The Edge can be a space and a program venue that exposes the research potential for these technologies and how students and faculty are using them. We are working with vendors in the cloud computing space to see if those services might be of interest to researchers. We are looking at deploying new wireless display systems to reduce the need for cables, and allow better collaboration inside project rooms.

Emory University: Learning Commons, Student Digital Life
Atlanta, Georgia, USA

Carnegie Classification	
Basic:	Doctoral Universities: Highest Research Activity
Undergraduate Instructional Program:	Arts & sciences focus, high graduate coexistence
Graduate Instructional Program:	Research Doctoral: Comprehensive programs, with medical/veterinary school
Enrollment Profile:	Majority undergraduate
Undergraduate Profile:	Four-year, full-time, more selective, lower transfer-in
Size and Setting:	Four-year, large, highly residential

Total Student Enrollment: 14,769
Year established: 1998
Year of expansion/renovation: 1999, 2014-16
Name: Learning Commons, Student Digital Life
Square footage of publicly available space associated with your facility: 40,000
Location: Main Library
Typical access hours per week: 149.5
Typical service hours per week: 93
Number of service points: 4
Number of desktop computers available for use: 142
Number of laptop computers available for use: 26
Other types of devices provided: Through the Music & Media Library, the library supplies access to many different types of equipment. This information is located on the Equipment Guide at http://guides.main.library.emory.edu/equipment/Welcome. This equipment includes the following: calculators (graphing and nongraphing), iPads, cell phone chargers, laptop chargers, external hard drives, Apple USB SuperDrives, 3D glasses, headphones, display adapters (laptops, tablets, and smartphones), cameras and tripods, microphones, projectors, multiregion DVD players, VHS players, cassette players, and phonographs.
Also, MediaLab provides flatbed scanners, Wacom Intuos Pro tablets, and microphones. More information can be found at http://it.emory.edu/studentdigitallife/spaces/medialab/index.html
Average monthly door count: n/a
Average monthly services transactions: n/a
Workstation sessions/logins: n/a
Library website: http://web.library.emory.edu/

Purpose

The Learning Commons, InfoCommons at the time, was designed as a comprehensive new public computing service program for the Center for Library and Information Resources (CLAIR), a 1998 expansion and renovation of the Robert W. Woodruff Library, Emory University's main library complex. The InfoCommons featured a much larger number of public workstations than the library had ever previously deployed, spread throughout all levels of the Woodruff Library, with support personnel integrated into and coordinated with traditional service points. The InfoCommons was designed to provide a new level of computing functionality for library users, enabling not only simple gathering of citations from online catalogs, but providing a comprehensive suite of software for learning and research.

Services

Learning Commons offers: computer workstations; print, copy, scanning, and faxing services; microform readers; BYOD support with the access to power, AV technology, and wireless network; group work support via 16 group study rooms (13 of which are equipped with AV technology) with online reservation system; collaborative work support through providing collaborative furniture and wall-mounted/mobile whiteboards; Presentation Practice and Web Conference room equipped with specialized technology; Tier 1 support of the above spaces and technologies through Library Service Desk staff; loaner technology available via the Music and Media desk; student personal technology support via the Student Technology Support desk; support of graphic design, video, audio, and image post production, poster printing, web development, and 3-D modeling in MediaLab. With the combined service points, the Library Service Desk includes not only the Learning Commons support but also circulation and reference services.

Software

All computer workstations have iMovie, Garageband, Audacity, Microsoft Office, SPSS, STATA, MatLab, Mathematica, R and Rstudio, and Xcode installed. Nine workstations have MaxQDA. MediaLab workstations have full Adobe Creative Cloud suite, Final Cut Pro X, Logic Pro X, Blender, and Sibelius. Emory Center for Digital Scholarship workstations have Aquamacs, MPEG Streamclip, SmartSVN, ArcGIS, ERDAS Imagine, Esri CityEngine, FME Workbench, Quantum GIS, SAS, and StatTransfer. The specialized applications in MediaLab and ECDS areas are supported by their designated staff.

Learning Commons
Source: Emory University

Print Resources

The Learning Commons is a distributed facility, with workstations located throughout the Woodruff Library and interspersed with the main primary collections of reference on Level 2, and government documents and microforms on Level 1. Current periodicals are located in the Matheson Reading Room on Level 3. Each level of the stacks tower has a catalog-only computer for quick access to the library's collection, although there are three Learning Commons group study rooms on Level 6 and three on Level 7. With more and more reference materials available online through the licensed e-resources, the library has reduced the reference collection by 75% and will reduce the collection even more in the coming year. The media collection is a closed collection; however, various pieces of equipment are available for the viewing patron in the Learning Commons on Level 4.

Staff

With four service points, staffing is provided through two primary divisions within the library. The Library Service Desk is a combined service point, staffed by the Library Service Desk team with the help of student workers. The reference portion of the desk is staffed by librarians, paraprofessionals, and graduate students. Student staff is trained on library operations by an LSD supervisor and on Learning Commons support by the Student Digital Life Learning Commons coordinator.

The Music & Media Library Service Desk is staffed similar to the Library Service Desk, using librarians, staff, and student workers to handle the different functions on the desk. The training on this desk includes in-depth training on the circulating equipment collection with minimal training on Learning Commons' tasks.

MediaLab desk is staffed with undergraduate and graduate students proficient in at least one graphic design application (e.g., Adobe Photoshop) and one video-editing application (e.g., Final Cut X Pro). Every shift, MediaLab student workers undergo professional development through either completing Lynda.com courses or working on multimedia projects. The student workers report to the Learning Commons Coordinator. MediaLab's regular staffed hours are Mon-Thu, 12-8 p.m., and Fri, 12-5 p.m.

STS desk is staffed with undergraduate and graduate students experienced in troubleshooting of Windows and MacOS. The student workers report to the SDL STS coordinator. The desk's regular staffed hours are Mon-Fri, 9 a.m.-5 p.m.

Funding/Budget

Learning Commons technology upgrades and operations are funded through the Learning Commons technology budget. MediaLab and STS student staffing is funded from the SDL student staffing budget. Library Service Desk and MUSME service desk are funded from the Access Services student staffing budget.

Publicity/Promotion

SDL spaces and services, including Learning Commons, MediaLab, and STS, are advertised to the incoming freshmen through printed materials during the annual Back to School event. New spaces, services, and technologies are marketed to the Emory community through the campus

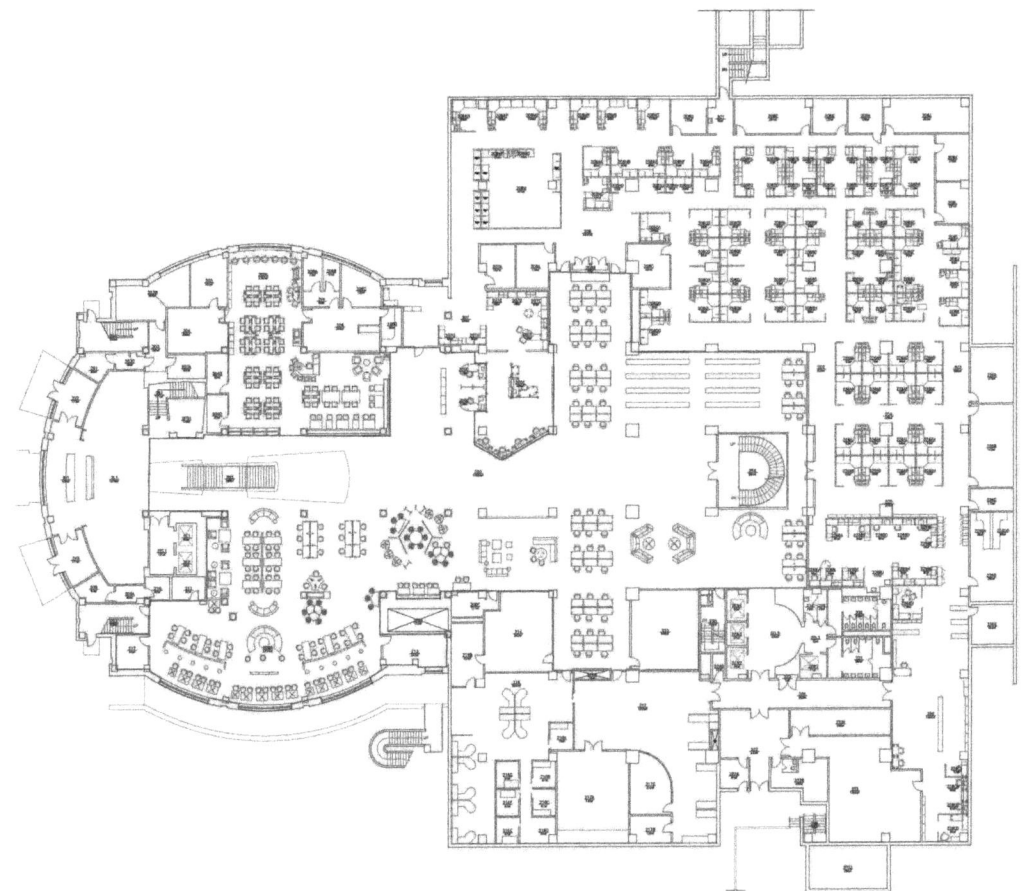

Learning Commons
Source: Emory University

newspaper, library scholarly blog, faculty outreach, digital and printed signage, Wonderful Wednesday events, workshops and other activities hosted in the appropriate spaces, and web resources.

Evaluation

Learning Commons metrics taken monthly include the number of computer logins, group study room reservations, Presentation Practice and Web Conferencing room reservations, and MediaLab door counts. Each instructor who conducted a workshop in MediaLab is asked to complete a satisfaction survey. The service desks record and categorize every work-related activity and interaction. Each semester, the metrics are analyzed and compared with previous years, and the results are taken into consideration for future planning.

Evolution of Facility

Learning Commons was created as a place purposed to combine library and information technology resources and support services in an accessible, welcoming space for student learning and research. As the technology and the needs of the students evolved, so did the Learning

Commons, expanding its space, technology, and service offerings. Latest renovations responded to the ongoing changes in both the technology available to students and in patterns of student learning and aimed at creating a comfortable and flexible environment that could effectively accommodate and support the increased use of mobile devices and the current patterns of student learning through collaboration and social interaction.

Future Steps

In looking toward the future, the library will continue to create a dynamic environment that will allow a variety of interaction modes between the library and users. The library will provide support that is easily accessible and tailored to meet the needs of its patrons. As students and faculty work in a variety of different ways, the environments in the library should continue to reflect that. That will be achieved through balancing the portfolio of spaces for collaboration and quiet reflection as well as through expansion of Learning Commons services to accommodate a broader range of needs of the library users.

Indiana University: Learning Commons
Bloomington, Indiana, USA

Carnegie Classification	
Basic:	Doctoral Universities: Highest Research Activity
Undergraduate Instructional Program:	Balanced arts & sciences/professions, high graduate coexistence
Graduate Instructional Program:	Research Doctoral: Comprehensive programs, no medical/veterinary school
Enrollment Profile:	High undergraduate
Undergraduate Profile:	Four-year, full-time, more selective, lower transfer-in
Size and Setting:	Four-year, large, primarily residential

Total Student Enrollment: 46,416
Year established: 2003
Year of expansion/renovation: 2014
Name: Learning Commons
Square footage of publicly available space associated with your facility: 28,000
Location: Main Library
Typical access hours per week: 168
Typical service hours per week: 168
Number of service points: 2
Number of desktop computers available for use: 75
Number of laptop computers available for use: 0
Other types of devices provided: tablets
Average monthly door count: 175,000
Average monthly service transactions: 7,000
Workstation sessions/logins: 90,000
Library website: https://libraries.indiana.edu/

Purpose

After 10 years of operation and millions of visitors, the Information Commons (open since 2003) was quite run down, and the staff who were responsible for the daily operation of the IC had learned quite a lot about the evolving needs of students and how services needed to change. The IC was a technology center with most of the technology configured like a computer lab space with rows of desktop computers. The IC lacked flexibility largely because the hardwired technology was immobile and the services were anchored to large service desks. The renovation that created the Learning Commons modernized the IC and made a more sophisticated environment for students that promotes BYOD.

Services

The Learning Commons offers research consultations, software and hardware support, reserve services, circulation, IT training, Writing Tutorial Services, and Financial Literacy.

Software

There are over 100 software applications on the fixed computer workstations in the Learning Commons.

Print Resources

The presence of book collections is limited to the new acquisitions for the Undergraduate Core Collection. There are usually no more than 50 books on the small book shelf at a time.

Learning Commons
Source: Indiana University, Bloomington

Field Guide

Staff

Indiana University Libraries, University Information Technology Services, and the Office of the Vice Provost for Undergraduate Education all provide a combination of full-time and part-time staff.

Funding/Budget

Indiana University Libraries and University Information Technology Services equally shared the cost of renovation.

Publicity/Promotion

n/a

Evaluation

People counts, space use surveys, and user surveys are used to gauge use and help to identify areas of improvement and change.

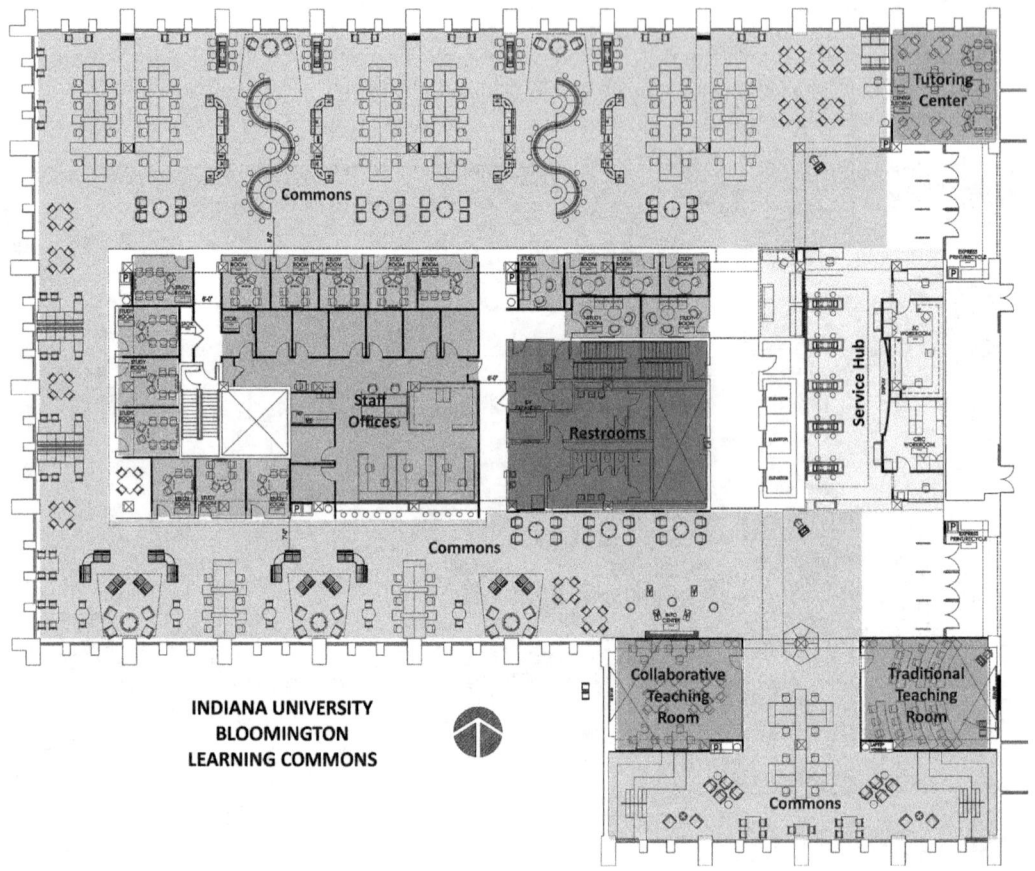

Learning Commons
Source: Indiana University, Bloomington

Evolution of Facility

n/a

Future Steps

n/a

Jackson State University: JSU Innovate
Jackson, Mississippi, USA

Carnegie Classification	
Basic:	Doctoral Universities: Higher Research Activity
Undergraduate Instructional Program:	Balanced arts & sciences/professions, some graduate coexistence
Graduate Instructional Program:	Research Doctoral: Professional-dominant
Enrollment Profile:	High undergraduate
Undergraduate Profile:	Four-year, full-time, inclusive, higher transfer-in
Size and Setting:	Four-year, medium, primarily residential

Total Student Enrollment: 9,508
Year established: 2014
Year of expansion/renovation: n/a
Name: JSU Innovate
Square footage of publicly available space associated with your facility: 2,000
Location: Main Library
Typical access hours per week: 80
Typical service hours per week: 60
Number of service points: 3
Number of desktop computers available for use: 10
Number of laptop computers available for use: 20
Other types of devices provided: iPads, smart boards, digital imaging
Average monthly door count: 1,000
Average monthly service transactions: 600
Workstation sessions/logins: 700
Library website: http://sampson.jsums.edu/

Purpose

This facility was created to help students, faculty, and staff use innovation in the teaching and learning process at Jackson State University. Utilizing state-of-the-art technology, the Jackson State University community is being exposed and utilizing cutting-edge technology to enhance the teaching and learning process.

Services

This newly built facility on the main floor of the Sampson library was completed to enhance and centralize academic information technology. Prior to the opening of the Innovate center all academic information technology was housed at the Mississippi e-center. This facility had a number of opportunities for faculty to enhance the learning experiences in their traditional and online class rooms. However, as the space became too small to allow all members of the JSU community to participate, the innovate center was opened to expand offerings and enhance the quality of digital learning at the campus.

Software

The innovate center offers both Mac and PC platforms for use by members of the community. All computers have a variety of software packages to assist community members in photo and movie editing as well as a number of software packages related to the performance of research.

Print Resources

Overall this facility has moved away from the traditional print and paper method of research. We have begun to enhance the digitization of all our materials to free up additional space in the library for conference rooms and other innovative approaches to enhance the teaching and learning experience

Staff

n/a

Funding/Budget

The funding from this project is a combination of state appropriations and grants related to the advancing of innovation at historically black colleges and universities.

Publicity/Promotion

Every semester public service announcements are produced and distributed via a multitude of channels. A number of faculty student and staff trainings are also held in this facility.

Evaluation

n/a

Evolution of Facility

n/a

Future Steps

n/a

Kansas State University: K-State InfoCommons
Manhattan, Kansas, USA

Carnegie Classification

Basic:	Doctoral Universities: Highest Research Activity
Undergraduate Instructional Program:	Professions plus arts & sciences, high graduate coexistence
Graduate Instructional Program:	Research Doctoral: Comprehensive programs, with medical/veterinary school
Enrollment Profile:	High undergraduate
Undergraduate Profile:	Four-year, full-time, more selective, higher transfer-in
Size and Setting:	Four-year, large, primarily nonresidential

Total Student Enrollment: 24,766
Year established: 2001
Year of expansion/renovation: 2015
Name: K-State InfoCommons
Square footage of publicly available space associated with your facility: 100,000
Location: Main Library
Typical access hours per week: 133
Typical service hours per week: 69
Number of service points: 2
Number of desktop computers available for use: 263
Number of laptop computers available for use: 0
Other types of devices provided: The entire main library is wireless enabled, with many additional wireless repeaters added in the summer of 2015. Library patrons bring their own laptops and wireless devices. The Media Development Center has a number of scanners and other equipment.
Average monthly door count: 80,000
Average monthly service transactions: 2,635
Workstation sessions/logins: 0
Library website: www.lib.k-state.edu/

Purpose

Students requested access to computing resources along with library resources to enhance writing papers and preparing other academic projects. K-State does not require students to own their own computers, so the university provides accommodations. K-State Libraries believe it is important to combine technology and library resources together to encourage students in information literacy and locating the best information regardless of format.

Services

Separate service points exist for library reference and information technology help, both in the main library. Assistance is available at both points in person, by phone, email, and via chat. A Media Development Center is also part of the InfoCommons and is located in the main library; however, it is administered and staffed by the university Information Technology Assistance Center.

Software

Applications include MS Office, course/discipline specific applications, library databases, RefWorks, technology programs, translation software, and adaptive technology programs. See http://lan.cns.ksu.edu/labs/software/software.htm for listings.

Print Resources

The K-State InfoCommons is scattered throughout the main library building and in two branch libraries. Computer workstations are located primarily on floors 1–4 of the main library, in the stacks, and in a technology classroom. A few workstations are "stand-up" (no chairs) to discourage "camping out."

Staff

Library staff and IT help staff are hired and administered through two different budgets, but cooperate and work together in partnership. Service points are primarily staffed by student employees with assistance of staff as needed. Peak hours include Sunday through Thursday—afternoons and evenings.

K-State InfoCommons
Source: Kansas State University, Manhattan

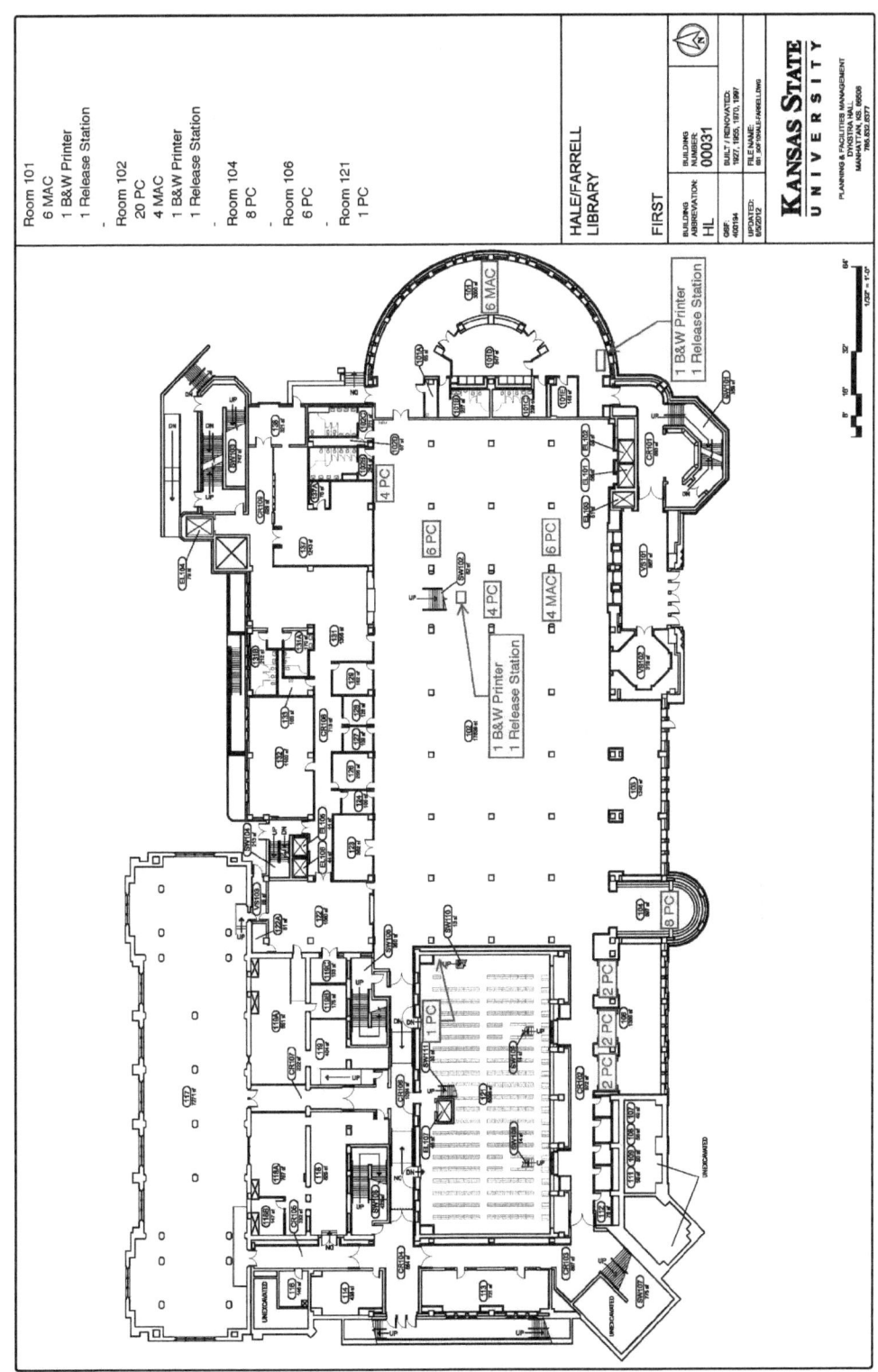

K-State InfoCommons
Source: Kansas State University, Manhattan

Funding/Budget

Staffing is provided by the library and the information technology units. Software and hardware is provided in part by a student technology fee. Planning and management of the InfoCommons is through a cooperative team of library and information technology administrators.

Publicity/Promotion

The facility opened in 2001, and the campus is now quite familiar with its location and offerings. This has eliminated the need for publicity other than listing on Library and iTAC web pages and Week of Welcome events at the start of each fall semester. Informative websites helping students find information about technology offerings are very important and are the best means of educating them about how we can assist.

Evaluation

Usability testing of the computer image and associated websites is done annually, with significant upgrades during the summer months and minor adjustments throughout the academic year. Communication of issues (complaints and problems) is ongoing through the cooperative team and among those staffing the library and IT service points to troubleshoot throughout the year.

Evolution of Facility

There were major furniture and wireless upgrades in 2015. The original 2001 furniture was still in use until 2015. The bandwidth needed to handle an ever-increasing load of mobile devices required the addition of more than 100 additional wireless repeaters.

Future Steps

Because major upgrades occurred last year, there are no short-term plans. There are long-range plans to convert all of the first floor of Hale Library into a learning commons. All stacks will be removed, and classroom and group and individual study spaces will be added.

North Carolina State University: Lake Raleigh Learning Commons
Raleigh, North Carolina, USA

Carnegie Classification	
Basic:	Doctoral Universities: Highest Research Activity
Undergraduate Instructional Program:	Professions plus arts & sciences, high graduate coexistence
Graduate Instructional Program:	Research Doctoral: STEM-dominant
Enrollment Profile:	High undergraduate
Undergraduate Profile:	Four-year, full-time, more selective, higher transfer-in
Size and Setting:	Four-year, large, primarily residential

Total Student Enrollment: 33,989
Year established: 2013
Year of expansion/renovation: n/a
Name: Lake Raleigh Learning Commons
Square footage of publicly available space associated with your facility: 5,600
Location: Main Library
Typical access hours per week: 146
Typical service hours per week: 146
Number of service points: 1
Number of desktop computers available for use: 75
Number of laptop computers available for use: 100
Other types of devices provided: We offer hundreds of devices including cameras (DSLRs, point and shoot, camcorders, 360 video cameras, camera traps, infrared camera), tablets (iPads, Microsoft Surface Tablets, Samsung Galaxy, Kindles), makerspace items (Arduino kits, Internet of Things kits, Raspberry Pi, programmable robots, EEG devices, 3-D scanners), audio production equipment (synthesizers, digital audio recorders, microphones), gaming controllers, projectors, virtual/augmented reality equipment, design and modeling equipment, calculators, and many power cables and accessories.
Average monthly door count: 117,728
Average monthly service transactions: 21,008 (includes 2,209 Circulation; 16,379 Technology Lending; 1,241 Textbook Lending; and 1,179 Reference, Print/copy, Computing, and Directional). Based on September 2016.
Workstation sessions/logins: n/a
Library website: www.lib.ncsu.edu/spaces/lake-raleigh-learning-commons

Purpose

The Lake Raleigh Learning Commons on the fourth floor of the Hunt Library provides 75 large collaborative workstations, most with fixed computing (PC, Mac, Linux), along with some table seating and some lounge seating along the perimeter of the space. A similar learning commons was opened at the D. H. Hill Library (the university's other main library) in 2007 and continues to be heavily used.

Services

We have a single service point two floors below called "Ask Us" that provides services throughout the building with a "we come to you" roaming model. Within the learning commons, we offer traditional reference services, data and GIS consultations, technology consultation on all aspects of digital media creation, and a 3-D printing service, all available through scheduled or ad hoc sessions. This single service point with roaming service model was created for the Hunt Library and is staffed by multiple departments. There is no traditional "reference desk" at the Hunt Library.

Software

We support multiple computing platforms, with several specialized capabilities in the commons including engineering workstations (Windows and Linux), design workstations (Mac and Windows), and data visualization and GIS workstations (Windows). The engineering software is managed by the College of Engineering while the other computing environments are managed by the Libraries' Information Technology department.

Print Resources

The Hunt Library houses 1,643,113 volumes of books, journals, microforms, media, and government documents in an automated retrieval system (the bookBot) and approximately 30,000 volumes on open shelving. Items in the bookBot may be searched and browsed online and through a visual "Virtual Browse" interface via a wall-mounted touchscreen on the first floor of the building. Virtual Browse also includes the Libraries' entire collection and can expand to include those of other regional and worldwide libraries. Items requested from the bookBot are delivered to the Ask Us center for pickup within five minutes. The NCSU Libraries has an additional two million print volumes available by three campus deliveries per day.

Staff

The Lake Raleigh Learning Commons is supported by the full-time Ask Us staff, roaming student advisors, and on-call librarians. The student advisors are selected for their technical abilities combined with excellent customer service and communication skills. We have an extensive student advisor training program and encourage their attendance at skills-based library workshops. We recruit and hire user-centered, full-time staff who manage the service point over three shifts, 24 hours a day, five days a week.

Funding/Budget

The Hunt Library received state-appropriated funding for the capital project that included design, construction, furniture (partial), and A/V (partial). The Libraries contributed private funding

Lake Raleigh Learning Commons
Source: North Carolina State University

(individual donors and corporate partnerships), student technology fee money, research overhead, and operating budget. The program plan for library spaces was developed by the Libraries' leadership team in consultation with library staff, faculty members, and students. The Libraries charged Service Model and Staffing Model Planning teams to develop operating plans and "service blueprints" for all library spaces, with the assistance of an external consultant.

Publicity/Promotion

We developed a comprehensive, award-winning Communication Plan for the Hunt Library, "Imagining 'The Library of the Future,'" with help from the University Communications team. Details are available at https://johncottondana.secure-platform.com/a/page/northcarolinastate2014. One successful example is "My #HuntLibrary," a creative initiative in which we engage our community to use their technology and design skills to "crowdsource" the story of the new building (https://red.lib.ncsu.edu/myhuntlibrary/). See www.lib.ncsu.edu/huntlibrary/about for more information, including a specially commissioned video.

Evaluation

Head counts are taken eight times per day in 40 separate locations throughout the library, including the learning commons. Monthly and annual trends are compared by day of the week and

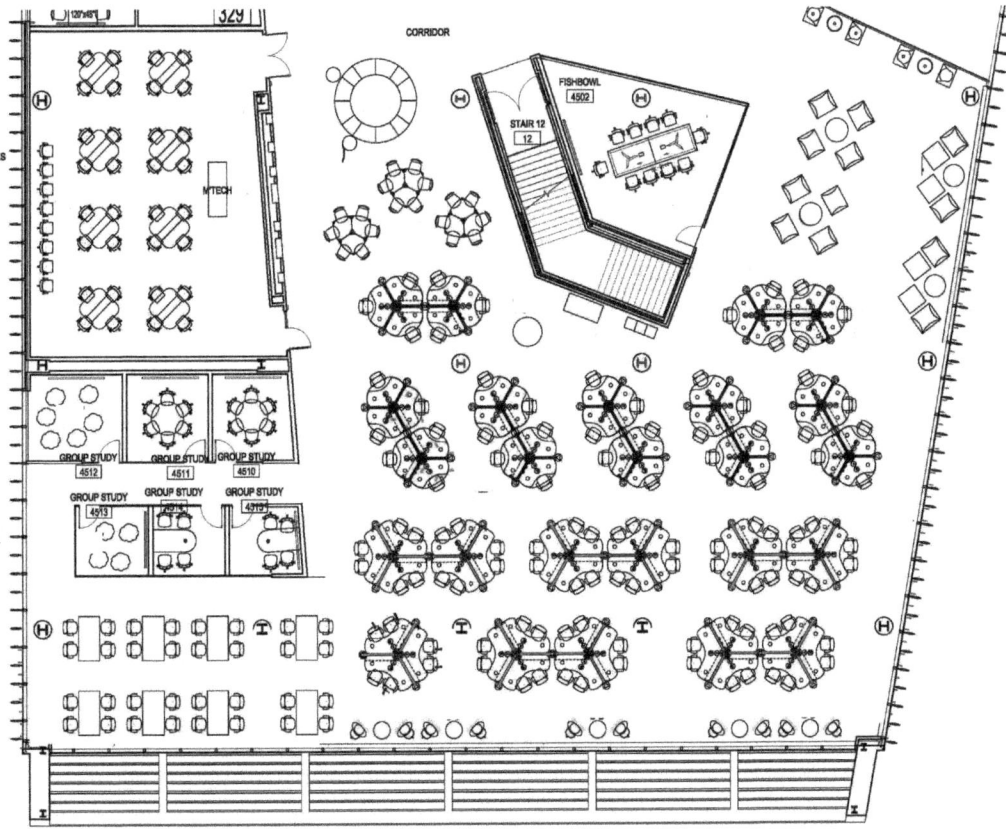

Lake Raleigh Learning Commons
Source: North Carolina State University

Field Guide

hour of the day. Overall, the average daily learning commons headcount increased by 5.2% between September 2013 and September 2016. The Libraries performs user studies in its spaces to assess the use of technology and seating as student use of the space (individual or group study). Frequent consultation with student and faculty advisory groups informs our decisions regarding space configuration, technology, and services.

The University surveys sophomores and graduating seniors on a regular basis. These surveys contain nine questions related to library use. The sophomore surveys issued prior to and after the opening of the Hunt Library showed a 7.6% increase in satisfaction with "space for individual student work" and a 12.9% increase for "space for group work." Over 75% of the sophomores surveyed were either "satisfied" or "very satisfied" with the space. The senior survey issued prior to and after the opening of the Hunt Library shows a 6.3% increase in satisfaction with "space for individual student work" and an 11.6% increase for "space for group work." Over 80% of the seniors were either "satisfied" or "very satisfied" with the space.

Evolution of Facility

There have been no changes to the layout, finishes, or furniture in the space since it opened in January 2013. The overall service model and approach have remained consistent. Library managers and staff have been able to apply their learning and observations of user needs and preferences to continually adapt and improve services and to ensure that the computing and technology capabilities remain robust and relevant.

Future Steps

As we approach the five-year anniversary of the opening of the building, we may make some adjustments to the type and location of furniture, perhaps reducing the amount of lounge seating in some areas and increasing the amount of standard-height tables and chairs and/or collaborative workstations. We will continue to analyze and adjust the ratio of general-purpose computer workstations to more specialized workstations that provide more processing power or access to advanced software applications. We plan to increase the number of workstations with GIS and data visualization software during Summer 2017.

Ohio University: Learning Commons
Athens, Ohio, USA

Carnegie Classification	
Basic:	Doctoral Universities: Higher Research Activity
Undergraduate Instructional Program:	Professions plus arts & sciences, high graduate coexistence
Graduate Instructional Program:	Research Doctoral: Comprehensive programs, with medical/veterinary school
Enrollment Profile:	High undergraduate
Undergraduate Profile:	Four-year, medium full-time, selective, higher transfer-in
Size and Setting:	Four-year, large, primarily residential

Total Student Enrollment: 29,217
Year established: 2004
Year of expansion/renovation: 2005
Name: Learning Commons
Square footage of publicly available space associated with your facility: 28,000
Location: Main Library
Typical access hours per week: 146
Typical service hours per week: 146
Number of service points: 1
Number of desktop computers available for use: 140
Number of laptop computers available for use: 25
Other types of devices provided: n/a
Average monthly door count: 160,000
Average monthly service transactions: 375,000
Workstation sessions/logins: n/a
Library website: www.library.ohiou.edu/

Purpose

Merge services and resources that promote student learning into the same physical space.

Services

When it opened a decade ago: reference department, open access computer lab, multimedia center, student writing center, group study rooms. Now: all of the above and café.

Software

n/a

Print Resources

The floor includes the print reference collection and the "leisure reading collection"—a collection of paperbacks and audiobooks. The Learning Commons is the only floor in the building open 24 hrs/5 days/week and pages from all other floors when the rest of the building is closed.

Staff

The reference department trains and supervises all students, staff, and librarians working the reference desk who support all IT and library operations on the floor. The Writing Center operates a separate tutoring center on the floor. Two permanent staff positions and student employees cover 8 p.m.–8 a.m.

Funding/Budget

Library operating budget.

Publicity/Promotion

Admissions and student orientation tours all stop on this floor of the building.

Field Guide

Evaluation

n/a

Evolution of Facility

Never-ending small adjustments of tech, study, collection, tutoring, group study spaces, and service points. Significantly downsized reference collection twice and moved multimedia closer to service point.

Future Steps

Hope to renovate to add additional tutoring space, as well as open another library floor overnight.

Pennsylvania State University: Knowledge Commons
State College, Pennsylvania, USA

Carnegie Classification	
Basic:	Doctoral Universities: Highest Research Activity
Undergraduate Instructional Program:	Professions plus arts & sciences, high graduate coexistence
Graduate Instructional Program:	Research Doctoral: Comprehensive programs, no medical/veterinary school
Enrollment Profile:	High undergraduate
Undergraduate Profile:	Four-year, full-time, more selective, lower transfer-in
Size and Setting:	Four-year, large, primarily residential

Total Student Enrollment: 47,040
Year established: 2012
Year of expansion/renovation: n/a
Name: Knowledge Commons
Square footage of publicly available space associated with your facility: 57,600
Location: Main Library
Typical access hours per week: 148
Typical service hours per week: 148
Number of service points: 9
Number of desktop computers available for use: 172
Number of laptop computers available for use: 90
Other types of devices provided: Calculators, cameras and media equipment, headphones, iPads, mobile device charging stations, dongles, 3-D printers, littleBits electronics
Average monthly door count: n/a
Average monthly service transactions: We average 7,500 monthly transactions across the service desks unique to the Knowledge Commons. These include reservation requests for group study rooms, technical assistance on lab computers and personal electronic devices, video and audio editing, and instruction on practice presentation studio.
Workstation sessions/logins: 19,750
Library website: https://libraries.psu.edu/knowledgecommons

Purpose

Three key factors moved Penn State Libraries to create the Knowledge Commons: assignments and study habits that required collaborative spaces; emerging technology and the technical support needed to assist students; and the growing trend at large academic libraries of these types of spaces, "Commons."

Services

Existing technical support services (pre-2012/pre-Knowledge Commons) were expanded. Information technology support went from supporting computer and printers to resolving problems on personal devices as well as peer tutoring on software and web-based application tools. In addition, multimedia support expanded with building presentation recording studios, known as One-Button Studios. In 2000, the Libraries eliminated its general reference desk and moved to subject specialties service desks. They maintained service desks for circulation of materials, lending of equipment, and directional.

Software

Technical support is provided by student workers, known as ITS Lab Consultants, employed by the Department of Information Technology and assigned to the Libraries. Campus computers have an extensive list of application suites that are accessible with Windows or Mac. This includes software applications for Microsoft Office, word processing, electronic publishing, digital imaging, spreadsheets and statistics, math and CAD and engineering, and assistive technology as well as a range of video and multimedia editing.

Knowledge Commons
Source: Pennsylvania State University

Print Resources

An underlying design principle for the Knowledge Commons was to create spaces that students would find inviting and welcoming. Included in the KC is the Leisure Reading Room holding current fiction, nonfiction, science fiction, comics, and other works that may have entertainment value for college students. Included in the Knowledge Commons is the Commons Services Desk where students go to check out items from the collection, equipment, and course reserves. The KC is on the first floor of a multistory building. On other floors students have access to most of the libraries' collection including periodicals, microform, rare books, and manuscripts.

Staff

There are three key services and each maintains one to three service desks. The Libraries staffs its entrances, a service desk in the Knowledge Commons, and its circulation desk, referred to as Commons Services. There is someone at each of these desks whenever the library is open (24/5 during the academic year). The Department of Information Technology provides student workers at three service desks. One is dedicated to providing technical support on the equipment in the Knowledge Commons, one assists with problems on personal electronic devices, and the third provides tutoring on software and web-based application tools. The first two are staffed until midnight most days of the week. The tutoring service has fewer hours. The third key service is multimedia support. Under the Department of Information Technology, the Teaching and Learning with Technology unit provides full-time workers to oversee its operations within the Knowledge Commons. Their service desk is available until 9:00 p.m. most days of the week.

Funding/Budget

The Libraries provides building operational and maintenance support for the Knowledge Commons. It also provides staffing for library services. The University's Department of Information Technology provides staffing for all IT and multimedia services within the Knowledge Commons.

Publicity/Promotion

The Knowledge Commons is very popular with students. Since it opened in January 2012, students have promoted the comfort of the space, the availability of services, being open 24/5, and its proximity to a coffee shop. In anticipation of the KC, the Libraries negotiated with public transportation to establish a bus stop near the entrance, making it more accessible for students who live off campus. A 2014 study found that one-third of Penn State students at the University Park campus (nearly 15,000 individual students) spent time at one of the Knowledge Commons computers during the Fall semester. The Office of Public Relations and Marketing ensures press coverage in campus, local, regional, and national publications. The Knowledge Commons is a stop for all campus tours. It is also included in new student orientation. And, annually the Libraries' Open House introduces 3,000–3,500 new students to it. It has been particularly rewarding to see how the Knowledge Commons has influenced new construction and renovations on campus, notably the Support Center for Student Athletes and the College of Nuclear and Mechanical Engineering's Commons.

Evaluation

Each service desk (library, ITS, multimedia) tracks desk transactions, tours, and classes. The library conducts hourly head counts. Computer usage reports (number of logins with length of time) are available from ITS upon request. Anecdotal data is collected as the Head of the Knowledge Commons office is located centrally. The library funded a graduate assistant for 2014-15 for more in-depth assessment. Seating sweeps, surveys, focus groups, field observations, as well as detailed computer use reports were examined. The new Office of Library Assessment has conducted field observations and student interviews.

Evolution of Facility

In April 2016 the Knowledge Commons opened its Makers Commons. It includes 32 3-D networked printers accessible to Penn State users across the Commonwealth. Located in the library, it has allowed students from any discipline, or campus, to create a 3-D object. In addition, a group study room was modified to become the Invention Studio, a space where students can use littleBits for rapid, hands-on prototyping of electronic devices.

Future Steps

The success of the Knowledge Commons has accelerated plans for further library renovations in the Pattee Paterno Libraries. Plans are to increase the number of group study rooms and provide more diverse study spaces. Construction is planned for 2019. More immediate, we are moving to a new service model. We are reducing, and concentrating, IT services into one central location and creating a peer2peer support center that will provide library research consultants, writing tutors, and technical tutors, Sunday-Thursday, 10-10, and Friday, 10-6, during the academic year. Throughout the school year special services will be offered in this space, such as personal financial guidance, explaining copyright and plagiarism, and promoting new digital services.

Simon Fraser University: Student Learning Commons
Burnaby, BC, Canada

Total Student Enrollment: 34,990
Year established: 2006
Year of expansion/renovation: Small renovations have happened along the way. A second staff/workroom and two small consultation offices were added in about 2008. Our open consultation space was enlarged and tables were wired for laptops/devices in 2014. Also in 2014, a classroom was added to an adjacent space, where we deliver many of our workshops and classes.
Name: Student Learning Commons
Square footage of publicly available space associated with your facility: 15,000
Location: Main Library
Typical access hours per week: 101
Typical service hours per week: 37.5
Number of service points: 1
Number of desktop computers available for use: 0
Number of laptop computers available for use: 0

Other types of devices provided: n/a
Average monthly door count: 0
Average monthly service transactions: 940
Workstation sessions/logins: 0
Library website: www.lib.sfu.ca/

Purpose

Our Student Learning Commons was created to provide centralized and easily accessible academic support for all students enrolled at our university, in the areas of writing, learning, and English language, through one-on-one consultations, group workshops, and self-access print materials. Our facility also provides work and staff room space for the approximately 75 members of our team, which includes part-time Peer Educators (student volunteers), part-time Graduate Facilitators (paid graduate students), and full-time program coordinators (professional staff members).

Services

Our services were available on campus prior to the opening of this facility. However, being held mainly in Student Services, they were less visible than this location in the Library and were, therefore, much smaller in scale.

Software

n/a

Print Resources

n/a

Staff

Peer Educators (student volunteers), 5 hours per week, varied schedules. Recruited from student (mostly undergraduate) body. Go through initial and ongoing in-house training. Graduate Facilitators (paid graduate students), 5–10 hours per week, varied schedules. Recruited from graduate student body. Program coordinators (professional staff members), 35 hours per week. Recruited from appropriate larger professional communities. Minimum requirement is master's degree and several years' experience in appropriate field. All of the above are on shift mostly during regular business hours. All receive initial and ongoing in-house training.

Funding/Budget

Initial funding for the Student Learning Commons came from the Vice-President Academic, as a support for student success and retention. The funding is now part of the Library's operating budget. The SLC service is managed by a Library Division Head, who reports to the AUL Learning and Research.

Student Learning Commons
Source: Simon Fraser University

Publicity/Promotion

We carry out a number of regular promotional activities, including submitting entries to the university student electronic newsletter; sending welcome emails to faculty each term; having a booth at numerous orientation events, both for students and instructors; visiting classrooms to give a miniorientation of our services; posting news and events on our Web site; and meeting with campus stakeholders formally and informally.

Evaluation

We collect student-satisfaction survey data both in-house and through the Institutional Research and Planning office at our university. We review this data and use it to inform policy and practice.

Evolution

n/a

Future Steps

No changes to our facility are planned at this time.

Texas Christian University: Information Commons
Fort Worth, Texas, USA

Carnegie Classification	
Basic:	Doctoral Universities: Higher Research Activity
Undergraduate Instructional Program:	Balanced arts & sciences/professions, some graduate coexistence
Graduate Instructional Program:	Research Doctoral: Comprehensive programs, no medical/veterinary school
Enrollment Profile:	High undergraduate
Undergraduate Profile:	Four-year, full-time, more selective, lower transfer-in
Size and Setting:	Four-year, medium, primarily residential

Total Student Enrollment: 10,033
Year established: 2000
Year of expansion/renovation: 2015
Name: Information Commons
Square footage of publicly available space associated with your facility: 9,000
Location: Main Library
Typical access hours per week: 138
Typical service hours per week: 138
Number of service points: 5
Number of desktop computers available for use: 110
Number of laptop computers available for use: 55
Other types of devices provided: 3-D printers, scanners, and standard printers
Average monthly door count: n/a
Average monthly services transactions: n/a
Workstation sessions/logins: 120,134
Library website: http://library.tcu.edu/

Purpose

The Library computer lab was staffed 24 hours/day and heavily used. The hours of availability and the breadth of hardware and software options contributed to the popularity. The intent was to offer a "one-stop" service center where computer lab, information technology assistance, and research support were colocated.

Services

The first version of TCU's IC combined the campuswide IT help desk, the Library's Reference Desk, and the Library's computer lab. At that time (15 years ago) and through today, the library computer lab is by far the largest computer lab on campus and the only one open 24 hours a day. With the library's major renovation in 2015, the newly configured Information Commons has a service desk that combines the Library's Computer Lab and the Library's Circulation Desk. The general campus IT help desk is on another floor near the 3D printing lab and the GIGA Lab (high-end software lab). New services include 3-D printing and high-end software.

Software

Adobe Creative Cloud, ArcGIS, Audacity, AutoCAD, ChemDraw, Eclipse, EViews, Firefox, GaussView, Geometer's Sketchpad, GIMP (Gnu Image), Google Chrome, Google Earth, Graph CALC, iLIFE, IE, Inventor, Komodo, MicroCase, MS Office, Mini Tab, NetBeans, QuickTime, PhotoStory, RefWorks, Revit Architecture, Safari, SAS, SPSS, and Windows Live Movie Maker software is accessible when TCU students log in using their campus network accounts. Staff support as needed.

Print Resources

The Information Commons is located on two floors. On one floor the IC adjoins the campus Information Services campuswide Help Desk and includes the GIGA Lab along with 3-D printing. It is separated from the book stacks. On the second floor the computer labs share a common service desk with Circulation (Access Services), and the Reference Desk is in close proximity. They too are separated from the books and from the microfilm services.

Staff

Staff for the Information Commons includes three shifts of employees covering 24-hour accessibility during the long semesters. Staff have job descriptions that use Information Technology skill sets and report to a Director of Library Systems. Staff may rove on occasion but for the most part are at fixed service desks. Supervisory staff from the Library and campus IT staff participate in the training.

Information Commons
Source: Texas Christian University

Field Guide

Funding/Budget

Funding for IC employees is included in the Library's budget. A planned replacement program, on a multiyear cycle for hardware and software, is funded through the campus Information Technology office. Management of the program is through the Library Dean's office by the Director of Library Systems with consultation as needed with campus IT employees.

Publicity/Promotion

Promotion and publicity includes: use of social media, inclusion in library brochures and the library newsletter, use of IC screensavers on hardware for campuswide announcements, and first-year orientation sessions for TCU students.

Evaluation

The Library moved into its current renovated space in Fall 2015. Evaluation was not in place during that time. Earlier evaluations no longer typify the current service offerings.

Evolution of Facility

The importance of the Information Commons cannot be underestimated on this campus. Its heavy use was one of the factors that persuaded campus administrators to renovate the library since it provides the only 24-hour computer lab that is always staffed and provides access to a host of networked software. It is a hub of student activity.

Future Steps

Implementation of data visualization resources

Trinity University: Information Commons
Fort Worth, Texas, USA

Carnegie Classification	
Basic:	Master's Colleges & Universities: Small Programs
Undergraduate Instructional Program:	Arts & sciences plus professions, some graduate coexistence
Graduate Instructional Program:	Postbaccalaureate: Education-dominant, with other professional programs
Enrollment Profile:	Very high undergraduate
Undergraduate Profile:	Four-year, full-time, more selective, lower transfer-in
Size and Setting:	Four-year, small, highly residential

Total Student Enrollment: 2,432
Year established: 2003
Year of expansion/renovation: 2007
Name: Information Commons
Square footage of publicly available space associated with your facility: 22,000
Location: Main Library

Typical access hours per week: 96
Typical service hours per week: 138
Number of service points: 5
Number of desktop computers available for use: 110
Number of laptop computers available for use: 55
Other types of devices provided: 3-D printers, scanners, and standard printers
Average monthly door count: n/a
Average monthly service transactions: n/a
Workstation sessions/logins: 120,134
Library website: http://library.tcu.edu/

Purpose

The Library computer lab was staffed 24 hours/day and heavily used. The hours of availability and the breadth of hardware and software options contributed to the popularity. The intent was to offer a "one-stop" service center where computer lab, information technology assistance, and research support were colocated.

Services

The first version of TCU's IC combined the campuswide IT help desk, the Library's Reference Desk, and the Library's computer lab. At that time (15 years ago) and through today, the library computer lab is by far the largest computer lab on campus and the only one open 24 hours a day. With the library's major renovation in 2015, the newly configured Information Commons has a service desk that combines the Library's Computer Lab and the Library's Circulation Desk. The general campus IT help desk is on another floor near the 3-D printing lab and the GIGA Lab (high-end software lab). New services include 3-D printing and high-end software.

Software

Adobe Creative Cloud, ArcGIS, Audacity, AutoCAD, ChemDraw, Eclipse, EViews, Firefox, GaussView, Geometer's Sketchpad, GIMP (Gnu Image), Google Chrome, Google Earth, Graph CALC, iLIFE, IE, Inventor, Komodo, MicroCase, MS Office, Mini Tab, NetBeans, QuickTime, PhotoStory, RefWorks, Revit Architecture, Safari, SAS, SPSS, and Windows Live Movie Maker software is accessible when TCU students log in using their campus network accounts. Staff support as needed.

Print Resources

The Information Commons is located on two floors. On one floor the IC adjoins the campus Information Services campuswide Help Desk and includes the GIGA Lab along with 3-D printing. It is separated from the book stacks. On the second floor the computer labs share a common service desk with Circulation (Access Services), and the Reference Desk is in close proximity. They too are separated from the books and from the microfilm services.

Staff

Staff for the Information Commons includes three shifts of employees covering 24-hour accessibility during the long semesters. Staff have job descriptions that use Information Technology skill sets and report to a Director of Library Systems. Staff may rove on occasion but for the most part are at fixed service desks. Supervisory staff from the Library and campus IT staff participate in the training.

Information Commons
Source: Trinity University

Funding/Budget

Funding for IC employees is included in the Library's budget. A planned replacement program, on a multiyear cycle for hardware and software, is funded through the campus Information Technology office. Management of the program is through the Library Dean's office by the Director of Library Systems with consultation as needed with campus IT employees.

Publicity/Promotion

Promotion and publicity includes: Use of social media, inclusion in library brochures and the library newsletter, use of IC screensavers on hardware for campuswide announcements, and first-year orientation sessions for TCU students.

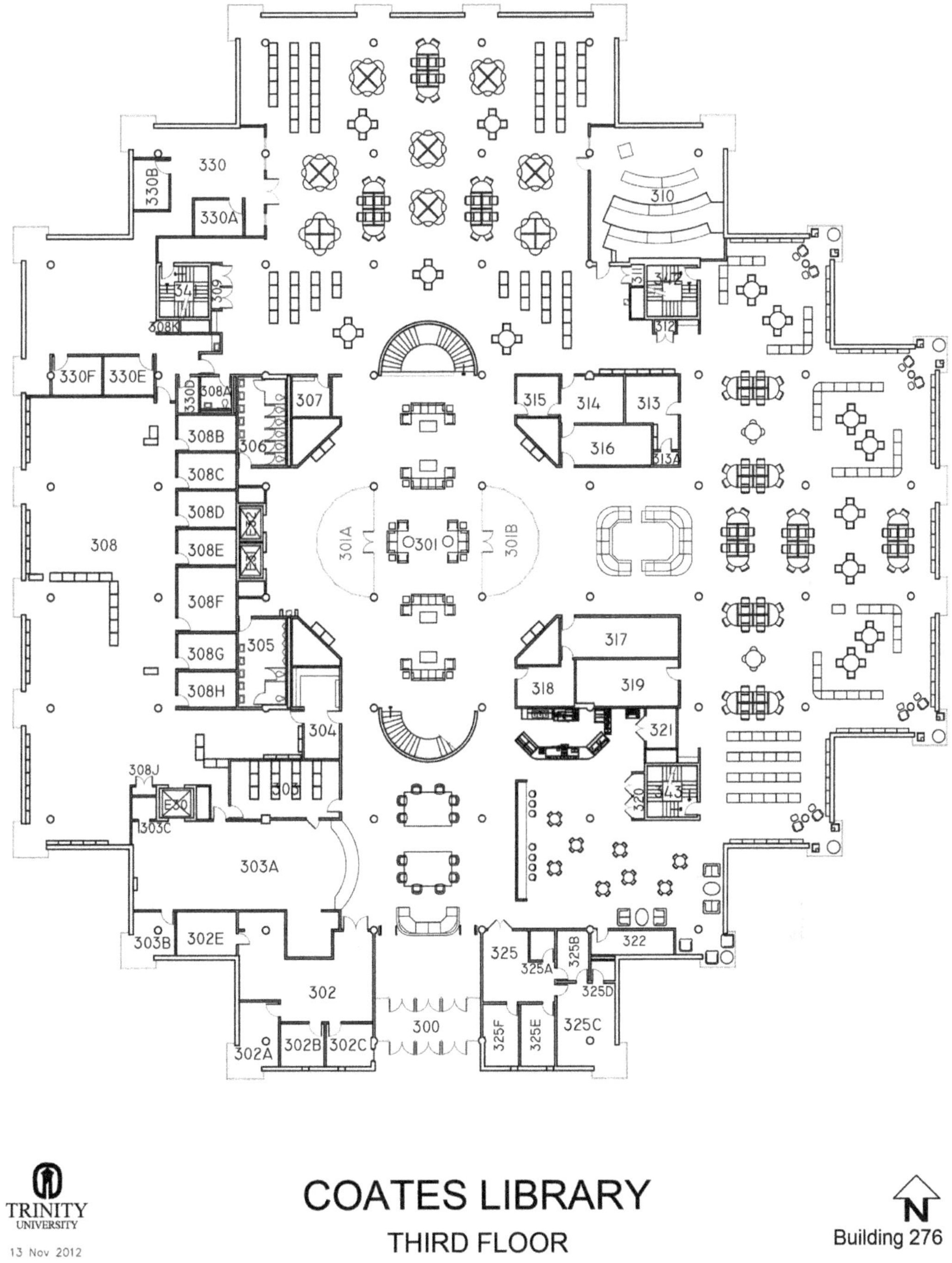

13 Nov 2012

Information Commons
Source: Trinity University

COATES LIBRARY
THIRD FLOOR

Building 276

Field Guide 117

Evaluation

The Library moved into its current renovated space in Fall 2015. Evaluation was not in place during that time. Earlier evaluations no longer typify the current service offerings.

Evolution of Facility

The importance of the Information Commons cannot be underestimated on this campus. Its heavy use was one of the factors that persuaded campus administrators to renovate the library since it provides the only 24-hour computer lab that is always staffed and provides access to a host of networked software. It is a hub of student activity.

Future Steps

Implementation of data visualization resources.

University of Cape Town:
Knowledge Commons, Research Commons, & Learning Commons
Rondebosch, Cape Town, South Africa

Total Student Enrollment: 26,357
Year established: 2002
Year of expansion/renovation: 2005
Name: Knowledge Commons, Research Commons, & Learning Commons
Square footage of publicly available space associated with your facility: n/a
Location: Main Library
Typical access hours per week: n/a
Typical service hours per week: n/a
Number of service points: n/a
Number of desktop computers available for use: 108
Number of laptop computers available for use: 25
Other types of devices provided: Printing facilities are available and so too are scanning facilities.
Average monthly door count: 35,000
Average monthly service transactions: 1,900
Workstation sessions/logins: 0
Library website: www.lib.uct.ac.za/

Purpose

To provide undergraduate support to students of the University. It is a one-stop shop.

Services

Access to internet database, library databases, and library soft skills. None of the services existed prior to the creation of this venue. Peer-to-peer is new as students prefer to engage with peers when they require assistance. The skilled library staff assistance still remain consistent. There is no reference desk facility—the library is working toward self-help through the creation of videos and such.

Knowledge Commons, Research Commons, & Learning Commons
Source: University of Cape Town

Software

Full MS Office suite, the online learning environment (Vula), and Statistica. First-level support is provided by peers via the peer-to-peer learning process.

Print Resources

The facility is designed to support virtual learning with a small collection of reference tools to support the virtual learning process. The print collection is literally a few meters away from the facility to students who would prefer to consult with the print collection.

Staff

There are two permanent library staff supported by 15 highly skilled students. These students receive an intensive three-day training session. Training is continuous over the year that they are employed by the Library. Recruitment of students is dependent on the knowledge of their catalogue and database skills and their MS Office skills. The students have to write a short exam before they are employed by the library.

Funding/Budget

The IT budget is in the region of $114,500. The budget for student assistants is $27,000.

Publicity/Promotion

Currently, the venue runs at full capacity. It is located at the entrance to the Library and is the venue of choice for undergraduate students.

Evaluation

We run user surveys—both quantitative and qualitative. We have focus group discussions for the qualitative data. We have a librarywide values project interrogating the efficiency of the library, its services, and spaces. The results of the recent survey have been published in an international journal.

Evolution of Facility

We seem to have hit a winning formula with this facility.

Future Steps

Given the popularity of the venue and its usage, the planning over the next year or two is to increase the number of seats, make the facility more "collaborative study" friendly, and make it into a 24-hour facility.

University of Central Florida: Knowledge Commons
Orlando, Florida, USA

Carnegie Classification	
Basic:	Doctoral Universities: Highest Research Activity
Undergraduate Instructional Program:	Professions plus arts & sciences, high graduate coexistence
Graduate Instructional Program:	Research Doctoral: Comprehensive programs, with medical/veterinary school
Enrollment Profile:	High undergraduate
Undergraduate Profile:	Four-year, medium full-time, selective, higher transfer-in
Size and Setting:	Four-year, large, primarily nonresidential

Total Student Enrollment: 60,767
Year established: 2010
Year of expansion/renovation: n/a
Name: Knowledge Commons
Square footage of publicly available space associated with your facility: 14,000
Location: Main Library

Typical access hours per week: 105.5
Typical service hours per week: 105.5
Number of service points: 2
Number of desktop computers available for use: 196
Number of laptop computers available for use: 100
Other types of devices provided: laptops, tablet PCs, iPads, calculators, digital cameras, digital voice recorders, flatbed scanners, headphones, projectors, video cameras, webcams, cables, chargers
Average monthly door count: 150,000
Average monthly service transactions: 28,909
Workstation sessions/logins: 268,496
Library website: https://library.ucf.edu/

Purpose

Design and repurpose areas in the main library to create more collaborative, flexible, and functional space. Meet the needs of patrons for more technology access, group study, individual study, research help, and instruction in using library resources, online and in print. Build on the success of Infusion, making the newly created area another place "where students want to be." It should be informal, inviting as well as highly functional.

Services

Reference desk was rebuilt and remains open
479 user seats, an increase from previous 263
196 desktop PCs, up from 94
116 seats with arm's reach access to power
167 additional seats in differing configurations including tables, upholstered chairs with tablet arms, soft seating, and group study settings
Rolling whiteboards and large-screen monitors sprinkled throughout
Major upgrades to electrical and network infrastructure
In total two-thirds of the seating on the floor has a desktop PC or easy reach to power
A new research assistance service point in the round to replace the existing reference desk
Two semienclosed consultation areas for in-depth research assistance and to accommodate complementary academic services such as from the University Writing Center
Improvements to the art wall and refacing of the Circulation desk
All new flooring and wall surfaces
In essence, an entirely new space with increased functionality and access to technology

Software

Adobe Acrobat XI Pro, Adobe Digital Editions 3.0, Adobe Flash Plugin, ArcGIS, ArcReader, Audacity, DjVu Viewer, EndNote X7, Google Chrome, Google Earth, Internet Explorer 11, iTunes, Java Plugin, Microsoft Forefront Endpoint Protection, Microsoft Office 2013 Suite (Word, Excel PowerPoint, Access, Publisher, Outlook, Lync, Visio), Microsoft Silverlight Plugin, Notepad++, Paint.NET, Pearson Lockdown Browser, ProQuest For Word, QuickTime Player, TestGen Plugin, VLC Media Player, Windows Media Player, Windows Movie Maker, Windows Photo Gallery, Wolfram CDF Player

Knowledge Commons
Source: University of Central Florida

Print Resources

Space for the project was made possible by relocating three-fourths of the print materials that had been on the floor. The book collection that remains constitutes a core reference collection and has a double benefit of providing additional visual screening.

Staff

Reference and information services desk is single staffed, double staffed during peak hours. Two "consultation stations" are located directly behind the reference desk for in-depth research assistance.

Funding/Budget

$1.4 million cost to build the Knowledge Commons including new power, data, floor and wall coverings, two new service desks, furnishings for 496 users, and carpentry work. Project was funded primarily by a student technology fee through a competitively awarded annual process. Facility is managed entirely by the Library. The project was planned entirely through collaboration between Library staff, a local professional architect, and design professionals with a leading national furniture company.

Publicity/Promotion

Twitter, Facebook, press release, web page, print flyers, social media. In truth, word of mouth was all that was needed. The KC is located on the main floor of the central library, which sits in the heart of the main campus.

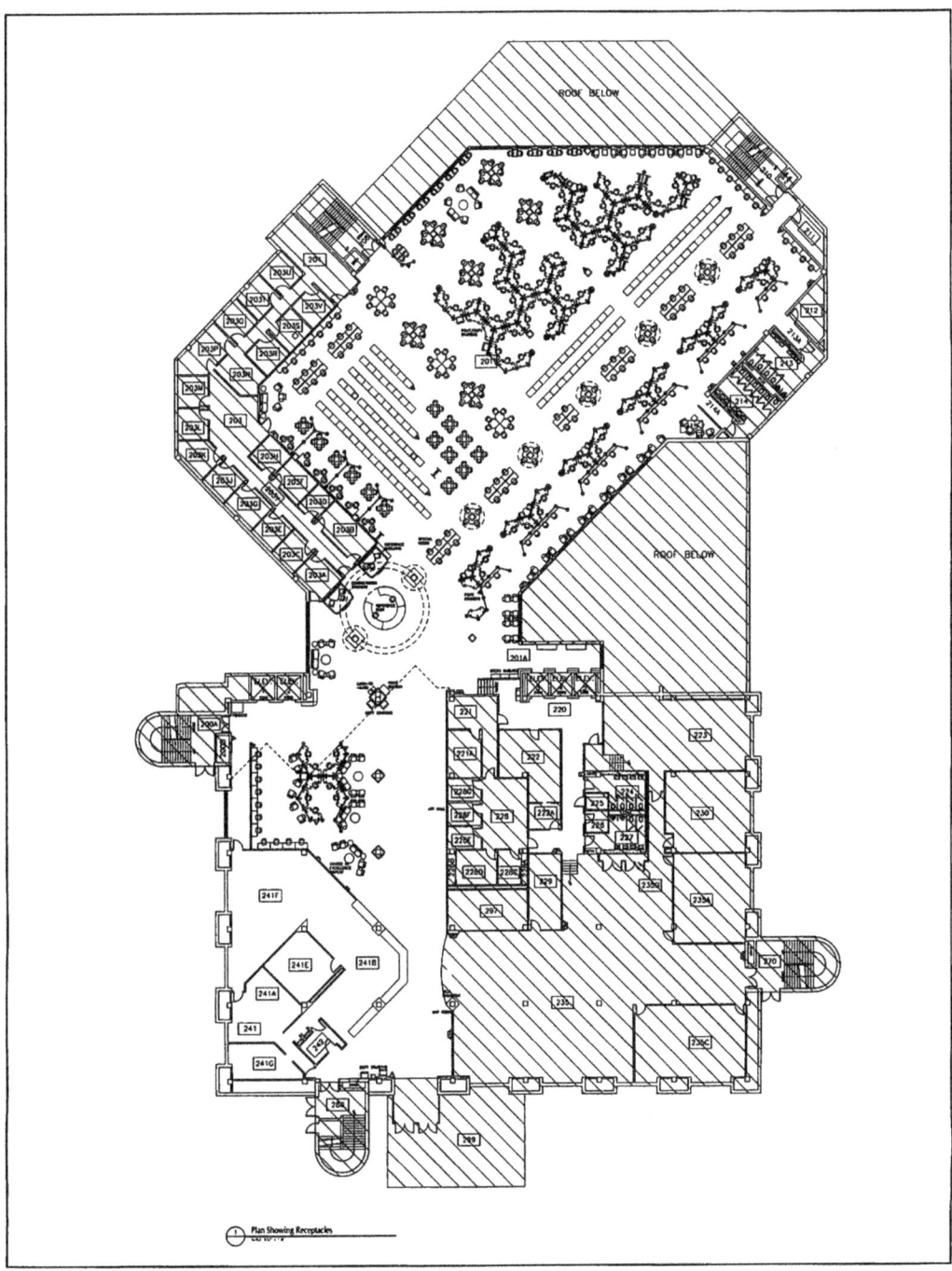

Knowledge Commons
Source: University of Central Florida

Evaluation

In the first full year of operation, gate count in the main library increased 8%. While this may seem modest, the KC encompasses only one of five floors, so an 8% gain was significant. Following opening, research questions at the reference desk increased 58% during the next 12 months.

Evolution of Facility

Tremendous success. Students are literally consuming it. Furniture is used so heavily that it is showing premature wear. We have swapped out wall-mounted monitors for larger ones with Teamwork 400 stations. This technology allows students to plug their laptops into the station and project from their laptop to the wall-mounted monitor.

Future Steps

Have just cleared an additional 7,500 square feet of stack space (10,800 linear feet of shelf space) to create an entirely new quiet study space on top floor with emphasis on individual study. Will seat about 175, 85% of which seats will have immediate access to power. Varieties of seating focusing on extended study.

University of Illinois at Urbana-Champaign: Scholarly Commons
Champaign, Illinois, USA

Carnegie Classification	
Basic:	Doctoral Universities: Highest Research Activity
Undergraduate Instructional Program:	Balanced arts & sciences/professions, high graduate coexistence
Graduate Instructional Program:	Research Doctoral: Comprehensive programs, with medical/veterinary school
Enrollment Profile:	High undergraduate
Undergraduate Profile:	Four-year, full-time, more selective, lower transfer-in
Size and Setting:	Four-year, large, primarily residential

Total Student Enrollment: 45,140
Year established: 2010
Year of expansion/renovation: 2012
Name: Scholarly Commons
Square footage of publicly available space associated with your facility: 742
Location: Main Library
Typical access hours per week: 40
Typical service hours per week: 40
Number of service points: 1
Number of desktop computers available for use: 11
Number of laptop computers available for use: 0
Other types of devices provided: Bookeye scanner; slide scanner; sheet-feed scanner; two flat-bed scanners (one optimized for images)
Average monthly door count: 150

Average monthly service transactions: 50
Workstation sessions/logins: 120
Library website: www.library.illinois.edu/

Purpose

The Scholarly Commons was created to provide a central place on campus where researchers can find help doing technologically advanced research. While some of this help was available from subject librarians before the Scholarly Commons was established, having the services available in one place made it possible to help researchers all over campus, and to form partnerships with other campus units that have similar missions in order to provide services in more depth than the library was able to offer.

Scholarly Commons
Source: University of Illinois at Urbana-Champaign

Services

The Scholarly Commons provides consultations in the following areas: copyright, research data management and curation, data finding and use, digital humanities, digitization, geographic information systems, scholarly communication, usability, and undergraduate research. The Scholarly Commons also manages a workshop series that encompasses all these topics. There was some activity in almost all of these areas before the Scholarly Commons opened, but it was by individual librarians to serve individual user groups.

Currently, the Scholarly Commons is the "public face" of two new library units: Research Data Service and Scholarly Communications and Publishing. It serves as a referral point for these units as well as for several services outside the library. We also have a mission to create an interdisciplinary community of scholars around each of the areas we cover, so we organize workshops, brown bags, special events, and outside speaker visits in order to bring researchers together so that they can network as well as from a presenter.

Until January 2015, the Scholarly Commons was a service point of the main reference department at the library; it is now an autonomous unit. Our front desk is an intake point rather than a traditional reference desk. Basic questions can be answered there, but almost every question is referred to a specialist inside or outside the unit.

Software

Other than the general productivity software that is available throughout the library, the Scholarly Commons has statistical, GIS, qualitative analysis, usability, optical character recognition, ARTstore, R, Python, and the complete Adobe suite. A complete list is available on the website: www.library.illinois.edu/it/helpdesk/groupspaces/main306sc.html. When possible, we try to provide an open source alternative in addition to expensive statistical and GIS packages. Scholarly Commons personnel are fluent in some of this software, and we rely on our reference collection to fill in gaps in our knowledge. Not every software package is on every workstation, to minimize the memory load on individual workstations and to save money on licenses if a package does not get heavy use.

Print Resources

We have a print reference collection that leans heavily toward tutorials and workbooks for the software we have in the space, but also contains some methodology texts for more general conceptual learning. Some of these books circulate from elsewhere in the library, but they are scattered across campus and are almost always checked out. We also are developing a collection of data sets as part of our data services mission. We keep this collection as current as possible and send older materials to the circulating collection.

Staff

Currently our staff consists of a Head, a Digital Scholarship Liaison and Instruction Librarian, a GIS Specialist, an office manager, and four graduate assistants. The manager of the campus's researcher information service and a digital humanities specialist also have offices in the space, though they are not technically part of the department. We rely on graduate assistants, who are MSLIS candidates, to staff our intake desk and to make referrals to specialists. The space is small enough that we only rove occasionally to check on a user's progress with a task they asked for help with. Both librarians have backgrounds in reference; one also

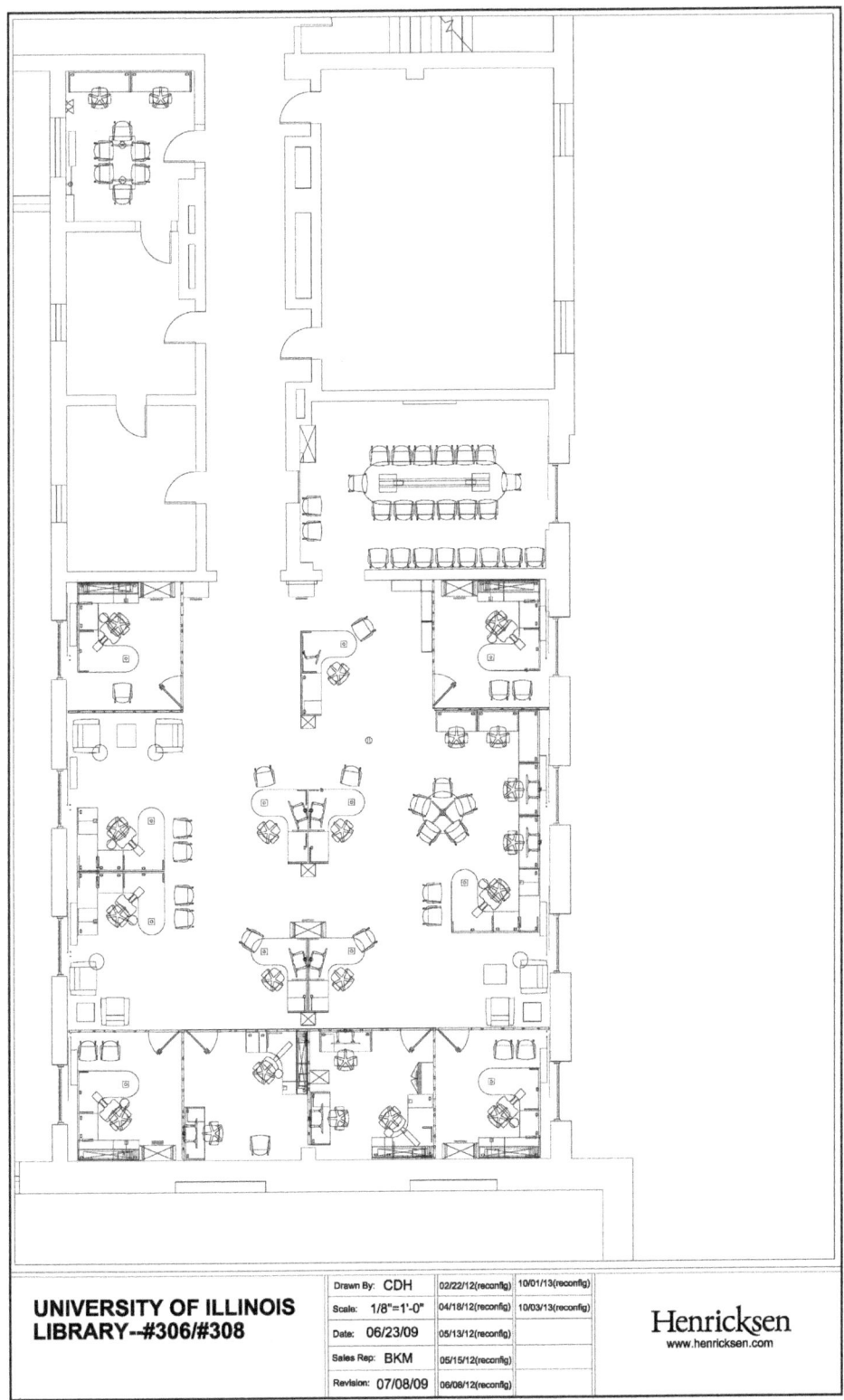

Scholarly Commons
Source: University of Illinois at Urbana-Champaign

has deep expertise in instruction and the other has expertise in data acquisition and use as well as government information. The GIS Specialist has an advanced degree in geography and experience working in a museum. We recruit staff and graduate assistants who have a strong service orientation as well as an understanding of how to explain technical information to nonexperts. Some of our graduate assistants also come in with expertise in one of our service areas, but primarily we look for interest in the types of services we offer and provide on-the-job training.

Funding/Budget

Our staff salaries, including stipends for graduate assistants, are part of the library budget. We fund our events and marketing from a gift account that the Scholarly Commons controls. We are part of the Library's Office of Research, and the Scholarly Commons works with the Associate University Librarian for Research on planning and facilities issues, particularly on any major needs like new positions or facilities changes. Program management is a collaborative endeavor between the Head and the Digital Scholarship and Instruction Librarian.

Publicity/Promotion

The events we host are a major source of student and faculty awareness of our work. We have electronic signs in the Library both for the department as a whole and for specific services we offer and events we sponsor, and we regularly speak at events on campus about how the Scholarly Commons can help researchers. We have a blog and a Twitter account where we promote services and events as well as other information of interest to researchers on campus. We do have printed promotional materials but use them primarily to hand out at events.

Evaluation

We have not yet done the formal service assessment that we would like to do. We do collect stories about the Scholarly Commons' impact on campus researchers and we use these on promotional materials with permission.

Evolution of Facility

When the Scholarly Commons opened, it was less than half the size it is now and offered consultations but no space for users to work on their own. It moved to its current location and opened a nearby usability lab once space became available.

Future Steps

The Head hopes that the Scholarly Commons can be moved from its out-of-the-way location in the Main Library to a space that is adjacent to humanities units and the main information desk and reading room. This would enable us to be more integrated into the other services offered in the Main Library and put us in a more welcoming and flexible space. We are hoping to host more of our larger events in our own space, which is extremely difficult in the quiet study and office space that we currently have. We also are always working to nurture new partnerships and deepen our services.

University of Iowa: Learning Commons
Iowa City, Iowa, USA

Carnegie Classification	
Basic:	Doctoral Universities: Highest Research Activity
Undergraduate Instructional Program:	Balanced arts & sciences/professions, high graduate coexistence
Graduate Instructional Program:	Research Doctoral: Comprehensive programs, with medical/veterinary school
Enrollment Profile:	High undergraduate
Undergraduate Profile:	Four-year, full-time, more selective, higher transfer-in
Size and Setting:	Four-year, large, primarily residential

Total Student Enrollment: 29,970
Year established: 2013
Year of expansion/renovation: 2012-13
Name: Learning Commons
Square footage of publicly available space associated with your facility: 3,200
Location: Main Library
Typical access hours per week: 120
Typical service hours per week: 120
Number of service points: 1
Number of desktop computers available for use: 90
Number of laptop computers available for use: 50
Other types of devices provided: We check out Lightning to HDMI and Mini DisplayPort to HDMI adapters, mice, PC and Mac computer chargers, HDMI, VGA and Ethernet, Ethernet cords, wireless presentation slide advancers, and microphones. Each group space has a large monitor to which students can connect their laptops. Three of the group spaces have Apple TVs.
Average monthly door count: 137,000
Average monthly service transactions: 8,377
Workstation sessions/logins: 175,756
Library website: www.lib.uiowa.edu/

Purpose

The Learning Commons was first envisioned by University leadership in a white paper published in 2007. In it, Nancy Baker, Tom Rocklin, and Steve Fleagle make a case for outfitting the academic library with spaces and resources that focus on the user, allowing them to learn how to interact with today's ever increasing digital landscape. The Learning Commons brought a much-needed facility and technology upgrade to the Main Library and cemented the Libraries' role as the academic heart of the institution in this century and set it up for continued worth into the future and the changes that will come with it. The Learning Commons was designed as a response to the drastic change in how users interact with the library over the last few decades with users spending more and more time working online using a variety of tools and output modes, and often collaboratively. The Main Library Learning Commons is also connected to part of the University of Iowa's strategic plan to support student success. The Main Library had always been a popular place for students to study for long periods of time, and the Learning Commons is a safe, welcoming space for students to spend hours on end studying, visiting, reading, eating, etc.

Services

The Main Library's multiple service desks were combined into one consolidated desk that sits in between the Learning Commons and the Main Library Collections. The last two service points to be combined were Circulation and Reference Services. When the Learning Commons opened, staff from both departments worked at the single service point. As time passed and data was gathered, we decided to staff it only with circulations staff. The research librarians would continue to monitor the Libraries' instant messaging service and would act as backup when needed. Staff primarily provide circulation-related services, basic technology troubleshooting support, basic reference support, and directional services. The service desk relies heavily on providing efficient and accurate referrals for everything else. We host several tutoring services including the Writing Center, the Speaking Center, the Statistics Tutoring Lab, and the Conversation Center, a brand new tutoring services that provides support for international students who are interested in improving their English speaking skills. The research librarians have two research consultation stations they may reserve when scheduling an in-person consultation with a library user. They also host office hours and monitor our instant messaging service at these stations. The Learning Commons houses one classroom that is managed by the Registrar's Office and 24 group rooms that are supported by the Learning Commons Coordinator and service desk staff. The Learning Commons is host to many workshops, classes, and events led by instructors, librarians, or other campus partners. Instructors often schedule class presentations in the Learning Commons to provide public speaking experience to their students. The Learning Commons is also home to the Food for Thought Café.

Software

All computers in the Learning Commons have Adobe Creative Suite, Microsoft Office Suite, ArcGIS, Virtual Desktop, and a variety of browsers and specialty software used in classes.

Print Resources

There are no book collections or stacks in the Learning Commons. Adjacent to the Learning Commons, and an original part of the renovations, is the Service Commons, which houses the media viewing equipment (microfilm, VHS, DVD, Blueray). The Service Commons also contains the browsable course reserves collection, new books, reference alcove, newspapers, public access computers (the only computers in the building that are open to community members), the One Button Studio (easy-to-use video recording studio), and a variety of study tables and lounge seating. There is one entrance between the Learning Commons and the rest of the Library, and it contains a security gate. All users must check out all library materials before they can bring them into the Learning Commons. Nonloanable items cannot be used in the Learning Commons. Librarians will often host programs highlighting various collections in the Learning Commons, called Pop-Up Libraries. These temporary collections must be monitored at all times and are checked out to a proxy card. If a user wants to check out a book from the Pop-Up Library, they can be checked out using a laptop and scanner. Recently, the Libraries renovated the Main Library Gallery Space, which is adjacent to the Learning

Learning Commons
Source: University of Iowa

Commons. The Gallery highlights many of our unique collections and has limited hours and is locked when not open.

Staff

A brand new FTE position, called the Learning Commons Coordinator, was created to coordinate support of the Learning Commons, including facilities and technology maintenance, programming, marketing and outreach, and services. The position is dual appointed to both the University Libraries (housed in Access Services) and Information Technology Services. The Learning Commons Coordinator collaborates with the Head of Access Services and the Head of Research & Library Instruction as well as staff supervisors to provide leadership for the Service Desk. The Service Desk is staffed by Access Services. The Research & Library Instruction (RLI) librarians provide backup while monitoring the instant messaging service at the research consultation stations.

Originally, both Access Services and Research & Library Instruction staff worked at the desk. After reviewing data showing that most interactions are circulation-related, we replaced RLI with the Interlibrary Loan staff. The Learning Commons is open 24/5 during the academic year. During the late- and overnight hours, one full-time staff (hired for that position) and two student workers work at the Service Desk.

At first, we tried having our student workers from Access Services rove, but the service was rarely used. While student workers were roving, they also were taking head counts throughout the first two floors. After one semester of roving, we discontinued the practice. This past December we have reinstated roving, with an effort to provide better printer and computer support. Each shift, a staff member or student worker must rove around the first two floors to check printers to make sure they are stocked. Student workers are peer trained by the Head of ILL, Learning Commons Coordinator, RLI, and Circulation. Staff are trained via training sessions.

Funding/Budget

The LC was created as a partnership between The Provost's Office, The University of Iowa Libraries, and Information Technology Services. Each department provides $5,000 a year for a budget of $15,000 to be used on professional development for the Learning Commons Coordinator, outreach and marketing, facilities maintenance, event planning, and hardware upgrades. The University Libraries maintains and supports all facilities issues, while Information Technology Services maintains and supports all technology issues. Both are coordinated by the Learning Commons Coordinator. Programming is coordinated via the Learning Commons Coordinator. Most programs are planned through the libraries, but the Learning Commons is available for any campus partner to host events.

Publicity/Promotion

During the planning and construction stages, marketing designed a half sheet filled with basic details about the new facility. Closer to opening, we provided sneak peek tours to Libraries and ITS staff. After the Learning Commons opened, we provided a series of "soft" open houses for new students, returning students, and the community. We sent out mass emails and attended many orientation and departmental meetings to promote the space. During the second semester, we hosted a grand opening. Currently we rely on word of mouth, a few mass emails to select departments, and we provide information at orientations for incoming students, faculty, and staff.

Evaluation

We look at gate counts (we get daily, weekly, and monthly numbers) and document interactions at the Service Desk. For the first two years we had a feedback board stationed at our heaviest entrance. Much of the feedback we obtained from the board was related to noise complaints (space was too loud), facilities issues (doors weren't working, group rooms too hot), and lack of available resources (all the computers and group rooms were full). In the spring of 2014, the university administered the Student Engagement in the Research University (SERU) survey, and we were able to include a series of questions about the Learning Commons. Approximately 67% of the respondents to these questions stated they use the Learning Commons in a typical week in an academic year. The median amount of usage was 1-5 hours a week. We took head counts for the first year. During the second year, we focused our head counts on what resources users were using and what they were doing. After the third year, we stopped taking head counts. We also collect usage statistics on computers and printers, and we look at reservation statistics.

Evolution of Facility

The facility is only a few years old—not much has changed. It took quite a bit of marketing and outreach to get campus partners and instructors interested in using the Learning Commons for educational events and one-shot classes. Most of our users were used to the library being a relatively quiet space and continued to treat it as such. After the first year, that began to change

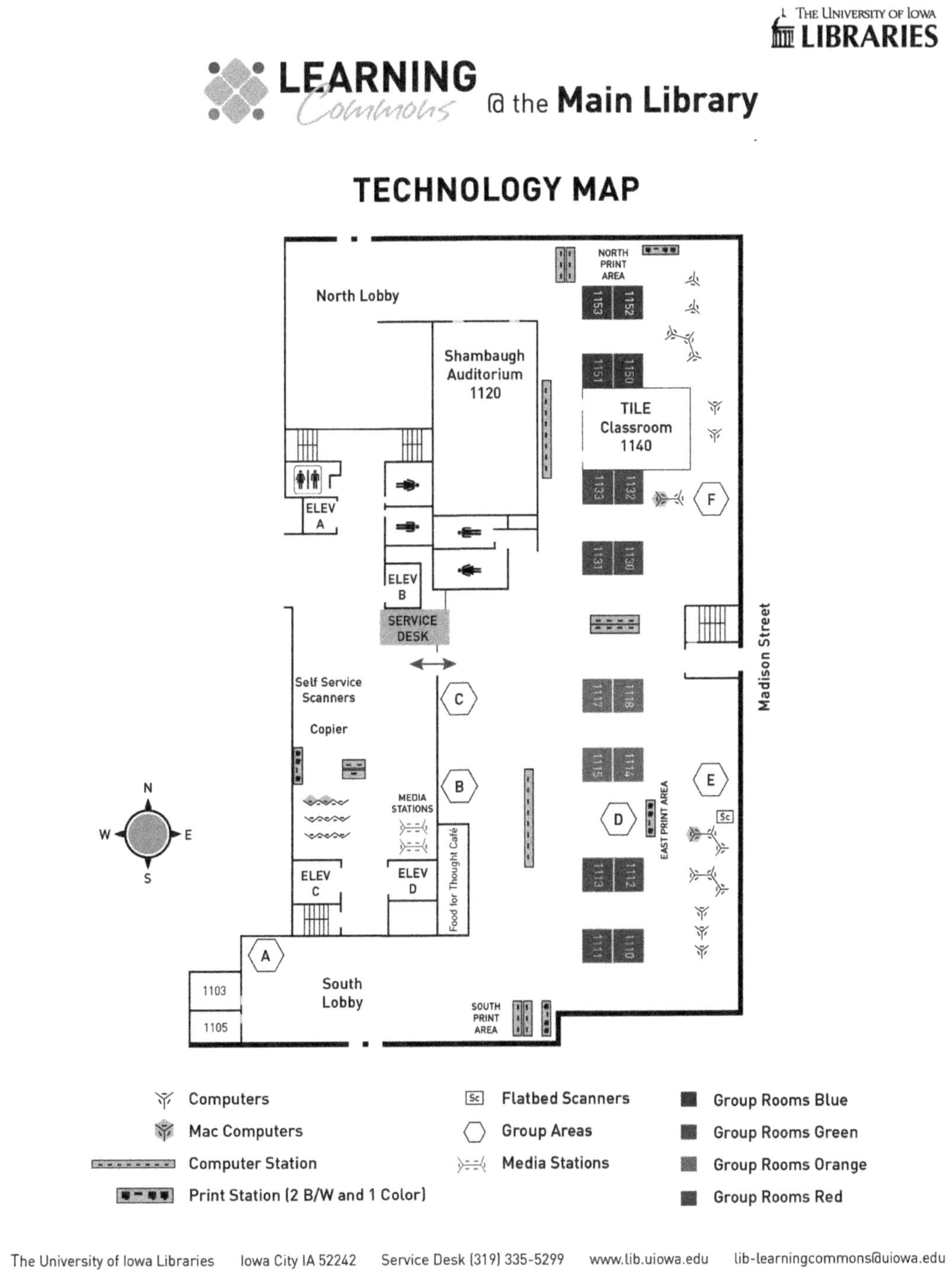

TECHNOLOGY MAP

Learning Commons
Source: University of Iowa

slowly. Now we focus our marketing and outreach efforts on incoming instructors. We have continued to add services to the service desk, including new peripherals available for checkout. Last fall, we added a One Button Studio, a very easy-to-use video recording studio. Out of the 24 group spaces we have, six of them are open group areas. These spaces weren't heavily used for student work and are now mostly used for events, activities, and class presentations. A couple of the spaces are rarely used by students and hopefully will be turned into digital exhibition spaces for student work. We have renovated the Main Library Gallery and have also renovated the entrance to the Digital Scholarship & Publishing Studio, which is adjacent to the Learning Commons.

Future Steps

We recently added a One Button Studio, an easy-to-use video recording studio. We are looking at how we can support video editing for users who are creating video content with the One Button Studio as well as other digital media support services. We are also looking at how we can use the Learning Commons to continue showcasing student work.

University of Maryland: Terrapin Learning Commons
College Park, Maryland, USA

Carnegie Classification	
Basic:	Doctoral Universities: Highest Research Activity
Undergraduate Instructional Program:	Balanced arts & sciences/professions, high graduate coexistence
Graduate Instructional Program:	Research Doctoral: Comprehensive programs, with medical/veterinary school
Enrollment Profile:	Majority undergraduate
Undergraduate Profile:	Four-year, full-time, more selective, higher transfer-in
Size and Setting:	Four-year, large, primarily residential

Total Student Enrollment: 37,610
Year established: 2009
Year of expansion/renovation: 2011
Name: Terrapin Learning Commons
Square footage of publicly available space associated with your facility: 17,222
Location: Main Library
Typical access hours per week: 132
Typical service hours per week: 132
Number of service points: 1
Number of desktop computers available for use: 93
Number of laptop computers available for use: 93
Other types of devices provided: 3-D printers, 3-D scanners, Apple Watch, batteries, binding and laminating equipment, button maker, calculators, circuit kits, digital audio recorders, DVD + Blu-Ray players, energy lamps, fax machine, flatbed scanners, Google Glass, headphones, keyboards, laptop and phone chargers, large-screen monitors, memory cards, mice, microphones, Oculus Rift headset, pixelstick, portable projectors, portable scanners, poster printers, printer/photocopiers, Sphero robots, still cameras, tablet computers, USB and FireWire hubs, video cameras, vinyl cutter, webcams, Xbox 360.
Average monthly door count: n/a
Average monthly service transactions: 8,827
Workstation sessions/logins: 30,000
Library website: www.lib.umd.edu/

Purpose

In response to feedback from students, the TLC was created to provide students with a "home away from home" where they could freely interact with their peers within the library. In contrast with the traditional "quiet" library research environment, the TLC was designed to encourage collaboration and the sharing of ideas through comfortable, nontraditional furniture which could be rearranged to meet their specific needs, whiteboards, computers, and ample outlets to facilitate student use of their own laptops and other electronics.

Services

Services offered at the TLC include equipment loan; reservable group study rooms; "self-publishing" services, including self-service printing and poster printing, binding, and laminating; event spaces; makerspace services, including 3-D printing and scanning; and makerspace training. Group study room reservations and collaborations with campus partners using our event spaces were new services, but the self-publishing services were formerly housed in a campus copy shop, and the equipment loan service was previously run through the library's main circulation desk. A new service unit was created for the TLC drawing staff from other units within the Public Services Department. The TLC Tech Desk was created as an additional service point, so the reference desk was unaffected by its creation.

Software

The TLC contains both PC and Apple computers. Both include office productivity, graphic, citation, and statistical software. The machines in the TLC are refreshed every four years with the best computers available that the Libraries can afford. The Libraries IT staff provides software support through consultations and by working with students as needs arise. The operating system and software on each computer is refreshed every summer. The following software is available on computers in the TLC: Internet Explorer, Mozilla Firefox, Google Chrome, Opera, Safari, Microsoft Office 2013 (including Word, Excel, Lync, PowerPoint, InfoPath, Outlook, and Publisher), Evernote, Endnote, RefWorks Write-N-Cite, Foxit Reader, Adobe Acrobat Pro XI, MATLAB 2014b, Maple 2015, SPSS 23, SAS 9.4, Wolfram Mathematica 9, Fathom 2, Chem Office 2015, Geometer's Sketchpad, Minitab 16, SketchUp 2015, Weka, QuickTime, Real Player, Microsoft Silverlight, Adobe Flash, Adobe Shockwave, VLC Media Player, Adobe Creative Cloud Suite, ArcGIS Desktop 10.3, ENVI 5.0, RStudio Desktop, QGIS, ArcGIS Explorer Desktop, Google Earth Pro, NASA Panopoly, Bioconductor, Anaconda, TightVNC, Microsoft Visual Studio 2013 Pro, Putty, WinSCP, Java, Camtasia Studio, Readcube, and Citrix client.

Print Resources

The TLC is located on the second floor of McKeldin Library, the University of Maryland's main library, where the bulk of the general collection of print and microform materials is housed. None of these materials are housed on the second floor, though. Despite the fact that the TLC is not primarily intended to provide access to print and other physical materials, we find that they are used frequently in the space, especially in connection with our scanners and printers.

Staff

The TLC is staffed by one librarian, four FTE exempt and nonexempt staff, and six FTE student worker staff (approximately 15 student workers at any given time). The space, like the rest of the

Terrapin Learning Commons
Source: University of Maryland

library, is open 24 hours/day Sunday through Friday at 8 p.m., and 10 a.m.–9 p.m. on Saturday. TLC staff are present from 8 a.m.–11 p.m. Sunday through Friday, and it is staffed jointly by TLC student workers and floating staff from elsewhere in the User Services & Resource Sharing Department, including late-night staff, the rest of the time.

Funding/Budget

The initial cost of developing the space was approximately $220,000, and the operating budget for the Libraries was increased by approximately $100,000 at the time it was created to pay for operating and maintenance costs. Staff salaries for the TLC equal approximately $300,000 per year. Equipment refresh and software licenses are paid for out of a general fund, so the amount of money dedicated to the TLC is not available.

Publicity/Promotion

We use a wide variety of means to make the TLC known to undergraduate students, including advertisements on the library website and social media accounts; promotions (last semester, for instance, we offered a "private study room" during finals week as a prize in a raffle); partnerships with other campus units such as the University Counseling Center, which conducts guided study sessions in our space, and Residence Life, which last year held an event called "The Amazing Race—Library Edition" there to make RAs and other Residence Life staff aware of our spaces and services; library instruction sessions for classes utilizing TLC equipment and services such as poster and 3-D printing; and a variety of other events, such as 3-D printing demonstrations and open houses. Last year, we also collaborated with another makerspace on campus to create 90 3-D-printed trophies for an event celebrating student innovators and entrepreneurs, which received positive feedback from attendees at the event, including the University president, and many great photos, all of which should be invaluable from a marketing standpoint. Honestly, though, the best publicity for the space is word of mouth!

Evaluation

Usage of the space is evaluated through circulation statistics, which tell us how often each type of equipment is checked out; RefAnalytics records of service desk transaction, where, most notably, we record turn-away statistics, our primary means of determining what new types of equipment we should make available; cash register statistics; and printer statistics. We do currently have a plan for evaluating user satisfaction, although we hope to develop one soon (see "Future Steps").

Evolution of Facility

Approximately a year after the TLC opened, a staffing presence was added to the space in response to feedback from students. A Tech Desk was created that offered reservable group study rooms, equipment loan, and "self-publishing" services including binding, laminating, and printing. Large-format printers were added shortly after that, followed by 3-D printers and scanners, and other emerging technologies, which were later collected together in a donor-funded makerspace. As a natural outgrowth of this evolution, the TLC has also become a locus for collaborations between the Libraries and other groups on campus who are attracted to the space and the services we offer in it.

Future Steps

New services and initiatives planned for the coming year include shifting to patron-managed group study room reservations, development of a new poster printing service whereby library users are encouraged to send print jobs to us to be vetted for proper formatting, development of a strategic/business plan for the John & Stella Graves makerspace, development of an emerging technologies lending program, development of a plan for displaying student-created artwork in the TLC, and creation of a plan to gather tangible feedback from users of the TLC on what specific things we're doing well and how we can improve their library experience. Subsequent initiatives include expanding both the makerspace and TLC, hiring new staff, and refreshing the furniture in the TLC.

University of Minnesota Twin Cities: SMART Learning Commons Minneapolis, Minnesota, USA	
Carnegie Classification	
Basic:	Doctoral Universities: Highest Research Activity
Undergraduate Instructional Program:	Balanced arts & sciences/professions, high graduate coexistence
Graduate Instructional Program:	Research Doctoral: Comprehensive programs, with medical/veterinary school
Enrollment Profile:	Majority undergraduate
Undergraduate Profile:	Four-year, full-time, more selective, higher transfer-in
Size and Setting:	Four-year, large, primarily nonresidential

Total Student Enrollment: 51,147
Year established: 2004
Year of expansion/renovation: 2008
Name: SMART Learning Commons
Square footage of publicly available space associated with your facility: 2,800
Location: Other
Typical access hours per week: 100
Typical service hours per week: 89
Number of service points: 3
Number of desktop computers available for use: 27
Number of laptop computers available for use: 0
Other types of devices provided: The SMART Learning Commons Media Services component does support a pool of digital cameras, audio recording devices, and associated peripherals (tripods, storage drives, and microphones) to support media production activities.
Average monthly door count: 53,884
Average monthly service transactions: 407
Workstation sessions/logins: 31,000
Library website: www.lib.umn.edu/

Purpose

The SMART Learning Commons as it exists today is the result of a collaborative effort by several campus units to create a universally accessible, comprehensive learning support center for undergraduates. In addition to new services, existing programs with varying histories and connections became part of SMART. Groups involved in the SMART collaboration include the University Libraries and Office of Undergraduate Education within the Office of the Provost.

Services

Services are primarily designed and targeted toward undergraduate students. SMART Learning Commons' services include: one-on-one consultations with an experienced peer across math, science, econ and liberal arts disciplines at the undergraduate level, writing support for native and nonnative speakers of English, facilitated group study sessions (PAL), and individual and group study spaces. Test Bank: Copies of previously administered exams are available to students as provided by professors and departments. The students request a test, which is sent to a library printer for the student to print out at 12 cents per page using a "U Card." Test preparation for high-stakes normed tests (MCAT, GRE, TOEFL, etc.). This includes both computerized and paper-based materials. Internet/library research assistance: Internet and research assistance is available through media consultants located in Walter Library, or through learning consultants with research methods background. Multimedia curriculum integration facilitation, technology education, multimedia equipment checkout, and production support: Multimedia equipment is available for check-out in SMART—Walter and SMART—Wilson, with assistance and tutorials available from media consultants scheduled in Walter as well. None of the services were entirely "new" upon incorporation into the SMART model but had already been offered in some fashion on the campus. The libraries continued to also have more traditional Reference Desks (later, Information Desks) as separate service points in the libraries that also house SMART Learning Commons sites (there are three such sites across the campus).

Software

SMART public computing has a few variants of computing profiles. The PCs generally follow the larger public computing profile including a basic Windows environment and utilities including the core Microsoft Office applications as needed for student use. The iMac computers are generally to support media production and so, in addition to a standard OS profile and general productivity tools, also include media production support programs such as Adobe Creative Suite, Final Cut Pro, iMovie, iPhoto, Audacity, and Screenflow.

Print Resources

The collections associated with the SMART Learning Commons are situated in the Walter location and consist of circulating media collections and a set of study materials for standardized preparatory tests such as the DAT, GMAT, GRE, LSAT, MCAT, and NCLEX tests. There is also a Test Bank Collection of previously administered tests, quizzes, or other assessment measures from many classes at the institution. These materials have been provided by faculty, are authorized for sharing, and are usually 2-3 years old so as to provide an illustration of the material to help students prepare, but not provide questions/answers currently in use. These materials have been scanned in and then SMART staff mediate access to prepare print-outs of these for student use.

Staff

Libraries staff include the SMART Student Media Consultants who staff the SMART Desk and provide support for media creation, media collections, Test Bank materials, and

SMART Learning Commons
Source: University of Minnesota Twin Cities

Field Guide

general service information regarding PRC and PLC tutoring Services; and Peer Research Consultants who provide library research tutoring support. Regular staff from the Libraries include a full-time SMART Media Site Manager, a full-time Media Outreach Librarian, and other Libraries Operation staff who provide some support to SMART activities in the SMART locations (but are not full-time devoted to SMART). The Office of Undergraduate Education staff includes three full-time staff, Peer Learning Consultants, and Peer Assisted Learning Consultants.

Funding/Budget

The Information Commons started with $180,000 in one-time funding, and the Libraries component of SMART Services has been operating with an $85,000/year annual budget that goes mainly for student staff support and computer and other technology replacement funding. Another $85,000 approximately for the two dedicated SMART Libraries regular staff as noted above.

Publicity/Promotion

The SMART Learning Commons has a set of public web pages describing services and resources (smart.umn.edu), utilizes a variety of printed promotional resources including a general brochure, specific support handouts, and posters, table-tents, and other signage for use in a variety of spaces in SMART, the broader Libraries, and other campus spaces. There is a communications and events plan for identifying specific activities for the year.

Evaluation

Tutoring services use postsession feedback instruments (immediate after session, another a few weeks out to further address impact). PAL uses pre and post surveys, and grade impact analysis. SMART media course support uses instructor feedback assessment. At

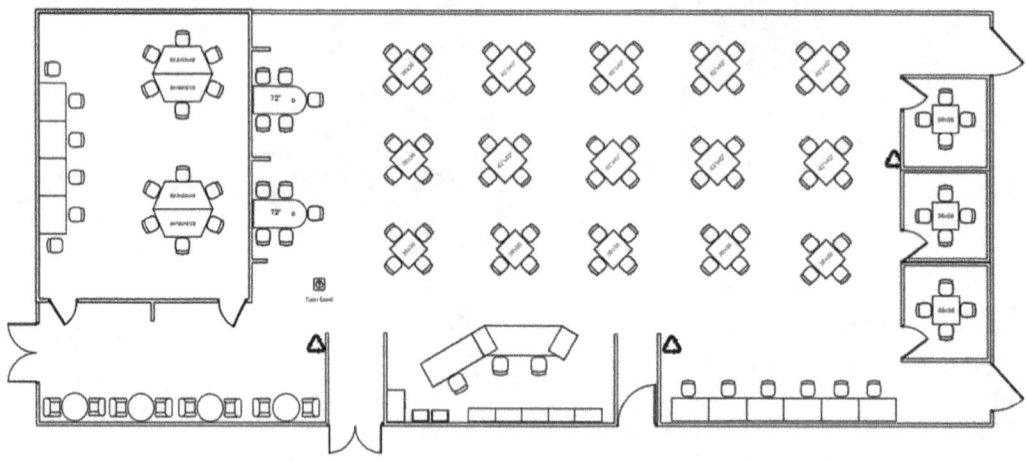

SMART Learning Commons
Source: University of Minnesota Twin Cities

present, do not have more robust feedback channels for SMART Media Service point or PRC services.

Evolution of Facility

Started as an Information Commons in one library (Wilson) in 2004. In 2006 the SMART partnership was founded, incorporated the Wilson site, and brings the Mcgrath site online. In 2008 the Walter site comes online. Wilson moved to a new location in the building in 2014. Walter had some refurbishment in 2016.

Future Steps

There is a potential colocation of a makerspace in the Walter space in 2016. There is currently an evaluation of the SMART model as part of a broader study of models for Academic Support underway in 2016 including further incorporation with other campus services, and development of online tutoring services, etc.

University of North Carolina at Greensboro: Digital Media Commons
Greensboro, North Carolina, USA

Carnegie Classification	
Basic:	Doctoral Universities: Higher Research Activity
Undergraduate Instructional Program:	Balanced arts & sciences/professions, high graduate coexistence
Graduate Instructional Program:	Research Doctoral: Comprehensive programs, no medical/veterinary school
Enrollment Profile:	High undergraduate
Undergraduate Profile:	Four-year, full-time, selective, higher transfer-in
Size and Setting:	Four-year, large, primarily residential

Total Student Enrollment: 18,647
Year established: 2012
Year of expansion/renovation: 2015
Name: Digital Media Commons
Square footage of publicly available space associated with your facility: 7,000
Location: Main Library
Typical access hours per week: 120
Typical service hours per week: 120
Number of service points: 2
Number of desktop computers available for use: 23
Number of laptop computers available for use: 16
Other types of devices provided: digital cameras, 3-D printers, HD video cameras
Average monthly door count: 300
Average monthly service transactions: 650
Workstation sessions/logins: 1,200
Library website: https://library.uncg.edu/

Digital Media Commons
Source: University of North Carolina at Greensboro

Purpose

The DMC was created to provide the space and resources for UNCG students, faculty, and staff to create and refine their multimedia projects.

Services

We help with digital images, digital video, digital audio, presentations, web pages, and 3-D printing/makerspace.

Software

Adobe Creative Suite, MS Office Suite, Makerbot, Sculptris, and Audacity.

Print Resources

n/a

Staff

The DMC has three full-time staff members, two student managers, and six student assistants. Full-time staff have staggered schedules. Our Tech Coordinator works M-F, 8-5. Our Digital Designer works Sat-Wed, 10-7. Our Department Head works M-F, 9-6.

– Naming Opportunities for the DMC and DACTS –

Legend:
- Digital Media Commons
- DMC Service Commons
- Gaming Lab
- Video, Imaging, Audio Lab
- Presentation Practice Room
- DMC Consultation Rooms
- Media Rooms
- Digital ACT Studio
- DACTS Consultation Rooms
- DACTS Service Commons

Digital Media Commons
Source: University of North Carolina at Greensboro

Funding/Budget

n/a

Publicity/Promotion

We have advertised in campus news, posted flyers, done digital signs, held promotional events for faculty and students, and we do tours and in-class presentations about the space.

Evaluation

We evaluate our program using usage data stats and direct consumer feedback.

Evolution of Facility

The program's space was expanded to make room for the Digital Rhetoric portion of our operation.

Future Steps

n/a

University of North Texas: Collaboration & Learning Commons
Denton, Texas, USA

Carnegie Classification	
Basic:	Doctoral Universities: Highest Research Activity
Undergraduate Instructional Program:	Balanced arts & sciences/professions, high graduate coexistence
Graduate Instructional Program:	Research Doctoral: Comprehensive programs, no medical/veterinary school
Enrollment Profile:	High undergraduate
Undergraduate Profile:	Four-year, medium full-time, selective, higher transfer-in
Size and Setting:	Four-year, large, primarily nonresidential

Total Student Enrollment: 36,486
Year established: 2010
Year of expansion/renovation: 2010
Name: Collaboration and Learning Commons (Eagle Commons Library)
Square footage of publicly available space associated with your facility: 5,630
Location: Branch/Special Library
Typical access hours per week: 88
Typical service hours per week: 88
Number of service points: 1
Number of desktop computers available for use: 24
Number of laptop computers available for use: 6
Other types of devices provided: desktop scanners, printer, copiers, study/meeting rooms, calculators, phone chargers, headphones, light tables, wireless presentation devices
Average monthly door count: 11,529
Average monthly service transactions: 7,061
Workstation sessions/logins: 2,785
Library website: www.library.unt.edu/

Purpose

The Eagle Commons Library is home to the government documents, law, political science, geography, and business collections and is also UNT's Funding Information Network location. The Collaboration and Learning Commons (CLC), housed within the Eagle Commons Library, is the ideal place on campus to study in groups featuring multiple whiteboards, movable furniture, and two study rooms to practice presentations and more.

Services

The CLC in the Eagle Commons Library offers a combination of hardware setups including Dell Windows workstations, Apple MacOS workstations, and Dell laptops as well as group study areas with movable whiteboards and furniture. Some other services available are desktop computing, laptop computing, scanners, group study, and wireless presentation devices.

The CLC used to hold "on-demand" technology workshops for the software that is in the instruction rooms as well as the smart boards. When the science and technology collection was moved out and the government documents collection moved in, services changed dramatically (besides basic circulation and reference service). A new GIS Librarian is available to respond to faculty requests for library assistance in this area, which complemented the map collection that moved over with the documents collection. Also, the foundation center collection was added along with access to those databases (restricted to ECL access only).

Software

The facility now offers a combination of hardware setups including Dell Windows workstations, Apple MacOS workstation, Dell laptops and MacBooks, as well as Mac Air laptops. The types of software offered at the Collaboration and Learning Commons is as follows: JAWS, MAGic, Microsoft Windows Ease of Access Center, Universal Access (Mac OS), Internet Explorer, Mozilla Firefox, Google Chrome, Google Earth, Safari (Mac), Adobe Creative Cloud, Paint.NET (Win), GarageBand (Mac), iDVD (Mac), iMovie (Mac), iPhoto (Mac), Readiris (Mac), AutoDesk 123D Design, AutoDesk, Meshmixer, iWork Pages (Mac), iWork Numbers (Mac), iWork Keynote (Mac), Microsoft Office, Write-N-Cite, ArcGIS, QGIS, SPSS, SAS, Wolfram, Mathematica, MATLAB, Adobe Acrobat, Google Earth, iTunes (Mac), VLC, ALEKS, Sassafras k2, Static IC 14, PuTTY telnet (Win), WinSCP (Win), 7-Zip (Win).

Print Resources

The Eagle Commons Library houses the libraries' large government document collection, which is available in multiple print formats as well as online. The print reference collection and the foundation center collection are across from the library services desk and the political science, public administration, law, geography, and business collections, which are housed on the mezzanine level. Microfiche and readers are on the lower level of the library.

Staff

When it first opened, the commons was staffed with two librarians (head of library learning services and a science librarian), four support staff (stacks manager, reserves/circulation supervisor, document delivery coordinator, and an outreach coordinator), two graduate assistants (one of

Collaboration and Learning Commons
Source: University of North Texas

these was a night manager), and several student assistants. After the science and technology collection was moved out and the documents collection was moved in, there are now four librarians (government information librarian/department head, GIS Librarian, Business Librarian, and Social Sciences Librarian), eight support staff, one GLA, and several student assistants.

Funding/Budget

The remodeling and staff of the Collaboration and Learning Commons are funded by the Library Use Fee.

Publicity/Promotion

There was a press release and a grand opening event in Spring 2011. The current state of promotions with the new collections at the ECL include regular blog, Twitter and Facebook postings, collaborating with External Relations to create print and online marketing materials, and press releases for events. Promotion also occurs through the Subject Librarians or Student Government Association for applicable events such as Constitution Day. The U.S. Pocket Constitutions are also a popular way of promoting the library, as are the Foundation Center workshops that occur off campus.

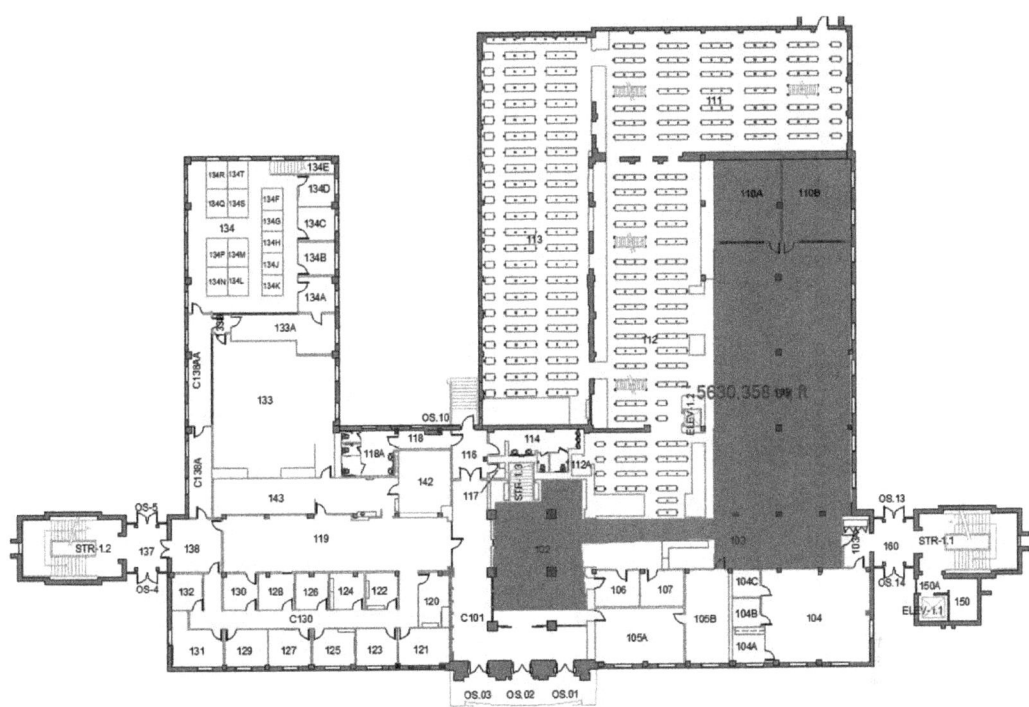

Collaboration and Learning Commons
Source: University of North Texas

Evaluation

The remodel was partially the result of feedback from LibQual. The first department head did a survey using iPads at the service desk. We also participated in a space study that the UNT Willis Library was doing.

Evolution of Facility

The Eagle Commons Library (ECL) was the first library on campus and was built in 1936. When the Willis Library was built in the 1970s and became the main library on campus, the ECL was divided up and renamed the Information Science Building, then later renamed to the Science and Technology Building. In 2010, the library closed for renovations to add the Collaboration and Learning Commons and, shortly after, the library housing the commons was renamed to Eagle Commons Library.

Future Steps

Probably the biggest change that is forthcoming for the space is an expansion of the business librarian services. We plan to continue listening to feedback from library users and to promote what the CLC has to offer through the Student Government Association and the Undergraduate Advisors meetings.

University of North Texas: The Factory
Denton, Texas, USA

Carnegie Classification

Basic:	Doctoral Universities: Highest Research Activity
Undergraduate Instructional Program:	Balanced arts & sciences/professions, high graduate coexistence
Graduate Instructional Program:	Research Doctoral: Comprehensive programs, no medical/veterinary school
Enrollment Profile:	High undergraduate
Undergraduate Profile:	Four-year, medium full-time, selective, higher transfer-in
Size and Setting:	Four-year, large, primarily nonresidential

Total Student Enrollment: 36,486
Year established: 2014
Year of expansion/renovation: 2016
Name: The Factory
Square footage of publicly available space associated with your facility: 1,778
Location: Main Library
Typical access hours per week: 64
Typical service hours per week: 64
Number of service points: 1
Number of desktop computers available for use: 5
Number of laptop computers available for use: 0
Other types of devices provided: Arduino, LaunchPad, Raspberry Pi
Average monthly door count: n/a
Average monthly service transactions: n/a
Workstation sessions/logins: n/a
Library website: www.library.unt.edu/spaces/factory

Purpose

The UNT Libraries' makerspace promotes the cooperative and creative use of technology. We provide the UNT community with access to equipment, software, and training that promotes innovative, cross-disciplinary learning.

Services

The Factory provides equipment and classes in each of the following categories:

Desktop computing

Audio/Visual—We have equipment that will allow you to record audio, video, and still photography in a variety of situations. cameras and lenses, microphones, recording, MIDI, synthesizers, digital sequencer, analog rhythm machine.

Electronics/Programming/Prototyping—Try everything from building your own robot to building your own computer or wearable electronic devices. Arduino, LaunchPad, MakeyMakey, Raspberry Pi, LittleBits, Robotics, Virtual Reality.

- Printing/Cutting/Replication—Wide range of advanced printing and replication services. 3-D printing, 3-D scanning, die cutting, large-format printing, laser cutting, milling, vacuum forming.
- Textiles—Several sewing machines, accessories, and a couple of portable looms available for use. Sewing machines, weaving.
- Tools—a number of hand and electric tools, measuring and soldering equipment, data loggers, and probes, some of which can be borrowed and others which can only be used in-space. We also offer a collection of books for you to use as a reference in your project creation. Various hand and electric tools, various scientific/probeware, soldering equipment.

Software

The software offered by The Factory is as follows: JAWS, MAGic, Microsoft Windows Ease of Access Center, Universal Access (Mac OS), Internet Explorer, Mozilla Firefox, Google Chrome, Google Earth, Safari (Mac), Adobe Creative Cloud, Paint.NET (Win), GarageBand (Mac), iDVD (Mac), iMovie (Mac), iPhoto (Mac), Readiris (Mac), AutoDesk 123D Design, AutoDesk, Meshmixer, iWork Pages (Mac), iWork Numbers (Mac), iWork Keynote (Mac), Microsoft Office, Write-N-Cite, ArcGIS, QGIS, SPSS, SAS, Wolfram, Mathematica, MATLAB, Adobe Acrobat, Google Earth, iTunes (Mac), VLC, ALEKS, Sassafras k2, Static IC 14, PuTTY telnet (Win), WinSCP (Win), 7-Zip (Win), Auduino, IDE 1.6.9, Blender, Makehuman, Pepakura, Sketchup 8, Steam, Solidworks Education Edition, Unity Pro.

Print Resources

We have a small collection of books that can be used as reference materials when working with our equipment. The remaining general collection is housed locally and in off-site storage.

Staff

Area is managed by 0.5 of an FTE; the remaining staff are student workers. There is a least two technicians on duty during operating hours. Staff is recruited by the campus student careers division. Looking for working knowledge of items in the space. All staff is cross trained on all equipment.

Funding/Budget

Area is funded from Library Fee. A small portion of revenue is used to buy consumables.

Publicity/Promotion

Many different kinds of publicity. Website, digital signage, Facebook, tours, personal outreach to campus clubs, maker fairs, outreach to area schools.

Evaluation

Items checked out, machine usage, print jobs, verbal feedback. During its pilot year, the Factory circulated a total of 1,549 items. Fiscal year 2016–2017 will serve as the baseline, with the goal of increasing items transactions by 10% the following year, and an additional 15% the year after that, to show that the items are in line with what the patrons desire while meeting the University's desire to engage students with innovative services.

The Factory
Source: University of North Texas

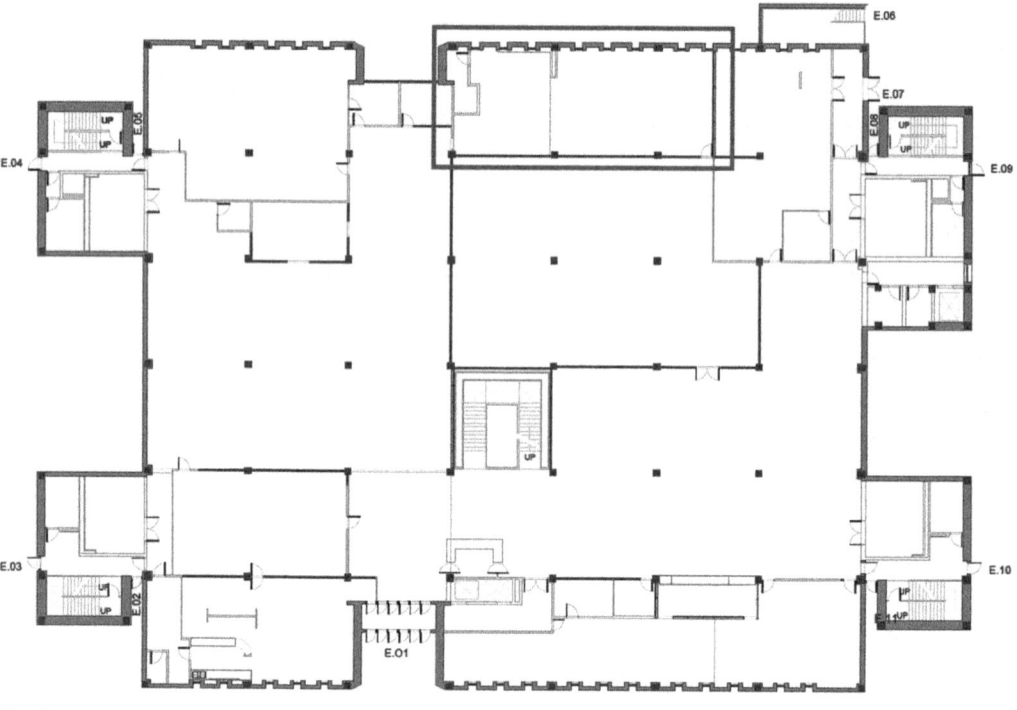

The Factory
Source: University of North Texas

Evolution of Facility

Fall 2016 added 1,117 sq. ft. to space.

Future Steps

Examining adding woodworking.

University of Oklahoma: Helmerich Collaborative Learning Center
Norman, Oklahoma, USA

Carnegie Classification	
Basic:	Doctoral Universities: Highest Research Activity
Undergraduate Instructional Program:	Balanced arts & sciences/professions, high graduate coexistence
Graduate Instructional Program:	Research Doctoral: Comprehensive programs, no medical/veterinary school
Enrollment Profile:	High undergraduate
Undergraduate Profile:	Four-year, full-time, more selective, higher transfer-in
Size and Setting:	Four-year, large, primarily residential

Total Student Enrollment: 27,261
Year established: 2014
Year of expansion/renovation: 2013-14
Name: Helmerich Collaborative Learning Center
Square footage of publicly available space associated with your facility: 18,000
Location: Main Library
Typical access hours per week: 121
Typical service hours per week: 121
Number of service points: 2
Number of desktop computers available for use: 6
Number of laptop computers available for use: 30
Other types of devices provided: Another 30 laptops as well as iPads are available on the main floor of the library, but they can easily be carried to the HCLC and also utilized there.
Average monthly door count: 3,000
Average monthly service transactions: n/a
Workstation sessions/logins: n/a
Library website: https://libraries.ou.edu/

Purpose

Our goal was to build a collaborative workspace where students, faculty, and staff could go beyond just finding existing knowledge, but could take that knowledge and analyze, synthesize, think about it and then use it as the basis for creating new knowledge. We wanted to provide them space that they could easily reconfigure and personalize to their needs and those of their collaborators and that was welcoming and encouraging of them engaging with the library on a continuing basis.

Services

As a library, we've always offered traditional library services. In the HCLC, we've expanded this by offering access to IT support, digital scholarship support, data research services, GIS, informatics, and research data management planning. Yes, we still have a traditional reference desk as well. The HCLC has its own coordinator and staff, which are assigned (depending on the position) to Access Services or Knowledge Services.

Software

Full Adobe suite, full MS suite, and Apple Pro applications. DSL, in addition, offers R and ArcGIS.

Print Resources

The HCLC area is located within the library, so it is surrounded by all the traditional library collections and resources. In addition, as we develop and/or plan programs within the HCLC spaces, we always try to leverage the other resources of the library during, or at the end of, such presentations.

Helmerich Collaborative Learning Center
Source: University of Oklahoma

Staff

One Coordinator, two Emerging Technology Librarians, and 16 student workers in HCLC. DSL has one Digital Scholarship Specialist, a post doc and student worker. Positions are part of either Public Access Services or Knowledge Services departments.

Funding/Budget

Funding is provided by the overall library budget. Planning is directed by the Senior Leadership Team of the OU Libraries.

Publicity/Promotion

We've utilized a full range of public awareness mechanisms from advertising in university newspapers, social media (Facebook, Twitter, Flickr), displays on the monitors in the Memorial Union, presentations to faculty liaisons, Deans, and Associate Deans, as well as tours. We've also worked with university tour guides who run student recruitment tours to ensure the HCLC is featured on the tours. Routinely we offer programs in the Community Room of the HCLC that are conducted by other colleges (but which link back to the libraries) so as to draw in students, faculty, and staff.

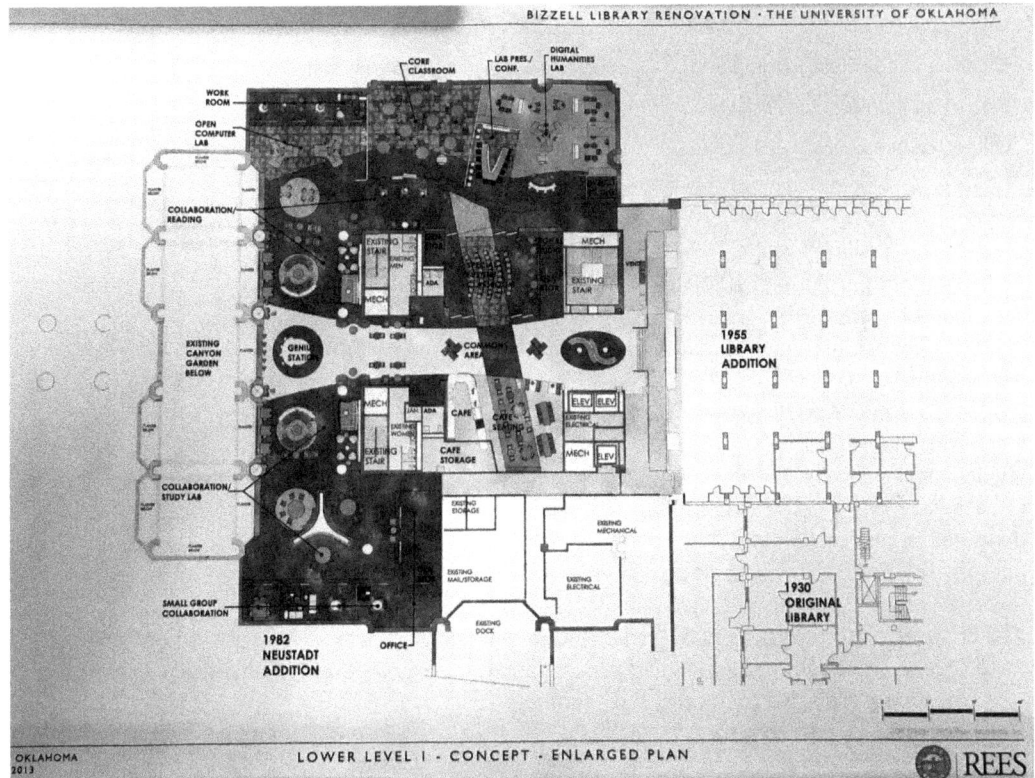

Helmerich Collaborative Learning Center
Source: University of Oklahoma

Evaluation

We have door counters installed, plus HCLC staff take hourly counts of people in the area. Counts of programs and presentations made are recorded, along with classes held in the Core Classroom. We also do counts in the Digital Scholarship Lab (within the HCLC) of recording sessions in the studios, meetings with faculty, number of programs sponsored or held in the DSL, presentations done across the campus by DSL staff, as well as courses in which DSL staff have become embedded.

Evolution of Facility

n/a

Future Steps

Expansion of the same basic concept to other floors of the library.

University of Tennessee at Chattanooga: Studio
Chattanooga, Tennessee, USA

Carnegie Classification	
Basic:	Master's Colleges & Universities: Larger Programs
Undergraduate Instructional Program:	Professions plus arts & sciences, some graduate coexistence
Graduate Instructional Program:	Research Doctoral: Professional-dominant
Enrollment Profile:	Very high undergraduate
Undergraduate Profile:	Four-year, full-time, selective, higher transfer-in
Size and Setting:	Four-year, large, primarily residential

Total Student Enrollment: 10,781
Year established: 2015
Year of expansion/renovation: n/a
Name: Studio
Square footage of publicly available space associated with your facility: 1,600
Location: Main Library
Typical access hours per week: 74
Typical service hours per week: 74
Number of service points: 1
Number of desktop computers available for use: 25
Number of laptop computers available for use: 0
Other types of devices provided: Audio/Video digitizing hardware, A/V equipment and accessories, microcontrollers, lighting room, audio recording room, VR headsets, electronics prototyping tools, 3-D printing, and scanning
Average monthly door count: 0
Average monthly service transactions: 0
Workstation sessions/logins: 0
Library website: www.utc.edu/library/

Purpose

Studio was part of an all-new construction project at UTC. The facility is partially the result of early focus groups for the new library project and partially the result of an internal library committee's ultimate planning decisions.

Services

Most services were not entirely new but had not been offered at nearly the same scale. Studio provides (1) access to high-spec PCs with a multitude of design and development software, (2) circulating equipment (A/V, VR, prototyping), (3) production rooms, (4) 3-D printing services, and (5) help/instruction/workshops/consultations. Studio became a new service point with its own dedicated staff. There is a service desk in the space.

Software

Studio offers suites for two major manufacturers—Adobe and AutoDesk—via UT system availability. In addition, Studio offers one-off licensed and free software including Unity, Arduino, Processing, Audacity, Apple Logic Pro, and Apple Final Cut Pro.

Studio
Source: University of Tennessee at Chattanooga

Print Resources

Studio does not maintain a print collection or budget, but has accumulated a small cache of resources that individual staffers use regularly. The library's print collections are on separate floors. Studio does make requests for one-time funds in print collections and recommends titles to the appropriate library liaisons. Librarians still refer to print as appropriate when teaching/consulting.

Staff

Studio reports through the library's Public Services area. It is made of of 2 librarians, 2.5 full-time staff, and a small cadre of student assistants (typically 7-9). Librarians and staff tend to work day or evening shifts staggered throughout the week. Librarians teach as needed and keep varying schedules. Staffers tend to have been or concurrently serve as practitioners or students in fields relevant to Studio activities. Staff have access to online training courses and are generally self-starters that can learn new applications or media quickly. New students are given comprehensive "assignments" to complete that require them to use a broad array of equipment and software. Ongoing training modules.

Funding/Budget

Studio is funded through the library—which maintains its own part of the university budget and takes in money from library fees. Given the recent new construction, the library is currently working on refresh cycles for technology throughout the library—Studio is part of this discussion.

Publicity/Promotion

At the time of this writing, Studio is just under a year old. Being part of an all-new library has been the most effective form of promotion and has generated a significant amount of publicity throughout the university and the community. Otherwise, Studio promotes the same as other library units: ads on the library website, outreach programming such as the library workshop series, word of mouth with faculty, and more. Librarians are engaged with faculty and have been able to quickly ramp up instruction efforts and help design assignments, which both generate users in Studio.

Evaluation

Studio tracks a combination of patron interactions and circulation numbers. In addition, librarians follow up with faculty to try to understand how reworking assignments and providing instruction sessions have affected students' work and related skills.

Evolution of Facility

n/a

Future Steps

Currently Studio is taking in its first full year and refining its processes. We would like to continue to offer more programming and find the most effective and engaging ways to introduce users to new media and design while continuing to support those that have intermediate and higher experience.

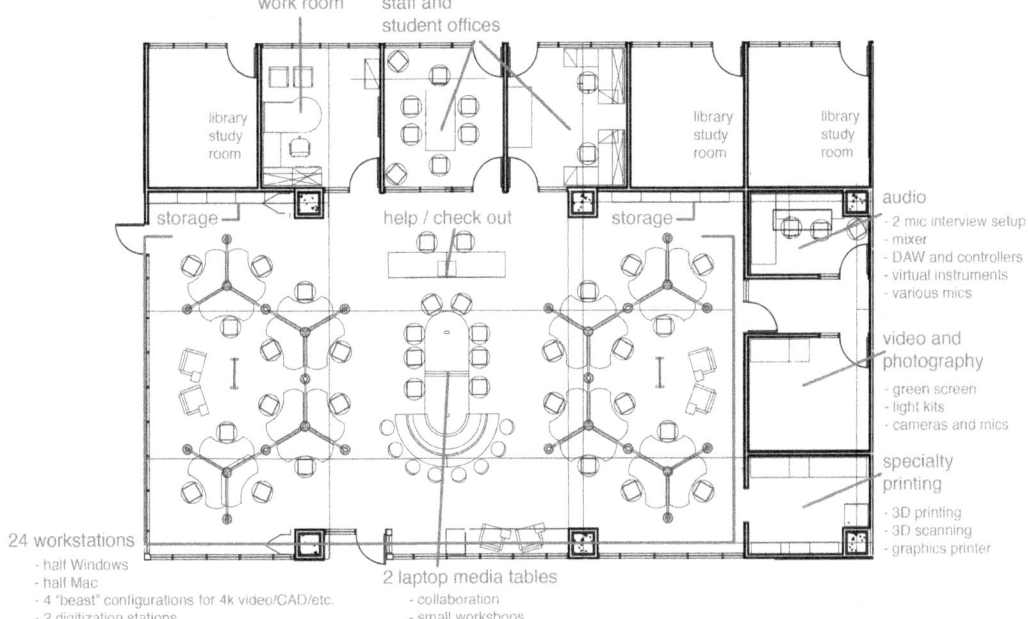

Studio
Source: University of Tennessee at Chattanooga

University of Texas: PCL Learning Commons
Austin, Texas, USA

Carnegie Classification	
Basic:	Doctoral Universities: Highest Research Activity
Undergraduate Instructional Program:	Balanced arts & sciences/professions, high graduate coexistence
Graduate Instructional Program:	Research Doctoral: Comprehensive programs, no medical/veterinary school
Enrollment Profile:	High undergraduate
Undergraduate Profile:	Four-year, full-time, more selective, higher transfer-in
Size and Setting:	Four-year, large, primarily nonresidential

Total Student Enrollment: 51,313
Year established: 2015
Year of expansion/renovation: n/a
Name: PCL Learning Commons
Square footage of publicly available space associated with your facility: 20,000
Location: Main Library
Typical access hours per week: 145
Typical service hours per week: 63
Number of service points: 2
Number of desktop computers available for use: 64
Number of laptop computers available for use: 120

Other types of devices provided: Crestron Air Media and flat panels, which allow students and instructors to wirelessly connect their mobile devices to a flat panel for collaboration. Students may also check out video cameras, superdrives, and microphones from the Check Out Desk in the Library to use in the Media Lab.
Average monthly door count: 218,282
Average monthly service transactions: 1,470
Workstation sessions/logins: 537
Library website: www.lib.utexas.edu/

Purpose

The Learning Commons is designed to support student academic success by enabling collaborative learning, supporting excellence in pedagogy, and facilitating deep collaborations between campus academic support units in information literacy and writing. It consists of offices for teaching and research librarians, the University Writing Center (UWC), a Media Lab, and five Learning Labs (active learning classrooms). When not in use for teaching or writing consultations, all spaces are open for study. This is phase one of the Learning Commons, and additional spaces and services to support student learning will be created, including a pilot Public Speaking Center opening in February of 2016.

Services

The Learning Commons brought together existing units, including moving the UWC into the Libraries. The Library still has a circulation and reference desk adjacent to but not currently a part of the Learning Commons. The following services are offered: Librarians provide in-depth research consultations to students, faculty, and staff and course and assignment design consultations to faculty and instructors (existing service). University Writing Center staff provide writing consultations to students (existing but newly expanded to graduate students) and writing groups for faculty and graduate students (new). Librarians provide instruction to students at faculty request (existing service now provided in Learning Labs). Librarians support faculty to integrate technology into their courses in Learning Labs and Media Lab (new). Library staff, University Writing Center staff, and other campus partners provide workshops and events to campus about research, writing, using technology, public speaking, and more (expanded service). Students, faculty, and staff use the Media Lab to create audio, video, 3-D animation, and visual media with consultation and workshops from Media Lab assistants (new). Students use Learning Labs as collaborative, technology-enabled study space between instruction reservations (new).

Software

The Media Lab includes software for digital media creation, including Adobe Creative Cloud, Final Cut Pro, Autodesk Maya, Autodesk Mudbox, Blender, Sketchup, ProTools, Audacity, Finale, Sibelius, Sublime Text, and Microsoft Office 2016. The lab is supported by proctors and a full-time lab manager, as well as by the desktop support staff of the Libraries. The Learning Labs use Crestron AirMedia, which enables students and instructors to connect their laptops wirelessly to flat panels to share and collaborate. We have a custom control system for instructors using the active learning teaching space as well as simple instructions for students to use the screens during collaborative study.

PCL Learning Commons
Source: University of Texas, Austin

Print Resources

The only print collection in the Learning Commons is a small resource library (one bookshelf) for Writing Center consultants. However, the Learning Commons is located in the main library building, which contains over 3 million print items, including some special collections such as maps. Librarians teaching information literacy sessions and providing consultations in the Learning Commons work with users to discover and access useful print collections. In addition, faculty who want to engage their classes with print collections may book a Learning Lab in the Learning Commons for up to three sessions per semester to facilitate this engagement.

Staff

Library staff from Teaching & Learning Services and Research & Liaison Services office in the Learning Commons provide research help and course design consultations. They include MLIS degree holders, graduate student assistants, and classified staff. Staff from across all library branches, UWC staff, and invited campus partners and faculty teach in the Learning Labs any time the building is open. The majority of classes are held during regular business hours. The Media Lab is coordinated by a Media Lab Manager who oversees nine student interns provided by a campus student success program. The Lab is staffed from 1 p.m. to 10 p.m. most days and is open all hours the building is open. The University Writing Center, open 10 a.m.–7 p.m. Monday through Thursday, 10 a.m.–3 p.m. Friday, and 1 p.m.–7 p.m. Sunday, is staffed by a faculty director, four staff members, and two post-docs from the Department of Rhetoric & Writing, and over 100 graduate and undergraduate students from across campus who serve as consultants, provide presentations, and run special programs. Technical and facilities staff from the Libraries provide support and management of the Learning Commons as needed. Writing Center staff and library staff are beginning to cross-train. Library staff train instructors to use the Learning Labs.

Funding/Budget

Initial funds for this $4 million project came from the Libraries, the College of Liberal Arts (administrative home to the University Writing Center), and the Provost. Library staff are funded by the Libraries and UWC staff by the College of Liberal Arts. The majority of facilities maintenance and technology costs come from the Libraries budget with some funds coming from the College of Liberal Arts. Planning and management of the facility is primarily the responsibility of Libraries staff with some oversight of the UWC consulting space offered by UWC staff. Planning and management of programs is a mix. The UWC continues to plan and manage its own consulting programs, and the Libraries continue to plan and manage their own teaching and research support programs. The Libraries support the UWC in use of the Learning Labs. Libraries and UWC staff work together to develop new, collaborative programs and invite each other to participate in traditional programs. This collaboration is facilitated by the Learning Commons Steering Committee made up of UWC and Libraries staff.

Publicity/Promotion

When the Learning Commons opened in 2015, we had a major ribbon cutting with the University President. Since that time, UWC and Libraries communication staff have worked to raise awareness of the Learning Commons on campus through the student paper, social media, campus tour guides, and other outlets. Libraries and UWC staff offer events in the Learning Commons to draw in the campus community. For instance, they convened the University of Texas Libraries Committee in the Learning Commons early in the Fall Semester. The Libraries and UWC have also invited some faculty in to teach semester-long classes in the Learning Labs to showcase technology-enabled pedagogy. Library staff have invited numerous faculty groups into the Learning Commons to learn about how to incorporate it into their courses, whether it is a visit to a Learning Lab to work with a librarian or a visit to the Media Lab for training on software for their class.

Evaluation

We are just finishing our first semester evaluation, and the report will be ready in February. We wrote an assessment plan as a guide that included assessments of use and assessments of satisfaction. Assessments of usage included such measures as Media Lab logins, Learning Lab bookings, research and writing consultations, and gate counts. Assessments of satisfaction included a user survey in the Media Lab, focus groups with staff who use the Learning Labs and staff the Media Lab, a "kindness audit," a poster survey of Learning Commons users throughout the space, and an analysis of the types of events and classes held in the Learning Labs. The UWC continues to assess user satisfaction through exit surveys, and the Libraries continue to assess student learning in information literacy classes through a pre- and posttest model and rubric analysis of assignments. When the first semester's report is complete, Libraries staff will begin working on the recommendations and begin the next cycle of assessment.

Evolution of Facility

n/a

PCL Entry Level

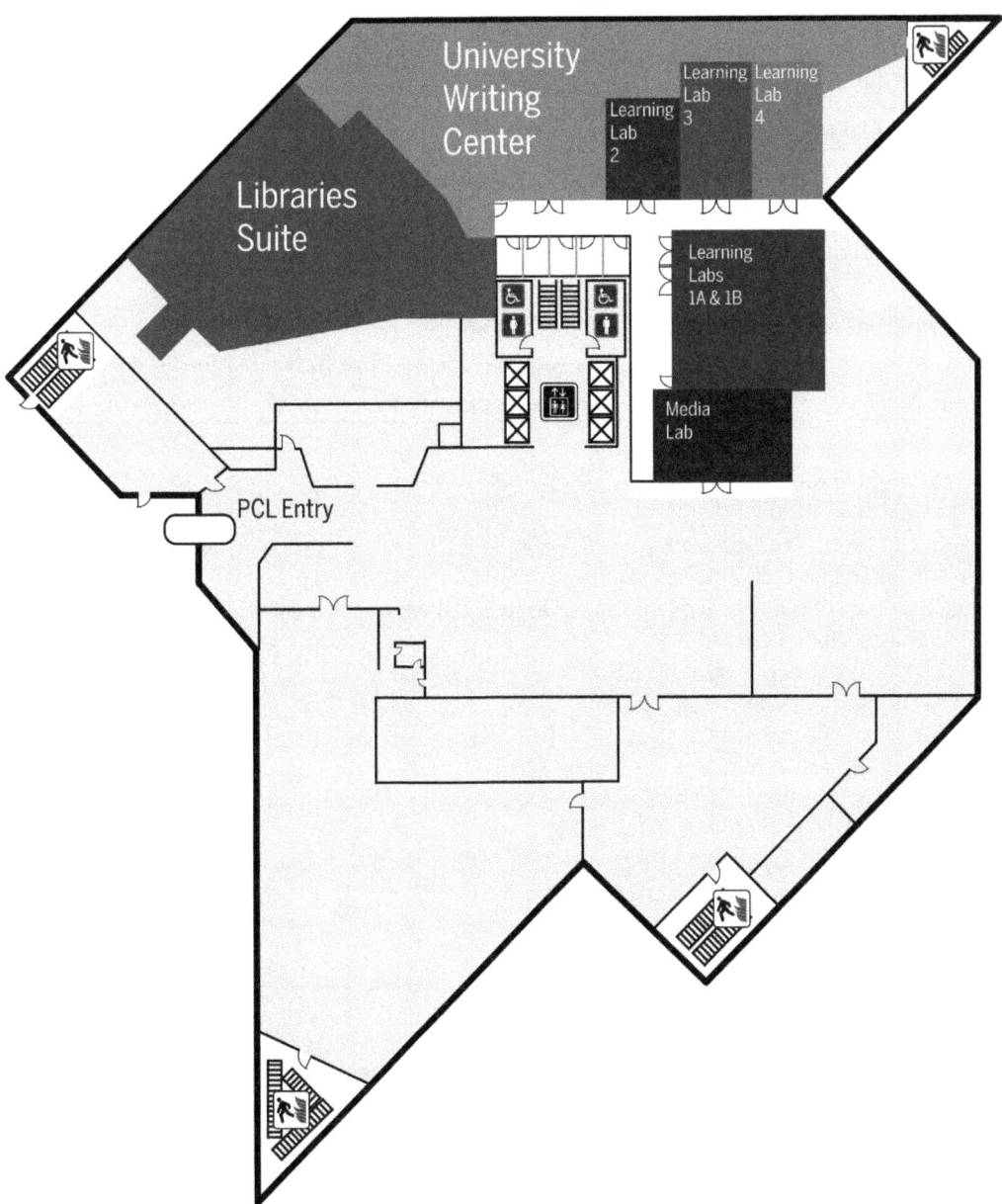

PCL Learning Commons
Source: University of Texas, Austin

Future Steps

Our plan is to raise money to convert the remaining 40,000 square feet of the library's entry level into the Learning Commons. We are piloting a Public Speaking Center and opening new STEM study areas in the spring. We have a vision document that includes more spaces for faculty to innovate with technology, more technology-rich spaces for all users such as a one-button studio and a green screen room, and more collaborative spaces.

Virginia Commonwealth University: Multimedia Collaboration Room
Richmond, Virginia, USA

Carnegie Classification	
Basic:	Doctoral Universities: Highest Research Activity
Undergraduate Instructional Program:	Balanced arts & sciences/professions, high graduate coexistence
Graduate Instructional Program:	Research Doctoral: Comprehensive programs, with medical/veterinary school
Enrollment Profile:	High undergraduate
Undergraduate Profile:	Four-year, full-time, selective, higher transfer-in
Size and Setting:	Four-year, large, primarily residential

Total Student Enrollment: 30,848
Year established: 1932
Year of expansion/renovation: 2012
Name: Multimedia Collaboration Room
Square footage of publicly available space associated with your facility: n/a
Location: Branch/Special Library
Typical access hours per week: 102.5
Typical service hours per week: 102.5
Number of service points: 1
Number of desktop computers available for use: 6
Number of laptop computers available for use: 8
Other types of devices provided: Two iPads
Average monthly door count: 3,052
Average monthly service transactions: 328
Workstation sessions/logins: n/a
Library website: www.library.vcu.edu/

Purpose

The Multimedia Collaboration Room was designed to create a dynamic space that students could configure to suit their needs. With whiteboard walls, students can map out ideas and work together to solve problems. Higher-end computing stations give users the power to unleash their creativity. The cafe booths and the movable seating/table provide a comfortable environment in which to study, create, and learn.

Services

The Multimedia Collaboration Room is not staffed. Additional graphics and audio software were added to higher-level computers. The health sciences library has a single point of service that is staffed by classified employees. Most reference work is handled through the active liaison program.

Multimedia Collaboration Room
Source: Virginia Commonwealth University

Software

GIS software, large-format printer (requires staff assistance), scanning, photo printer, photo scanner, Adobe CS6, dual-cassette tape digital archiver, plasma TV, Blu-ray player, VCR, PC and Macintosh computers, analog to digital converter, DVD/CD burner, DVD/CD duplicator, microform viewer/scanner, Adobe Acrobat, GarageBand, and Photoshop.

Print Resources

The room is adjacent to the journal collection and on the same floor as the audiovisual collection. For the most part, there is little interaction with the print resources of the library.

Staff

The area is not staffed.

Funding/Budget

Does not have an allocated budget.

Publicity/Promotion

n/a

Evaluation

n/a

Meeting Flooring Pattern

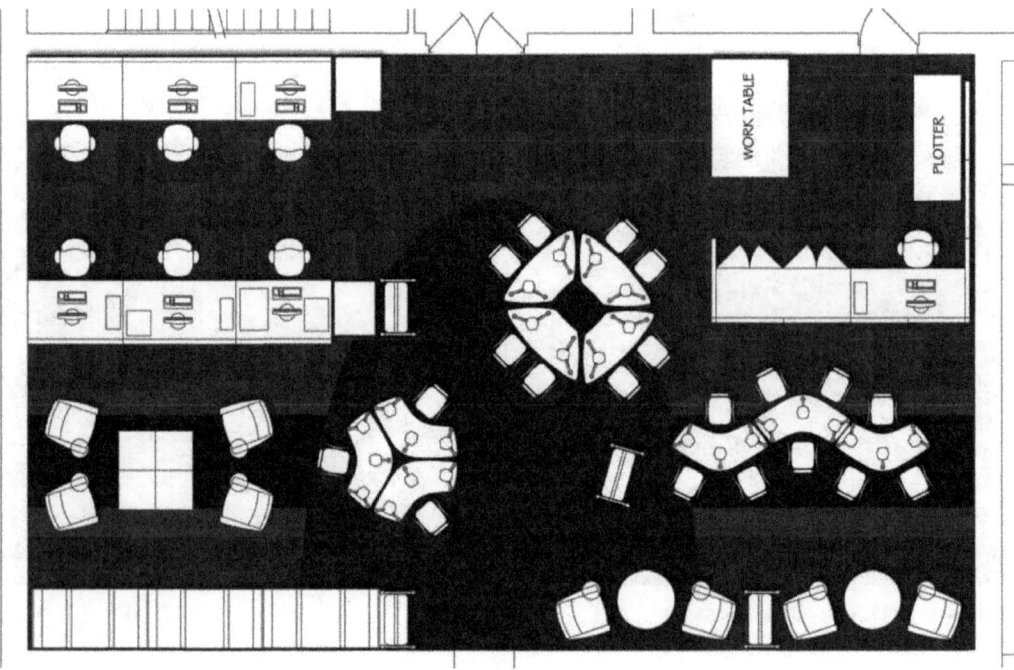

Multimedia Collaboration Room
Source: Virginia Commonwealth University

Evolution of Facility

n/a

Future Steps

n/a

Virginia Tech University: Learning Commons
Blacksburg, Virginia, USA

Carnegie Classification	
Basic:	Doctoral Universities: Highest Research Activity
Undergraduate Instructional Program:	Balanced arts & sciences/professions, high graduate coexistence
Graduate Instructional Program:	Research Doctoral: Comprehensive programs, with medical/veterinary school
Enrollment Profile:	High undergraduate
Undergraduate Profile:	Four-year, full-time, selective, higher transfer-in
Size and Setting:	Four-year, large, primarily residential

Total Student Enrollment: 30,848
Year established: 1955
Year of expansion/renovation: 1981, 2009
Name: Learning Commons
Square footage of publicly available space associated with your facility: 70,000
Location: Main Library
Typical access hours per week: 143
Typical service hours per week: 143
Number of service points: 2
Number of desktop computers available for use: 24
Number of laptop computers available for use: 85
Other types of devices provided: Laptop and phone peripherals, cameras, recording equipment, calculators
Average monthly door count: 91,823
Average monthly service transactions: 9,900
Workstation sessions/logins: n/a
Library website: www.lib.vt.edu/

Purpose

The learning commons is intended to provide library users with a variety of flexible work spaces, both individual and collaborative in nature. With reconfigurable tables and a range of furniture options, the commons supports the diverse array of needs of university students, faculty, researchers, and staff.

Services

The learning commons encompasses Circulation and Reference Desks as well as a Writing Center and a Comm Lab. In 2016, we added a 3-D printing studio and the Fusion Studio, an interdisciplinary undergraduate research project space. We are in the process of merging our Circulation and Reference desks; the merger should be complete by Fall 2017.

Software

Microsoft Office and Adobe Acrobat.

Print Resources

Commons area exists on two floors (2 and 4), while print collection is shelved on alternating floors (3 and 5). Microform and remaining print collection are located at Library Service Center (Remote Storage).

Staff

Circulation department, consisting of roughly twenty staff and student workers, is staffed in three shifts—library is open 24 hours 5 days a week. We have roughly 12 student rovers (Student Services Team). Circulation and Reference report to the same person, who oversees training in both areas. Recruitment is carried out primarily through university HR website.

Learning Commons
Source: Virginia Tech University

Funding/Budget

We receive our budget from the Provost's office and, beyond that, the state.

Publicity/Promotion

We have a Creative Services team that coordinates marketing efforts within the library. Events, new services and resources, and other marketing items are displayed on digital signage throughout the building, in campus news outlets, and on the library website when needed. We also have a liaison council that serves as a means of relaying information to library liaisons, who can then disseminate information and news to their constituencies.

Evaluation

In addition to individual or departmental assessment goals and priorities, which may overlap with the evaluation of our learning spaces, we have a library space assessment coordinator who is responsible for leading programmatic needs and outcomes assessment of our commons and related areas.

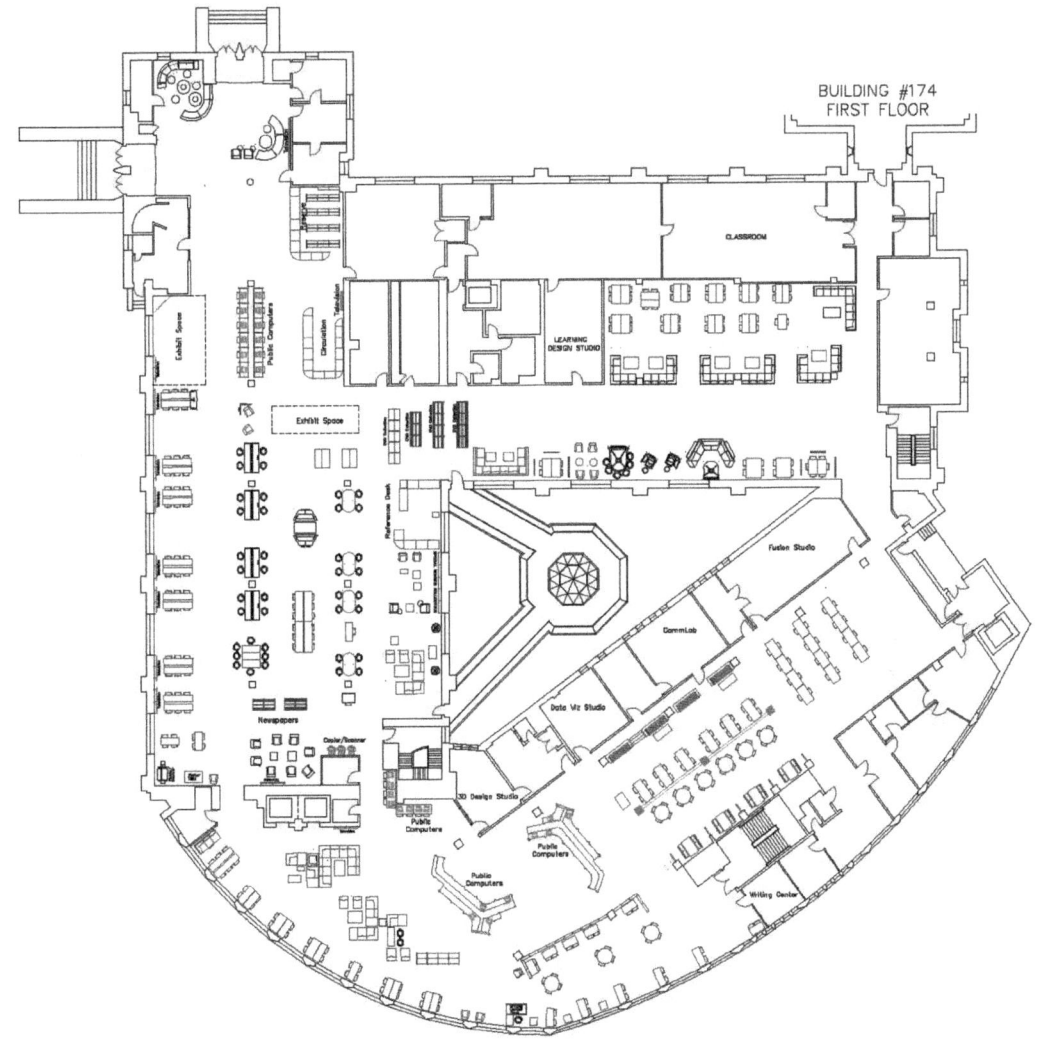

Newman Library: Second Floor

Learning Commons
Source: Virginia Tech University

Evolution of Facility

We are in the process of consolidating our reference and circulation service points into a single desk. This will take place over the summer and will open in Fall 2017. We added a café in 2009, a SCALE-up classroom (partnership with College of Science) in 2012, and a public exhibits initiative in 2015.

Future Steps

We continue to build strategic partnerships with departments and academic units on campus to produce innovative spaces. These include digital/data literacy classrooms, a digital humanities lab and classroom, and a media production studio. We are opening a Virtual Environments studio in Fall 2017 and a Data Visualization studio in the spring.

Field Guide

Afterword

Designing for Laughter

Seven Concepts for Inventing the Future of Academic Communities

Marie S.A. Sorensen, AIA

On an ordinary morning in Cambridge, Massachusetts, I bicycle at 5:00 a.m. down Harvard Street to Kendall Square and MIT. At Portland and Main, the traffic thickens and I watch for construction vehicles, workers in yellow vests dashing across Main, and semitrailers delivering gases to labs. This morning there's a sprite in jeans and spiked hair playing on rollerblades outside the Google headquarters. He stops at the intersection and smiles, I imagine, at the dawn and the sudden street-side companionship, witnesses to his creative night. In five minutes I'm over the "salt-and-pepper" bridge and in the boathouse with coach and teammates, signing out a single scull. We bring oars to the dock and shove.

Research, regalia, and rowing: three reference points for Cambridge, a liberal American university town bracketed by Harvard and MIT.

Massachusetts Avenue runs northwest into Harvard Square like the quay to an academic harbor. The edge is filigreed with shop fronts. Tourists and students on errands buy eyeglasses, scented soaps, magazines, heraldic neckties, and rare books. Behind glass, feet shuffle—computer bags, designer coats, and hands with smart phones—in queues for falafel, soba, and croissants. They laugh around a ten-seat rough-sawn table and squeeze side by side for political-themed hamburgers. By the river, the mood softens into the life of the Houses. Athletes return from practice to dining halls and second-floor library perches. Suits and flowing dresses disappear behind courtyard gates. Instruments in backpacks migrate to subterranean sound studios. This is a snapshot of one of the most productive and admirable academic communities in the nation.

I'm an architect and master planner in Cambridge. I'm a college professor teaching architecture studio, history, and building science, and I run my own firm. Our office is located just off

Massachusetts Avenue, two blocks from Harvard's Widener and Lamont Libraries and around the corner from Le Corbusier's only U.S.-built work, the Carpenter Center for the Visual Arts.

For me, to design buildings for colleges and universities, I want to be immersed in the culture. I talk to a lot of researchers, scholars, and librarians about how they're doing their jobs and what they're trying to discover. I want the world to be a cooler, more humane, more enriched place, and I think libraries have a really important role in doing that. In the notes that follow, I've named seven categories that structure my thinking about what matters when designing academic communities: tribe, power, crossroads, subject, detail, den, and skunkworks. These are not purely architectural, technological, or pedagogical themes. They are cognitive, anthropological, social, style-based, and formative: the DNA of this realm.

Tribe

Tribes are cohesive groups that advertise their activities and purpose in a way that permits you to see the potency of their community. The architecture firm Snøhetta constructs this togetherness with a massive cafeteria table instead of a lobby at its New York City office. The table doubles as a sandbox for design charettes with drawings and models spread out across the long surface and chairs filled with experts. Metropolis magazine promotes the Snøhetta tribe by publishing the memorable image of the company table.[1]

Shirts, furniture, and behavior matter. Some librarians are reluctant to act like tribe members because their identities are built on distinguishing themselves, even (or especially) from those in their own discipline. Librarians I've talked to describe an interest in unifying their attire so that they are recognizable. Many libraries have done away with reference desks, and so these librarians are looking for ways to interact with students, for example, using text-message and then geo-locating students who need help at their seat. I understand that a few libraries have tried this. It is something like a retail model of customer help. Why don't we study and model retail, then? There are things we can learn from Apple and from the new experience-driven shopping culture. Tribe membership clues indicate common language, knowledge, or status, and make it easy for strangers to interact. Apple, like Snøhetta, uses a piece of furniture to show you how to find the Genius Bar. Geniuses wear blue shirts with a small corporate logo. They make eye contact and small talk.

The Genius Bar in Boston has seventeen seats. I've seen up to ten Geniuses behind the bar. A football team is eleven players. NC State's SCALE-UP and MIT's TEAL active learning classrooms have multiple tables for nine students,[2] and typical seminar classes have between eight and fourteen students. Numbers shape tribe dynamics. While a tribe may have hundreds of at-large members, the number that can interact well and feel comfortable sitting together for long periods of time is usually much smaller. San Francisco–based clothing retailer Everlane divides its converted factory office into intimate seating areas for ten, each framed by columns and ringed with plants.[3] There are several dozen seats in the Grand Reading Room at OSU's Thompson Library, but they are divided into groups of four to twelve, and the chairs typically look different in each cluster.

These numbers are just a small part of a much larger discussion about psychological comfort, productivity, and participation. Susan Gibbons, Yale's university librarian, found that sociology PhDs have a higher completion rate when they study in a departmental reading room.[4] Librarian Daniel Sheehan reports that MIT students prefer one-on-one instruction for skill acquisition, a part of the school's "DIY culture."[5] Writer Susan Cain reports that introverts will not participate

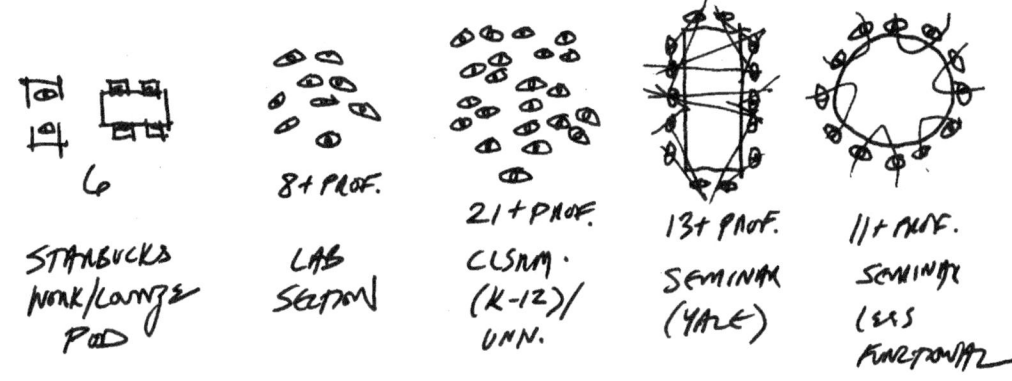

Tribe group size—What feels comfortable? (2017)
Source: Marie S. A. Sorensen, AIA

in group sizes above three.[6] These details are grounds for abandoning the open-plan office and library floor in favor of intimate right-sized spaces where social bonding can happen. Workspace design expert Evelyn Lee says even top companies are still building open plan—but only to save money.[7] The myth is that open plan builds group spirit and promotes idea exchange. This may be true, but typically open plan is used in corporate offices as a strategy to seat more employees in less space, reducing overhead. Architects either created or abetted this organizational trend in the early large floor-plate office buildings (only made possible in the 1950s due to the invention of air conditioning) by designing partitioning systems. Early glass-walled cubicles were touted as innovation in a 1961 issue of *Progressive Architecture*: "Two to four designers share an office—which provides 95 sq ft per person (as opposed to the customary 125). However, this minimal work space seems to be larger because of the use of clear glass panels, and the partitions tend to reduce distracting sounds from other offices."[8]

Numbers, furniture, and shirts are obviously not enough for a tribe to bond. Claude Lévi-Strauss or any first-year anthropology professor will tell you that behaviors and rituals cement group membership. Every August, hundreds of creatives from major U.S. metropolitan areas take an oath of participation at the gate of Burning Man where Greeters spank first-timers and say to everyone "Welcome home." A long-time attendee writes: "It is a place where you don't fuck with the people who fuck with you and if you do, you fail the test."[9] Similarly countercultural, college fraternities have the script of ritual coded in their OS. Streaking through a college quadrangle without clothing along with ten other initiates, laughing about it together afterwards, and letting the rumor mill turn is a taboo-breaking rite-of-passage that cements frat tribe membership.

Tribes build their culture through storytelling and in-jokes, and bond through laughter. As Sophie Scott has said recently on NPR and TED, authentic laughter is a stress reducer and social glue, with neurological effects that make us like each other.[10] Table size is quantifiable, but laughter is so different from a table. What else do we need to do to convert those chairs into a place where a tribe hangs out? If only it were simple enough to say that seven chairs and a denlike atmosphere

Afterword

will produce laughter. And so we have to zoom out and see the whole: we're not just placing chairs. We're designing for laughter and intellectual growth.

Power

Power is commanding resources in a socially visible way. In academia, faculty with sufficient power win grants and start labs, "centers," and institutes to enlarge their influence and fund capital costs for buildings or leased space. The University of Chicago, for example, has over 140 research institutes and centers. These include "The Center for Decision Research," "The Crime Lab," and "The Paleographic Atlas Project."[11] Stanford University lists 93 research centers, from "Re-Inventing the Nation's Urban Water Infrastructure" to "Nanocharacterization Laboratory" and the "Center for Medieval and Early Modern Studies."[12] Yale has 86 centers and institutes including "The China Center," "The Global Institute of Sustainable Forestry," and "The Center for Statistical Genomics and Proteomics."[13]

People in communities will tend to group themselves so that those who want social and organizational power can have it, at least some of the time. Good leaders shape environments around a worthy vision and marshal resources—including territory, information access, and technology. The many institutes at Stanford, Yale, and Chicago show that the physical space and resources defined by departmental and other hierarchies did not accommodate the number of good leaders present in those academic communities. The flourishing on the institute-and-center ecology shows that these schools acknowledge and allow healthy power seeking.

Creating a space around a mission is one of the most affirming aspects of intellectual identity formation. Perhaps something like this could exist in academic libraries for students. Tom Hickerson, one of the figures behind the Taylor Family Digital Library at the University of Calgary, proposes a lab-in-library concept of "dynamic hubs" that are "joining and unjoining." These would be application-based spaces where occupants would work for a week or a month. They'd apply for tools, machines, and resources to be placed in their workspace, and they'd be surrounded by the information-rich and socially supportive environment of the library and its skilled staff.[14]

Autonomy is a dream most people are afraid to chase. In a YouTube video targeted to university students, Tesla founder Elon Musk brags about telling his girlfriend she'd have to sleep on the couch with him in their office, since he had no apartment. Subtext: but he did have an office, his office. Jason Ankeny reports: "Entrepreneurial Americans rank 'launching a company' second on the countdown of the scariest life-changing events they may face, trailing only concerns about retirement savings."[15]

Pecking-order power struggles (aka "politics") are the flour of work-life for most recent college graduates. I drive to the White Mountains on weekends with friends on iPads completing work requested Friday at midnight until the last cellular signal bar disappears. Every employee who wants to keep his job knows whose e-mail he has to answer at what time of day or night. In Silicon Valley, where flat office culture was invented, Scott Hassan—after designing the software for Yahoo! Groups, Google, Alexa Internet, and the Stanford Digital Library—created telepresence robot Beam to "[give] people the power to choose when and where to be present, regardless of geographic location." But while freeing for some, Beam may be perceived as an extension of corporate hierarchy to those who are required to be physically present, as one office worker describes: "'To come into my office they bang the Beam against my door...I have to open it, and they come rolling in.'"[16]

The new generation of librarians fills me with optimism. It is widely known amongst anthropologists and historians of urban planning that a territory assigned to leadership by a specific person will become more personalized and welcoming. The socially aware and highly skilled new generation of librarians can show leadership in the library by creating communities anchored around themselves as conveners and "superusers." The university is a critically important place for students to test nascent leadership skills by setting a vision, shaping territory, convening peers, and securing resources. But not all students are equipped to do this. Many students are good at learning by imitating and through socialization. "Convener-librarians" would be more like a friend or peer rather than a "shushing" authority figure. They'd definitely not sit behind a desk. They would be the tribe, cultural denizens with an attitude and an approach that models what is possible.

Crossroads

A crossroads is an open space to meet people in the routine path of a day.

In the Peruvian Amazon, our naturalist took us to a field behind the lodge that the staff used for soccer. I was slightly annoyed; I was there to see the forest. "But it's easier to see animals in an open space," our guide said. "They sit on the trees overlooking the field, and they can see their prey."

It is easier for everyone to see in a field.

At Cornell University—a friend told me while we were walking around at his reunion a few years ago—one of the most boring spaces in the library is the most popular. It's called the "Fishbowl." A pedestrian bridge close to the main entrance to the library overlooks this relic of a room packed with side-by-side solid wood study carrels. Students sit in the Fishbowl to finish an assignment quickly before class, and they can easily be found there.

"Fishbowl," Cornell University Library, Ithaca, NY (2014)
Source: Marie S. A. Sorensen, AIA

Afterword

In the rural northeast United States, road intersections in remote areas with a gas station and a convenience store are called "four corners." If "four corners" is how I find my neighbor in Downeast Maine, how do I find my friends on campus? Does every university have or need a "Fishbowl"? Or do they always have one—but only the students know where it is?

Last January, I walked around the first of the reopened spaces of the Boston Public Library Johnson Building with director David Leonard. The two main street-side halls have been humanized and enriched by Rawn Associates and by the programming direction of David and the library team. The first floor is one acre in size, David tells me; it is the only floor where a person can stand at the center, see, and walk to any point on the periphery. In this sense, it is a "field"—but it is not a crossroads, as programming and pathway connections do not link through it. Perhaps in a future reinvention the BPL could suspend a "floating" deck in the center of the atrium, coplanar with the second floor, and ring it with seating overlooking the floor below, leaving openings for people to overlook. Doorways could be enlarged in the first-floor atrium walls to create visible destinations accessed from the building's center. A café serving breakfast and lunch could be located in the center of the first floor. This would make a crossroads.

The architectural complement to a "field" is an "edge." Architects can help people find each other at crossroads by making distinct edges, landmarks, overlooks, and meeting points. In late eighteenth-century Paris, the "field" was the streets and the "edges" were the first restaurants, a key contributor to the city's flourishing public life. Economist Ed Glaeser writes: "Restaurants, like pubs or coffeehouses, are...a way of adapting to the high price of urban space. City apartments often have tiny kitchens and no dining room. Eating or drinking out is a way to share common space so that the urbanite isn't confined by a compact flat. In a sense, then, cities pull people out of private space into public areas, which helps make them centers for socialization."[17] Translating this lesson to campus design, we could make small dormitory rooms and many "public" places for students to study and socialize.

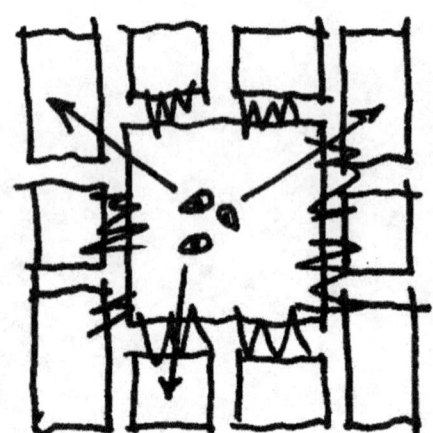

Boston Public Library Johnson Building Reimagined: Field, Edges, and Periphery (2017)
Source: Marie S. A. Sorensen, AIA

If we're not getting to know each other at a restaurant on a neighborhood shopping street in Paris, we may be able to use even simpler orientation clues to make and find friends. My firm worked with Benjamin Franklin Institute of Technology (BFIT) in Boston to create a "learning commons" on their main floor. The Institute operates out of one dense citylike building bordering Chinatown and the South End. The ground floor has fifteen-foot ceilings with one large lobby, two entrances from well-trafficked city streets, and two cross-axial halls, each about twenty-five feet wide.

BFIT has a great first-floor plan that is easy to understand and works like a crossroads with an obvious gathering spot in the center (the lobby). But beyond the main halls, the rooms are illegible and overcrowded. Our renovation is tactical and simple: removing walls and ceilings to ensure that the programs have enough space; creating unique design attributes in each space to improve function and make it memorable; and making sure spaces on the cross-axial halls have transparent storefronts and clear signage.

In the Peruvian Amazon, I thought about where the crossroads is on the river. There are no city streets or internet connections to create orientation—and so the "information highway" and the "world wide web" would be poor metaphors for how locals find each other and share information. The gathering points are the square hut living room with a perimeter bench; the hut's dock and front porch visible from the river; the town green, where people come for daylong festivals; and the fishing grounds, a lagoon off of a tributary where canoes gather.

In larger public buildings, crossroads spaces perform the work of urban plazas and boulevards, bringing hundreds of people together. Moshe Safdie's airport concourse in Tel Aviv is a circular agora with a fountain surrounded by pavilion cafes with individual roofs—small communities of patrons within the larger light-filled space.

Rotunda at Ben Gurion Airport, Tel Aviv, Israel (2013)
Source: Marie S. A. Sorensen, AIA

Afterword

Departing for a flight, passengers descend gradually on a wide inclined walkway—a format reminiscent of sacred Islamic processional space. The walkway pours into the rotunda where passengers wait in a place that feels like a city plaza. Arriving passengers walk along "a mezzanine overlooking the concourses and the rotunda and then descend toward passport control through the connector, crisscrossing departing passengers."[18] The ballet is logical and symbolic, creating a coherent sense of togetherness amongst arriving and departing passengers.

Subject

Subjects are the content and theses that active research communities consume, generate, and perform. For some time I have been talking to library directors about the absence of visible subject matter specificity in university libraries. University libraries today are too general. They advertise "books" or "media"—but not topics. Library directors say to me, "Yes, departmental libraries have been consolidating. Now only a very few libraries with diverse format collections like art and music are kept separate. It's a matter of reducing costs."

I would like to walk into a library and be provoked to consider the many possible subjects I might research in that library. I would like to see "subject-matter dens"—areas of the library set up with artifacts, media, books, and a "convener-librarian." These spaces could be designed around the core academic disciplines, or they could be curated to gather together people with subtly related interests. For example, there could be a subject-matter den designed to convene musicians and physicists. There might be acoustic or visual clues (either symbolism or what architects call "materiality"—designed combinations of textures, shapes, and colors) to stimulate expansive thought connecting these disciplines. The convener-librarian might select instrumental music to be played softly into the space—though perhaps it would be louder around certain seats to accommodate differences in acoustic preference. There might be a window from this space onto a courtyard with a small pond so that while writing or coding and listening to the music one might also look out at the pond and watch the wind move the water.

Fifteen years of recession have left us anxious for the university to be relevant to job acquisition and preparedness. The World Economic Forum Future of Jobs Report warns that over five million job losses between now and 2020 will occur for people who do not upgrade technical skills, and for those in clerical jobs.[19] MIT researcher and author Andy McAfee says only certain jobs will not be automated in the "second machine age": "The least threatened jobs may well be those that involve human skills beyond the simply technical, to physical, creative, and social skills."[20] And so what the Future of Jobs Report says to me in this context is that it matters that we are not generalists—but rather that we know subjects in great detail. Jesuit scholar Richard Rohr says he felt comfortable expanding the dialogue of Catholicism because he had been so thoroughly immersed in it.[21] Knowing a subject matter well permits us to creatively break its rules. And knowing one or more subjects well lets us combine ideas from across territories of knowledge.

One of the people I talked to about subject matter specificity was Susan Gibbons. "Oh yes," Susan said in response to my gripe. "Sociologist Andrew Abbott represented the faculty in the reorganization of the University of Chicago's libraries [from 2005 to 2011]. He bemoaned the death of departmental libraries. He felt the disciplines had a stronger sense of self and community when you had a common canon and gathered in those libraries."[22]

Indeed Abbott shows—in his comprehensive social and institutional history of university research libraries, "Library Research Infrastructure for Humanistic and Social Scientific Scholarship in the

Twentieth Century"—that faculty and graduate students saw each other and shared references regularly and directly when departmental libraries existed. Most volumes in departmental libraries were duplicates of university library holdings. The libraries were typically maintained by a designated graduate student. They were located a short walk down the hall, and they were used.[23]

To me, it is a revelation—and a relief—to learn that the large, anonymous, centralized library I encountered as an undergraduate was not a result of pedagogical design. Rather, as Abbott describes, its size and generality reflect the economics and bureaucratic efficiency of housing the superabundance of scholarly material published in the postwar period.[24]

What if there were an opportunity to design a university from scratch? Could we put a library at the center and have that library provoke students to understand and distinguish between the academic disciplines?[25] Let's imagine that there is a new urban university that encompasses an entire city block. The center of the university is a long, rectangular atrium four or five stories high. This atrium-cum-agora is run and staffed by convener-librarians who create the distinct cultures of a number of pavilions, mezzanines, and podia, and other memorable architectural enclosures. At one end of the atrium you enter from the main street outside the university and at the other you find a dining concourse with a varied and wondrous universe of restaurants and cafes accessed by meal plan. (Of course, the dining functions could mix easily with the agora.) To work in a lab, attend class, or visit a faculty office, you walk through the departmental library for that subject or subjects. These departmental libraries could take all shapes and forms as subject-matter dens. Naturally, each department would have a second entrance to the street outside. Provided the university is new construction rather than renovation, this design solves the cost-reduction-by-consolidation-of-media issue (the issue that spurred academic librarians to call for the abolition of departmental libraries in the postwar period) since the libraries are all adjacent to each other.

If we were designing a whole university and a library from scratch, what would it look like?

Detail

Detail is nuance—fine-grained, plural, entropic, and variable—and is the threshold of complexity.

I left Calgary by car last fall and drove two hours across the plains toward the Rocky Mountains. A commercial break in my music set promised more content "streaming to my device," and I pondered that phrase while leaving civilization for the trail and a remote hut six miles into the mountains. Two concepts the first humans understood: a stream, which carries objects from a place far away, and a device—a tool—which defines me as human. When I arrived at the trailhead, I acknowledged and took some time to read the signs about bears. Carrying bells and walking in groups was advised. I was alone. I had no bell.

I did have plenty of time to think while I approached the Asulkan Glacier on a trail cut (as is typical) alongside a stream. I thought about how to sing sounds that would be perceived by bears as a warning. I tried every consonant and vowel in the alphabet in combination and with varying volume and rhythm until I settled on two that seemed right and alternated between them for the remainder of the hike.

Why does walking stimulate thought? Is it because memories are related to physical sensations and we rekindle these through movement?[26] Is it because walking gives us visual access to more details in the environment? The National Library of France is organized as a broad hall ringing a wooded courtyard and surrounded by reading rooms. The hall is populated with groups of seats facing the interior promenade and the trees. If I were to study here rather than just visit, I would walk between chapters or problem sets.

The Victorians loved detail. Their worlds were filled with objects, rugs, and furniture from places across the world. The objects gave them an understanding of other places, as images do for us now. Why is the Victorian detail-filled atmosphere of curios and shelves so appealing and calming? Architect Lisa Heschong has a theory: "Other than a fire or the sun, we are generally the warmest thing in our environment, our own source of heat …. Places that remind us of the presence of people, of the life and activities that they generate, capture some of this sense of warmth. The Victorian parlor, with all of its clutter, its remnants of people's lives, its deep upholstered chairs and layers of rugs and curtains and hangings and pictures, has this sense of warmth."[27]

With desktop fabrication tools, today, more of us can make details. Chris Anderson, former editor of *Wired*, and founder, in 2015, of *Make* magazine, says that desktop fabrication means there is "no cost to complexity." One robot can have multiple tool-heads. Designers work in small batches making changes to each prototype rather than having it produced overseas and waiting weeks to see a mistake that it's then too late in the product delivery cycle to correct.[28] While digital fabrication is creating more detail for us to enjoy, I am concerned that the switch from tangible to digital book content is impoverishing our visual field.

Researchers have anecdotally told me they find it cumbersome to scroll back and forth between pages in a digital book. I wonder if people are keeping fewer pages "open" in front of them because they have only one screen, whereas previously a researcher would have spread open many books on a desk, each marked to the pages most relevant to their work. There is reason to believe we need this visual comparison of media to understand the characteristics that distinguish one instance of a situation from another. Science, math, architecture, and art all require comparative analysis. Famously (to his many generations of students), Yale architectural historian Vincent Scully had his exam study materials mounted at eye level in a corridor in the Art History building, each image and description mounted on a separate page in sequence with the curriculum.

I have been photographing researchers' desks and asking them about their information-gathering habits to unpack this concern. Christopher Wardman, a Boston-based freelance electronics engineer, describes his ideal research workspace as "a big flat monitor to fit everything on." He has come to terms with lots of cable everywhere but doesn't want drawers. "Everything I want would be visually in front of me. Looking for stuff wastes time."[29]

A great way to get ideas for future environments is watching sci-fi movies. I just watched *Interstellar* (2014) and noted a low-tech toggle lever the lead character uses to flip quickly back and forth between a 24-inch LCD and a whiteboard mounted on the back. Yes, I realize that SMART Board technology lets us annotate straight on top of specialized screens, but SMART Boards are expensive. Here's a low-cost space-saving tool that Christopher Wardman might even use.

Den

Why does everyone want to be "immersed" in everything these days? Gloria Sutton, speaking at Harvard's Carpenter Center for the Visual Arts in 2015, described a renewed interest in Stan Van Der Beek's 1967 Movie Drome, which was recreated in the 2012 New Museum exhibit Ghosts in the Machine. The Movie Drome, Sutton said, was an "immersive spectatorship experience" that demanded audience participation and "ameliorated the alienating effect of technology." Further, it was a political tool to critique war and the "computing industrial complex."[30]

Edward O. Wilson's "biophilia hypothesis" may provide an explanation. Humans seek interactions with nature, Wilson states.[31] In their uninterrupted form, ecosystems can be expansive and immersive, with natural patterns continuing over large areas, and the topography of mountainous areas giving us an experience of being surrounded by nature. Kent Bloomer and Charles Moore also wrote about the calming psychological effect of being surrounded by nature, mountains, or architecture in their 1977 primer for Yale freshmen, *Body, Memory and Architecture*.[32]

I think it's fine if the '60s are back. It was an era of discontent, and the artists and intellectuals of this period set up some worthwhile formats for critique—including the den, the personalized object- and image-rich social environment where a tribe is at ease to debate. Plus, I never lived through them, so for me it's new.

But I'm twenty years older than today's college students and twenty-somethings, and their experience is worth looking at in its native format. When I do this, I see a trend toward living well and small and low-cost, enjoying each other's company, and being surrounded by experience and beauty, without a lot of commitments. One of my graduate students in thesis studio at MassArt designed the smallest possible space a human could live in. He, at the time, had turned a closet in a friend's apartment into his bedroom. *The New York Times* and *The New Yorker* have written about #Vanlifers Foster Huntington, Emily King, and Corey Smith[33] who left behind city jobs to live together in a treehouse or a van, traveling from surf spot to hot spring. They support themselves through product endorsements on their social media feeds. And then there's my cousin, who two years ago decamped Boston for Portland, Oregon.

Like Burning Man, Portland seems to be a place you go because there are different rules for everything. The main rule in Portland is to enjoy life, to enjoy life with your tribe, and to take the time to do that. Last January when I visited, I experienced the city as a sensory-rich place where every door is open. Yes, the doors are open for retail—but you don't quite experience it this way. I walked down Northwest Third Avenue and saw in a shop window a trio of dresses—red, green, and lilac—billowing like flowers. I stepped in and there was a dog resting on the floor and two racks of clothes on either side, purple and brighter red and multicolored blouses and A-line dresses—all silk. I asked if the dressmaker was there, and she was: Lena Medoyeff. We talked for nearly an hour and I learned how she is manufacturing these custom garments in small batches and who her audience is. After visiting Lena's shop, I walked into Tender Loving Empire, and the tables were filled with hand-sized objects. The walls and ceiling were illustrated, and the shelves were filled. I talked to the staff, and they smiled and made eye contact, and I felt welcome and happy, like I'd just found a new living room to visit whenever I wanted. Hand Eye Supply, another Portland store with an alluring name, is equally nuanced with visual and tactile objects for stimulation and/or for purchase. Work aprons are displayed on a radial arm turnstile, the way rugs are typically shown. I left the store with an apron that I've never used.

Skunkworks

So a great academic community considers the social dynamics of Tribe and Power and has the characteristics of Crossroads, Subject, Detail, and Den. What else do we need? How can we make an academic library or other targeted space on campus productive and enjoyable for students? How do we design for learning, laughter, creation, and growth?

Skunkworks are temporary participant-formed think tanks fueled by the energy of individuals who want to see their ideas changed and shaped with others they respect. They are special, maybe even secret, places.

MIT Library Director Chris Bourg says students in the library should feel, "These are my resources. This is my identity."[34] Can library space be skunkworks? Can the space and territory of the library be one of the "resources" that students command in order to test and ideate with others?

One of the most successful buildings that ever existed on the MIT campus was called Building 20. To an architect working in Cambridge, understanding Building 20 is like knowing what Thanksgiving is. Building 20 was a three-floor temporary structure built in 1943. Many labs and people were moved in and out over its 55-year life. Because it was temporary, the occupants knocked down drywall at will and popped holes to run additional power cables through. The cheap nature and abundance of space meant that "'many quite risky projects got off the ground,'" says former building occupant Morris Halle. Space was so cramped that researchers would prop their doors, explains Walter E. Morrow. "The result: 'as you wandered down the corridors, you saw what was going on in the rooms... In that process, you learned of many wondrous things in addition to your own work.'" Labs in Building 20 developed interaircraft detecting microwave radar; liquid helium and its application to the creation of MRI imaging in hospitals; and the field of linguistics—under the direction of Noam Chomsky.[35]

Airbnb has allowed latent social conveners to express themselves, and, with a capitalization greater than any hotel chain, is the most successful hospitality business in the world today. Chuck, an involved participant in multiple work and place-based communities, hired us to design a house in New Hampshire's White Mountains. He'd lined up his contractor Jason, a hub of the local economy he'd found by talking to folks and knocking on the workshop door behind the sandwich shop in town. Chuck is a Duke graduate who did his master's thesis on the environmental psychology of views of nature and wrote about the Appalachian Trail while hiking it. Chuck works at the office of an outdoor education organization based in New Hampshire and Boston and chose his house site because the Appalachian Trail crosses through less than a quarter of a mile away. He plans to host hikers who want an Airbnb night, a hot shower, and a dose of camaraderie, comfort, and beauty. The Airbnb piece is a studio under the same single-pitch roof as the house but separated by a breezeway. Chuck has created a comfortable working group between owner, architect, and contractor, bringing us together with encouragement and prompts. I love that the potential of Airbnb has allowed him to dream of creating one more community where he can bring people together around his interests.

Really creative people can have vastly different work styles. Two I admire are fiction writer Jonathan Franzen and scientist Tim Crain. I read Franzen's *The Corrections* when it came out in 2001. I had to read it because it was billed as the next "great American novel," and I like epics. It proved to be a great story, set in the Midwest, which I knew little about, and satirizing the suburban family and the intellectual—so, basically, me. I researched Franzen before buying and read that he'd committed himself to a small room in a derelict building in Harlem to write the book. I thought this was admirable. I also suspected immediately that he'd leaked this detail.

I heard about Tim Crain from two bright aerospace scientists I interviewed in Cambridge. They both told me I had to talk to Tim if I wanted to know what workspace design and planning details are likely to spawn research breakthroughs. We met at aerospace robotics startup Intuitive Machines' headquarters in Houston. It's a suburban office building owned by Boeing with a row of sports cars parked out front. NASA is a short drive away. Tim has an office at the window with a view of his car and a view of the "mosh pit," a social workspace where fifteen or more people can get together. His door is always ajar. "I can't work without buzz," he says. He hands me a Raspberry Pi and says, "As you turn the object around, you visualize what you could do with it and you think of alternate uses for it—this could be an autopilot. Turning the object around stimulates the thought process." If he could add any room to his new office/lab workspace, Tim would want "an extensive parts junkyard filled with boards, nuts and bolts and clamps and wires. I may just let an engineer go in there and pick up things and start soldering them into place. This is Thomas Edison's idea—to innovate you need a great imagination and a pile of junk."[36]

When asked about the most inventive and prolific work environment he's ever been in, Tim tells me about a place he calls a "skunkworks"—"the bunker"—a 10,000-square-foot high-bay space where he and five others were located for three months to fast-track the development of an integrated hardware and software product that would function as the brains of a spacecraft for NASA. "The project team was ten people but really five or six of us ended up being there all the time. The sense of urgency and the isolated location helped us cut through the unnecessary stuff."[37]

Tim's description of "the bunker" is inspiring. So inspiring, in fact, that it was likely on my mind the following spring when I walked into the boathouse across the "salt-and-pepper" bridge to learn to row. It's a modest Victorian building with three bays of boat-racks stacked to the ceiling, a bookcase for lights and cleaning supplies, a shop, and locker rooms. An old-timer took a minute, on that beautiful spring cleanup day, to show me how to sign out a boat and pointed to the training scull.

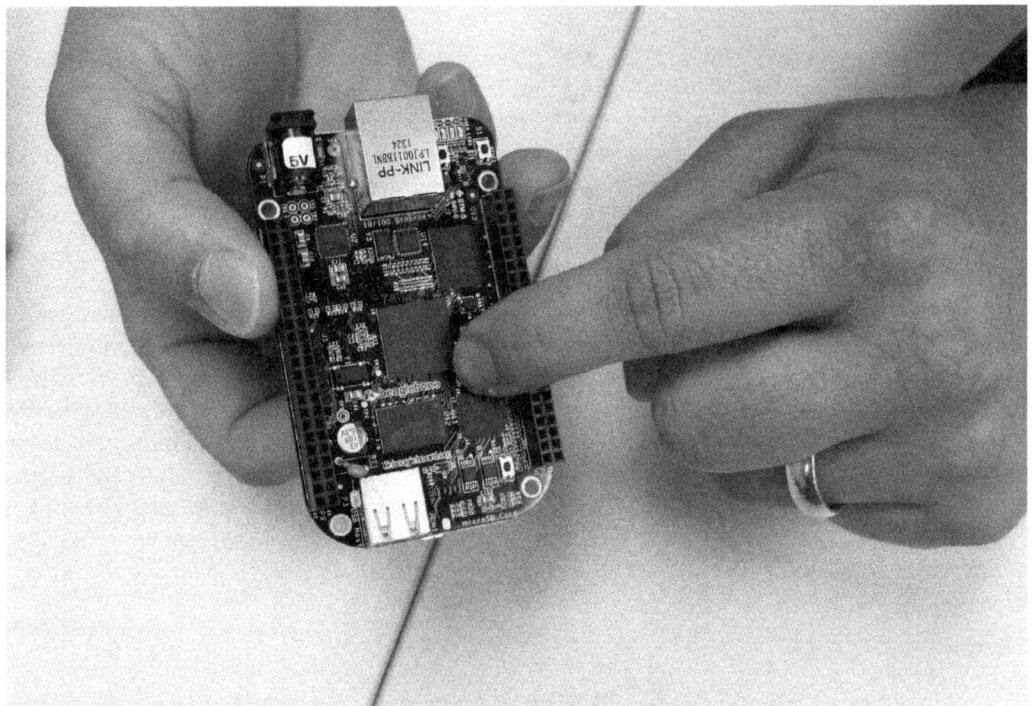

"Raspberry Pi" explained by Dr. Tim Crain of Intuitive Machines, Houston, TX (2013)
Source: Marie S. A. Sorensen, AIA

Afterword

"Mosh Pit" at Intuitive Machines office move-in, Houston, TX (2013)
Source: Marie S. A. Sorensen, AIA

I was assigned a locker, which I filled with headbands and water bottles. For weeks and then months the rowing shell stabilized as I learned how to move on the water. Every day, someone different took a minute to teach me a skill—how to carry my boat, how to square blades just as the handles pass over my laces, how to catch the water and match its speed and accelerate. And I learned that the river moves with its own playbook—travel patterns, shore-based landmarks, practice sequences, and crossing protocols. Quickly I began to learn most by just watching and imitating the other rowers.

Cambridge is famous for the Head of the Charles Regatta. MIT, Harvard, Boston University, Tufts, Boston College, Northeastern, and numerous prep schools all practice daily on the river. There is in rowing, as in the academic community as a whole, a quiet logic to its prosperity: the boathouse tribe, the convener-coach, the riverine crossroads, the sport itself and the nuance of technique, the provisioned clubhouse, and the 5:00 a.m. meeting of people working together, and individually, to break through. This admirable community has developed and thrived over many decades, yet it is still open to newcomers wanting to join, learn, laugh, and grow. When I think about how I want students to feel when they step onto campus, it is this sense of potential, wonder, and camaraderie that I want to foster with the buildings I design.

Notes

1. Anthony Paletta, "Setting the Table," *Metropolis* (Nov 2015): 89–93.
2. "SCALE-UP FAQs," scaleup.ncsu.edu/FAQs.html (accessed April 30, 2017). "Education Transformation through Technology at MIT—TEAL," web.mit.edu/edtech/casestudies.teal.html (accessed April 30, 2017).

3. Mikki Brammer, "Truly Transparent," *Metropolis* (June 2016): 92-99.
4. Susan Gibbons, Yale University Librarian (Interview—phone—May 4, 2015).
5. Daniel Sheehan, "How MIT Library Decided Not to Build a Data Visualization Lab Now," in Preconference 2: Digital Displays for Visualization, Engagement, and Learning, *5th Annual Designing Libraries Conference* (University of Calgary, September 18, 2016)
6. Susan Cain, *Quiet: The Power of Introverts in a World That Can't Stop Talking* (New York: Penguin Books, 2012).
7. Evelyn Lee, Corporate Managing Director, Workplace Strategy & Analytics, Savills Studley. (Interview—phone—March 16, 2017).
8. "Partitioning Systems," *Progressive Architecture* (July 1961): 124-27.
9. "Initiations and Salutations | Burning Man Journal," journal.burningman.org/2011/07/philosophical-center/spirituality/initiations-and-salutations/ (accessed April 30, 2017).
10. Sophie Scott, "Sophie Scott: Why we laugh," www.ted.com/talks/sophie_scott_why_we_laugh/transcript?language=en (accessed April 30, 2017).
11. University of Chicago: Research: Institutes and Centers. www.uchicago.edu/research/centers/ (accessed May 1, 2017).
12. Stanford University Research Centers. www.stanford.edu/research/centers (accessed May 8, 2017).
13. Yale Centers and Institutes. www.yale.edu/research-collections/centers-institutes (accessed May 8, 2017).
14. Tom Hickerson, Vice Provost (Libraries and Cultural Resources), University of Calgary, "Closing Remarks," *5th Annual Designing Libraries Conference* (University of Calgary, September 18, 2016).
15. Jason Ankeny, "Do Not Fear the Fear; You Can Beat It," in *Entrepreneur* (March 2016): 29.
16. Parmy Olson, "Let's Fake a Meeting: Telepresence Robots Could Change the Way Your Office Works—If You Don't Mind a $20,000 Price Tag," *Forbes* (July 15, 2013): 51.
17. Edward Glaeser, *Triumph of the City: How our Greatest Invention Makes us Richer, Smarter, Greener, Healthier, and Happier* (New York: The Penguin Press, 2011): 124.
18. Safdie Architects: Ben Gurion International Airport, www.msafdie.com/projects/bengurionairport (accessed May 1, 2017).
19. Nora Young, "What Will You Do When a Robot Steals Your Job?" *Spark with Nora Young, CBC Radio Podcast* (January 21, 2016).
20. Nora Young, "What Will You Do When a Robot Steals Your Job?" *Spark with Nora Young, CBC Radio Podcast* (January 21, 2016).
21. Richard Rohr, "Living in Deep Time," in *On Being with Krista Tippett podcast* (April 13, 2017).
22. Susan Gibbons, Yale University Librarian (Interview—phone—May 4, 2015).
23. Andrew Abbott, "Library Research Infrastructure for Humanistic and Social Scientific Scholarship in the Twentieth Century," in *Social Knowledge in the Making*, ed. Charles Camic, Neil Gross, and Michele Lamont (Chicago: University of Chicago Press, 2011).
24. Andrew Abbott, "Library Research Infrastructure for Humanistic and Social Scientific Scholarship in the Twentieth Century," in *Social Knowledge in the Making*, ed. Charles Camic, Neil Gross, and Michele Lamont (Chicago: University of Chicago Press, 2011).
25. In my 2015 talk to the Association of College and Research Libraries New England Chapter, I presented a diagram for an urban university organized around a library. Marie S. A. Sorensen, "The History and Future of Collaboration," co-keynote address at The Association of College and Research Libraries New England Chapter Conference (May 8, 2015).
26. Krista Tippett, "Bessel van der Kolk: How Trauma Lodges in the Body," *On Being, Podcast* (March 9, 2017).
27. Lisa Heschong, *Thermal Delight in Architecture* (Cambridge, MA: The MIT Press, 1979): 26-27.
28. Chris Anderson, "Makers: The New Industrial Revolution," at Romeconfluence (February 21, 2013).
29. Christopher Wardman, VXM Design (Interview—in person at Aurora Flight Sciences, Cambridge, MA—July 31, 2013).
30. Gloria Sutton, Assistant Professor of Contemporary Art History and New Media, Northeastern University, *Talk + Screening*, Carpenter Center for Visual Arts (May 12, 2015).
31. Edward O. Wilson, *Biophilia* (Cambridge, MA and London, UK: Harvard University Press, 1984).

32. Kent Bloomer and Charles Willard Moore, *Body, Memory and Architecture* (New Haven: Yale University Press, 1977).
33. Rachel Monroe, #Vanlife, the Bohemian Social-Media Movement.
34. Chris Bourg, "Future of Libraries" lecture sponsored by Arts at MIT (February 11, 2016).
35. "Building 20 denizens say farewell to former home." *MIT News*, news.mit.edu/1998/b20main-0401 (accessed May 2, 2017).
36. Dr. Tim Crain, Vice President of Research & Development, Intuitive Machines, Houston, TX (Interview—in person—October 10, 2013).
37. Dr. Tim Crain, Vice President of Research & Development, Intuitive Machines, Houston, TX (Interview—in person—October 10, 2013).

Appendix A

Field Guide Entry Survey Form

Information Commons Survey

How to complete this survey: This survey is to be used to enter descriptive information for an entry in the second edition of the book by Scarecrow Press, *The Information Commons: A Field Guide*, hereafter simply referred to as "the field guide." Descriptive entries in the field guide characterize library integrated service programs or facilities termed either as "Information Commons" or other related terms such as "Technology Commons," "Knowledge Commons," "Learning Commons," or "Makerspace." If you have received an invitation to complete this survey, we believe that you have such a program or facility that meets the criteria for inclusion in the field guide. All entries submitted will become the property of Scarecrow Press.

Answering the Questions: The entries are divided into two parts: summary data and narrative response descriptions. Please fill out all of the questions to the best of your ability. In case you lack the specific information requested, please make an informed estimate and indicate that it is an estimate. If you are uncertain about how to answer a question and need guidance, please send an email to the email address infocommons2@unt.edu. Someone will get back to you with a response or a phone call, whichever is more appropriate.

Institution: Please provide the name of the university or parent institution to which your library belongs, as well as the city, state (or territory), and country in the space below.

Picture/Photo: Please provide as a separate attachment a representative digital photograph of your Information Commons facility. Images should be provided as either JPEG, PNG, or GIF files, each less than 1 MB in size.

Floor plan or diagram: Please provide as a separate attachment a representative floor plan or diagram of your Information Commons facility. If you do not have a floor plan, you may include typical furniture/workstation diagrams or other relevant spatial layouts. Images should be provided as either JPEG, PNG, or GIF files, each less than 1 MB in size.

Name: Please indicate the name by which your service program or facility is typically referred to.

[ ]

Year established: Please indicate the year in which the facility or service first became available to the public.

[ ]

Years of expansion/renovation: Please indicate the year(s) that the facility underwent expansion or major renovation.

[ ]

Square footage: Please indicate as an integer the most accurate figure you have for the square footage of the publicly available space associated with your facility.

[ ]

Location: Please indicate which of the following options best describes the location of your facility.

- ⦿ Main Library
- ○ Branch/Special Library
- ○ Space shared with other campus organizations
- ○ Other

Typical access hours per week: Please indicate as an integer the typical number of hours that the program or facility is available to its clientele during a typical academic school-year week, with or without any service staff. If there are multiple service points or distinct locations, list the figure for the primary location.

[ ]

Typical service hours per week: Please indicate as an integer the typical number of hours that the program or facility is available to its clientele during a typical academic school-year week, with service staff. If the facility always has service staff available, this will be the same number as the previous response. If there are multiple service points or distinct locations, list the figure for the primary location.

[ ]

Number of service points: Please indicate as an integer the number of service points that you associate with this program or facility.

[ ]

Number of desktop computers available for use: Please indicate as an integer the number of desktop computers that are available for use by the clientele of this program or facility.

[ ]

Number of laptop computers available for use: Please indicate as an integer the number of laptop computers that are available for use by the clientele of this program or facility.

[ ]

Do you provide access to any other types of devices? If so, please describe.

[ ]

Average monthly door count: Please indicate as an integer the average door count during a typical month of the academic school year.

[ ]

Average monthly service transactions: Please indicate as an integer the average number of service transactions of any kind during a typical month of the academic school year, as well as any additional details of clarification.

[ ]

Workstation sessions/logins: Please estimate as an integer the average number of sessions (tracked by login or otherwise recorded or estimated).

[ ]

Field Guide Entry Survey Form

Purpose: Please describe the reason(s) for creating the facility in 50-200 words of narrative.

Services: Please describe the services offered in the facility in 50-200 words of narrative. Which services were new? Which ones existed prior to the establishment of the facility? Were some services a combination of new and old? Was a new service unit created? Do you still have a reference desk?

Software: Please describe the software offered in the facility in 50-200 words of narrative, including applications and utilities, as well as associated support and infrastructure.

Print resources: Please describe in 50-200 words of narrative the relationship with and proximity to print, microform, and other collections, resource integration philosophy, and practice. Try to describe any ways in which the facility interacts with the print resources of your library.

Staff: Please describe in 50-200 words of narrative the staffing patterns and schedules for the facility, where positions come from, if there are rovers, and how staff are trained and recruited, what their background is, etc.

Funding/Budget: Please describe in 50-200 words of narrative the source(s) of funds, budgeting, planning, and management for the program or facility.

Publicity/Promotion: Please describe in 50-200 words of narrative any processes you have established to make the program or facility known to students, any public awareness programs, or faculty liaison publicity activities. Generally, describe any means that you undertake to make your clientele aware of the program or facility.

Evaluation: Please describe in 50-200 words any measures of usage, user satisfaction, or other measures of impact that you have undertaken. How do you evaluate the program or facility?

Evolution of Facility: If your facility has been in operation for several years, please describe any significant changes or evolution in the facility.

Future Steps: What are future plans for the facility? What subsequent initiatives are being considered for your facility?

Appendix B

Timeline

1969	ARPANET (Department of Defense)
1981	IBM PC
1984	Apple Macintosh
1989	World Wide Web invented
1990	Coalition for Networked Information (CNI) established
1991	World Wide Web goes public
1992	First ever photo posted
	University of Iowa (Iowa, USA) opens the Information Arcade in the Main Library
1993	Early web browser "Mosaic" released by University of Illinois
1994	Yahoo
	Leavey Library, University of Southern California (California, USA), opens the Information Commons
	University of North Carolina, Chapel Hill (North Carolina, USA) opens the Electronic Information Service
1995	Web-based email launched
1996	University of Iowa (Iowa, USA) opens the Information Commons in the Health Sciences (Hardin) Library
1997	Google
	Lehigh University (Pennsylvania, USA) opens the Information Commons
	University of North Carolina, Chapel Hill (North Carolina, USA) expands its Electronic Information Service area and renames this comprehensive area the Information Commons
1998	Emory University (Georgia, USA) opens the Information Commons
	Oregon State University (Oregon, USA) opens the Valley Library Information Commons
1999	Bucknell University (Pennsylvania, USA) opens the Information Commons
	University of Calgary (Alberta, Canada) opens the Information Commons
	University of Iowa (Iowa, USA) expands the Information Commons in the Health Sciences (Hardin) Library
2000	Y2K
	University of Cape Town (South Africa) opens the Knowledge Commons

2001	Wikipedia
	Ferris State University (Michigan, USA) opens the Information Commons
	Kansas State University (Kansas, USA) opens the K-State InfoCommons
	Saint Martin's University (Washington, USA) opens the Information Commons
	University of Nevada, Las Vegas (Nevada, USA) opens the Lied Library
2002	Georgia Institute of Technology (Georgia, USA) opens the Library West Commons
	Texas Christian University (Texas, USA) opens the Information Commons
	University of Arizona (Arizona, USA) opens the Information Commons
	University of Cincinnati (Ohio, USA) opens the Info Commons at Langsam Library
2003	LinkedIn
	MySpace
	Skype
	Indiana University, Bloomington (Indiana, USA) opens the Information Commons
	Kent State University (Ohio, USA) opens the Information Commons
	Simon Fraser University (British Columbia, Canada) opens the Information Commons
	University of Auckland (Auckland, New Zealand) opens the Kate Edger Information Commons
	Trinity University (Texas, USA) opens the Information Commons
	University of Newcastle (New South Wales, Australia) opens the Auchmuty Information Commons
2004	Facebook
	Brigham Young University (Utah, USA) opens the Information Commons/General Reference
	Northwestern University (Illinois, USA) opens the Information Commons
	Ohio University (Ohio, USA) opens the Learning Commons
	University of Auckland (Auckland, New Zealand) opens the Grafton Information Commons
	University of Minnesota, Twin Cities (Minnesota, USA) opens the Information Commons
	University of Waterloo (Ontario, Canada) opens the RBC Information Commons
2005	California State Polytechnic University (California, USA) opens the Learning Commons or Digital Teaching Library
	University of Cape Town (South Africa) renovates the Knowledge Commons, Research Commons, & Learning Commons
2006	Twitter
	Simon Fraser University (British Columbia, Canada) opens the Student Learning Commons
	University of New Mexico, Albuquerque (New Mexico, USA) plans construction of a Student Research Plaza
2007	iPhone
	Trinity University (Texas, USA) renovates the Information Commons
2008	University of Minnesota Twin Cities (Minnesota, USA) renovates the SMART Learning Commons
2009	Virginia Tech University (Virginia, USA) renovates the Learning Commons

2010	Instagram
	University of Central Florida (Florida, USA) opens the Knowledge Commons
	University of North Texas (Texas, USA) opens the Collaboration and Learning Commons
2011	Snapchat
	University of Maryland (Maryland, USA) renovates the Terrapin Learning Commons
2012	Pennsylvania State University (Pennsylvania, USA) opens the Knowledge Commons
	University of Illinois at Urbana-Champaign (Illinois, USA) renovates the Scholarly Commons
	Virginia Commonwealth University (Virginia, USA) opens the Collaboration Room
2013	North Carolina State University (North Carolina, USA) opens the Lake Raleigh Learning Commons
	University of Iowa (Iowa, USA) renovates the Learning Commons
2014	Indiana University, Bloomington (Indiana, USA) renovates the Learning Commons
	Jackson State University (Jackson, Mississippi, USA) opens JSU Innovate
	University of Oklahoma (Oklahoma, USA) opens the Helmerich Collaborative Learning Center
2015	Dartmouth College (New Hampshire, USA) renovates the Jones Media Center
	Kansas State University (Kansas, USA) renovates the K-State InfoCommons
	Texas Christian University (Texas, USA) renovates the Information Commons
	University of North Carolina at Greensboro (North Carolina, USA) renovates the Digital Media Commons
	University of Tennessee at Chattanooga (Tennessee, USA) opens the Studio
	University of Texas (Texas, USA) opens the PCL Learning Commons
2016	Claremont Colleges Library (California, USA) opens the Collaborative Commons
	Duke University (North Carolina, USA) renovates The Ruppert Commons for Research, Technology and Collaboration ("The Edge")
	Emory University (Georgia, USA) renovates the Learning Commons, Student Digital Life
	University of North Texas (Texas, USA) renovates The Factory
2019	World Wide Web -- Happy Thirtieth Birthday!

Index

3D printing, 34, 112. *See also* MakerBot

Abbott, Andrew, 176-177, 183
academic advising, 27
academic commons, 11, 13, 19, 67
academic community, xviii, 3, 11, 14-16, 179, 182
academic computing center, 8, 27
accessibility equipment, 28
active learning, 15, 30, 56, 158, 170
active learning classrooms, 158, 170
adaptive technologies, 29
Adobe (software), 80, 83, 89-90, 113, 115, 121, 126, 130, 135, 139, 142, 145, 149, 152, 155, 158, 163, 165
Albanese, Andrew Richard, 17
Anderson, Chris, 178, 183
Ankeny, Jason, 172, 183
ArcGIS (geographic software), 83, 89, 113, 115, 121, 130, 135, 145, 149, 152
Arduino, 101, 148-149, 155
artificial intelligence (AI), xii
artwork, 28, 137
assessment, 14, 32, 37, 78, 81, 85, 109, 128, 139-140, 160, 166
Association of College and Research Libraries (ACRL), 5, 21-22, 183
Association of Research Libraries (ARL), 14, 17, 21
Atlanta University Center, 71
augmented reality, xii, 47, 101
automated retrieval system (ASR), xi, 102
Avila University, 59-61

Bailey, D. Russell, 24, 31
Barr, Robert B., 6, 17
Battin, Patricia, 16
Beagle, Donald, 10, 13-15, 18-22
Bechtel, Joan, 5, 17
Benjamin Franklin Institute of Technology, 175
Bennett, Scott, 9-11, 18-19
Bible, Brice, 31
Bird Library, 12
Blackburn, Janette, 19
Bloomer, Kent, 179, 184
Blue Ocean Strategy, 42
Bostock Library, xix, 69, 83
Boston Public Library, 174

Bourg, Chris, 180, 184
Brammer, Mikki, 183
Brigham Young University, 27
bring your own device (BYOD), 50, 75, 89, 93
Brody Learning Commons, 48
Brooklyn College, 6
Brown, Malcom, 18-19, 83, 126
Bruffee, Kenneth, 6, 17
Bryson, Tim, 21
Budd, John M., 4, 16
Burke, John, 22
Burns, Kristi, xv, 73

café, 11, 20, 24-25, 29, 47, 105, 130, 167, 174
Cain, Susan, 170, 183
cameras, 28, 48, 50, 78-79, 88, 101, 106, 121, 134, 138, 141, 148, 158, 165
Camic, Charles, 183
capital expenditure, 45
career center, 27
Carlson, Scott, 11, 17, 19
catalyst, xi, xix, 14
Cawthorne, Jon E., 22
Center for Teaching and Learning, 27
Center for Teaching Excellence, 69
Chomsky, Noam, 180
circulation desk, 58, 108, 112, 115, 121, 135
circulation statistics, 5, 137
Claremont Colleges Library, 75-77
Cline Library, 56-57
Coalition for Networked Information (CNI), 7, 21
coffee shop, 11, 108
Collaboration & Learning Commons, 144
collaboration room, 62, 82, 162-164
collaboration space, 67
Collaborative Commons, 15, 75-78
colocation, 7-8, 26, 140
Commings, Karen, 18
Commons 2.0, 11, 19
computer aided design (CAD), 51, 54, 60, 107
computer labs, 24-25, 48, 113, 115
Conaton Learning Commons, 68
Conkey, Christopher, 20
consultation, xx, 27, 29, 36, 64, 76, 101, 103-104, 109, 114, 116, 121-122, 130-131, 158
consultation space, 64, 109

195

Cook, Summer, xv, xxi, 53-61
cooperation, 5, 8, 26
Cornell University, 173
Crain, Tim, 180-181, 184
Creth, Sheila D., 18

D. H. Hill Library, 101
Daniels, William, 20-21
Darch, Colin, 20-21
Dartmouth College, 27, 78-79, 81
data visualization, xiii, 24, 30, 49, 69, 80, 83-84, 101, 104, 114, 118, 167, 183
Davis, Jinnie Y., 16
de Jager, Karin, 20-21
design thinking, 32, 38
destination commons, xxi, 68
Dewey, Barbara, 6, 31
digital commons, xxii
digital humanities, 13-14, 20-22, 84, 126, 167
Digital Media Commons, 141-143
digital scholarship, xxii-xxiii, 13-14, 18, 20-22, 30, 69, 83, 85, 89, 126, 128, 134, 152-154
digital scholarship center, xxii, 69
digitization, xix, 96, 126
distributed commons, xxi, 68-69
Doucette, Don, 7, 18
Dougherty, Richard M., 16
Dowson, Rebecca, 14, 20-22
Duke University, xix, 67, 69-70, 82-86

E-Science, xix, 21
Edison, Thomas, 181
Edge, The. *See* Ruppert Commons
Emory University, 12, 20, 35, 88-89, 91
Eng, Susanna, 11, 19
Epstein, Jennifer, 20
Estrella Mountain Community College, 7-8
event space, 29, 82
exhibit, xx, 29, 78, 178
exhibit space, 78
exhibits, xx, 28, 30, 36, 49, 167

faculty research commons, xii-xiii, xviii
Factory, The (UNT makerspace) 148-150
Fenwick Library, 69
Fishbowl, 173-174
flexibility, xix, 28, 36, 38, 43, 47, 53-54, 56, 62, 64, 93
Forrest, Charles, xvii-xviii, 18-19
Franzen, Jonathan, 180
Freeman, Geoffrey, 11, 19

gate counts, 5, 11, 17, 124, 132, 160
Gen Y, 62

Gen Z, 62, 65, 72
George Mason University, 69
Georgia Institute of Technology, 11, 23, 35
Gibbons, Susan, 170, 176, 183
Ginsberg, Sharona, 22
Glaeser, Ed, 174, 183
Goldenber-Hart, Diane, 21
Gordon, H. Scott, 16
Gottesman Libraries, 66
graduate student commons, xii-xiii, xviii, 30
Grand Valley State University, 27
Gray, Dave, 39
Gross, Neil, xx, 183
group studies, xii, 11, 23, 28-30, 46, 89-91, 104-106, 109, 121, 135, 137-138, 145
"guide on the side," 6-7

Halbert, Martin, xvii-xviii, 12, 18-19
Halle, Morris, 180
Hardin, Garrett, 16
Hartman, Craig, 17
Harvard Libraries, 37
Hassan, Scott, 172
Helfer, Doris S., 18
Helmerich Collaborative Learning Center, 20, 151-153
help desk, 27, 69, 112-113, 115
Hesburgh Libraries, 70-71
Heschong, Lisa, 178, 183
heuristic model, 6
Hickerson, Tom, 172, 183
hotel, 66, 180
Howe, Neil, 19
Hunt Library. *See* James B. Hunt Jr. Library
Huntington, Foster, 179

iMovie, 80, 89, 139, 145, 149
Indiana University, 13, 21, 92-94
infocommons, xvii, 18, 31, 88, 97-100
Information Arcade, 8, 18
Information Commons, 112-114, 114-117
information desk, 128
infrastructure, xi, 44, 50, 53, 57, 65, 121, 172, 176, 183
Innovation Commons, 67
intellectual center, 8
interactive computing, xii
interdisciplinarity, xii, 14
Internet, 5, 9, 24, 29, 101, 118, 121, 135, 138, 145, 149, 172, 175
iterative prototyping, 32

Jackson State University, 95
James B. Hunt Jr. Library, xi, xviii, 36

Johns Hopkins, 48
Jones Media Center, 78-81
Jones, C. Lee, 16, 78-81
JSU Innovate, 95

K-State InfoCommons, 97-99
Kansas State University, 97-99
Kaser, David, 16, 19
Kiley, Kevin, 20
King, Emily, 179
Kirschenbaum, Matthew G., 21
Kleinschmit, Matt, 72
Knowledge Commons, xviii, 15, 26, 75, 106-109, 118-120, 122-123
knowledge creation, 14
knowledge market, 27
knowledge production, 15
Kranich, Nancy, 16

Lake Raleigh Learning Commons, xii, xviii, 100-103
Lamont, Michele, 170, 183
language lab, 69
large format printer, 28
large-scale visualization, xii-xiii
LaunchPad, 148
Learning Commons, xii, xviii, xxii, 9-11, 13, 15, 18-19, 22-23, 25, 27, 30, 39, 42-43, 46, 48, 52, 58-61, 64, 67-69, 71, 75, 88-94, 100-105, 109-111, 118-119, 129-134, 136-141, 144-147, 157-161, 164-167, 175
learning community, xx
learning experience, 6-7, 96
learning space, xviii, 19, 25, 36, 56, 66-67, 76
learning studio, 56-57
learning styles, 6-7, 10, 25, 28
learning-focused space, xxi
Leavey Library, 8, 11, 18
Lee, Evelyn, 16, 171, 183
Leighton, Philip D., 4, 16
Leonard, David, 174
Lessig, Lawrence, 4, 16
Lévi-Strauss, Claude, 171
Lewis, David W., 16-17, 22
Lewis, Vivian, 16-17, 22
library as place, xviii, 17-19
library commons, xx-xxi, 30, 57
library-centric, 24, 32
Link, The (Duke teaching center) 67, 69
Lippincott, Joan K., xv, xx, 8, 10, 15, 17-19, 23-24, 26, 28, 30
littleBits (electronic building blocks), 106, 109, 148
Long, Phillip D., 19

machine learning, xii
MakerBot, 15, 142
makerspaces, xii-xiii, xxii-xxiii, 15, 22, 30, 46, 49, 52, 65, 75, 101, 135, 137, 140, 142, 148
Makey Makey electronics kit, 148
Maricopa County Community College District, 8
Martell, Charles, 17
Massachusetts Institute of Technology (MIT), 169-170, 176, 180, 182-184
Math Lab, 69
MatLab (software), 83, 89, 135, 145, 149
Mcafee, Andy, 176
Medoyeff, Lena, 179
Merritt, Stephen R., 19
Microsoft products, 76, 80, 89, 101, 107, 121, 130, 135, 139, 145, 149, 158, 165
Millennials, 9, 11, 19, 62, 65
Miller Learning Center, 30
Molholt, Pat, 16
Monroe, Rachel, 184
Montclair University, 48
Moore, Charles Willard, 43, 179, 184
Moran, Barbara, 5, 16-17
Morris, Jeff, 19, 180
Morrow, Walter E., 180
Mulligan, Rikk, 21
Multimedia Collaboration Room, 162-164
multimedia workstations, 8
Muñoz, Trevor, 22
Murr, Lawrence E., 5, 16-17
Murray, David, 18, 31
music production studio, xii

Naisbett, John, 5, 17
National Endowment for the Humanities (NEH), 14
Neff, Raymond K., 16
Net Generation, 11, 18
network, 5, 24-25, 34, 37, 46-47, 50-51, 64, 71, 89, 113, 115, 121, 126, 145
networking, xiii, xx, 17
networks, 18, 24, 47, 65, 72
Neville, Shelley, 19
North Carolina State University (NCSU), xi-xii, xviii, 28, 30, 36, 81, 100-103, 182
Northern Arizona University, 56-57
Nowviskie, Bethany, 22

Oblinger, Diane G., 18-19
Oblinger, James L., 18
Odegaard Library, 27
Ohio State University, 30
Ohio University, 104
Olson, Parmy, 183
open seating, 23, 76

operating budget, 103, 105, 110, 136
operations, 37, 45, 80, 84, 90, 105, 108

Paletta, Anthony, 182
pedagogy, 7, 15, 23, 33, 158, 160
peer tutoring, 107
Pennsylvania State University, xviii, 17, 26, 106-109
Penrose Library, 13
Perini, Michael, 21
perpetual beta, 46, 49, 51
Perry, Susan, 17, 58
Perry-Castaneda Library (PCL) Learning Commons, 58, 157, 159, 161,
plotter, 28
Posner, Miriam, 21-22
Post-Millennials, 62, 65
presentation practice, xii, xx, 28-29, 67, 89, 91
problem-solving, 44
project work room, 65
projectors, 28-29, 50, 78, 82, 88, 101, 121, 134
Purdue University, 30

QGIS (geographic software), 83, 135, 145, 149

rapid prototyping, xx, 46, 49
Raspberry Pi (small single-board computer), 101, 148, 181
reading lab, 69
reference desk, 71, 101, 105, 107, 112-113, 115, 118, 121-122, 124, 126, 135, 152, 158
Research Commons, xii-xiii, xviii, xxii, 13-16, 20-22, 67, 69, 118-119
research-focused environments, 62
Richardson Jr., John, 16
Ridley, Michael, 19
Ringling College of Art and Design, 65
Robinson, David G., 4, 16
robotics, 148, 180
Rohr, Richard, 176, 183
Roszkowski, Beth, 21
Rumsey, Abby Smith, 14, 21
Ruppert Commons for Research, Technology and Collaboration (The Edge), xix-xx, 30, 67, 69, 82-87, 169

Sack, John, 17
Safdie Architects, 183
Safdie, Moshe, 175
"sage on the stage", 6-7
Salem State University, 64
sandboxes, xx, 15, 46, 49, 170
SAS (statistics software), 83, 89, 113, 115, 135, 145, 149
SCALE-UP (NCSU active learning classroom), 56, 167, 170, 182

scanning, xii, 24, 29, 87, 89, 118, 135, 149, 154, 163
scanning stations, 24, 29
Scholarly Commons, 124-128
Scholarly Communication Institute, 14, 21
Scott, Anthony D., 16
Scott, Sophie, 171, 183
Scully, Vincent, 178
service delivery, 9, 30, 35, 37
service philosophy, xx, 35
service portfolio, 35
service providers, 34-36
sewing machines, 49, 149
Sheehan, Daniel, 170, 183
Simon Fraser University, 109, 111
Sinclair, Bryan, 19
Skype, 51, 67
Slepitza, Ronald, 60
SMART board, 178
SMART Learning Commons, 137-141
Smith, Corey, 179
Smith, Kathlin, 19
Smith Learning Theater, 66
social commons, 11
Soehner, Catherine, 21
Sorenson, Marie S.A., 171, 173-175, 181-183
Spiro, Lisa, 22
SPSS (statistics software), 80, 89, 113, 115, 135, 145, 149
St. Pierre, Alain, 21
Stanford University, 172, 183
Steam (computer game distribution service by Valve Corporation), 149
Steeves, Catherine, 21
Strauss, William, 19, 171
Student Digital Life, 88, 90
student government, xiv, 146-147
Student Learning Commons, 109-111
student success, 21, 25, 27, 36, 110, 130, 159
student success initiative, 27
Studio, 154-157
Sutton, Gloria, 178, 183
Syracuse University, 11-12

tablets, xii, 28, 47, 50-51, 55, 78, 88, 92, 101, 121, 134
Tagg, John, 6, 17
Taylor Family Digital Library, 172
Teachers College, Columbia University, 66
TEAL (MIT active learning classroom), 170, 182
technology commons, 75
technology-enabled, xvii, xix, 25, 30, 76, 158, 160
technology-rich, xii, 8, 11, 25, 62, 65-66, 68-69, 162

Terrapin Learning Commons, 134, 136
Texas Christian University, 112-113
"the library is the commons", xxi, 68, 70
Thompson Library, 170
Tippett, Krista, 183
Tompkins, Philip, 7-8, 17-18
Total Advising Center, 36
Tramdack, Philip, 19-20
Trinity University, 114, 116-117
tutoring, 25, 27, 36, 105-108, 130, 140

ubiquitous computing, 15
undergraduate learning center, 11
University of Calgary, 172, 183
University of Cape Town, 118-119
University of Central Florida, 120, 122-123
University of Chicago, 172, 176, 183
University of Denver, 13
University of Georgia, 30
University of Illinois at Urbana-Champaign, 124-125, 127
University of Iowa, 8, 18, 25, 57-58, 129-133
University of Kansas, 38
University of Maryland, 17, 20, 134-136
University of Minnesota Twin Cities, 137, 139, 141
University of North Carolina Greensboro (UNCG), 141-143
University of North Texas, 144, 146-148, 150
University of Notre Dame, 70-71
University of Oklahoma, 20, 30, 151-153
University of Pennsylvania, 30, 65
University of Southern California, 8, 18
University of Tennessee, 27, 154-155, 157
University of Tennessee at Chattanooga, 154-155, 157
University of Texas, 58, 157, 159-161
University of Virginia, 20-21, 36
University of Washington, 20, 27-28
user experience, 37-38, 43, 49, 85, 87
user needs, xx, xxiii, 32-33, 37-38, 85, 104
user-centered, xiv, xviii, 102
user-centric, 32, 39
user-focused, 55

Van der Beek, Stan, 178
Van Horn, Richard L., 16, 18

variations of names for information commons, 23, 27, 67. *See also* academic commons; collaborative commons; Commons 2.0; destination commons; digital commons; digital media commons; digital scholarship center; distributed commons; faculty research commons; graduate student commons; infocommons; innovation commons; knowledge commons; learning commons; learning space; learning-focused space; library commons; makerspaces; research commons; scholarly commons; social commons; technology commons
Varner, Stewart, 21
vending, xx, 24, 29
videoconferencing, xx, 28-29, 51
Virginia Commonwealth University, 65-66, 162-164
Virginia Tech University, 20, 164, 166-167
virtual reality, 49, 66, 87, 148
visual disabilities, 28
Vitale Digital Media Lab, 30
Vygotsky, Lev, 6, 17

Wang, Xuemo, 22
Ward, Jennifer, 21
Wardman, Christopher, 178, 183
wayfinding, xx, 47
Webb, T. D., 19
Weber, David C., 4, 16
Webex (Cisco Webex), 51
Wedge, Carole, 11, 19
Weigle Information Commons, 30, 65
Williams, James B., 5, 16-17
Wilmeth Active Learning Center, 30
Wilson, Edward O., 138, 140, 179, 183
wireless network, 47, 89
Woodruff Library, 71, 88, 90
Workshop, The (VCU makerspace) 65, 85, 180
World Wide Web (WWW), 5, 175
writing center, 25-28, 69, 105, 121, 130, 158-160, 165

Xavier University, 68

Yale University, 9, 183-184 Young, Nora, 183

Zoom, 51, 172

About the Editors and Contributors

Charles Forrest has more than 35 years of experience in academic and research libraries. After nearly a decade with the University of Illinois libraries in both Chicago and Urbana-Champaign, he came to Emory University in Atlanta, Georgia, in 1988 where he held a series of administrative positions in the Library, including director of instructional support services, director of planning and budget, and most recently director of library facilities. He served as library project manager for many library construction and renovation projects at Emory, including the Center for Library and Information Resources, a major addition to and renovation of Emory's main library. Charles retired from the University in May 2016. Charles has served as a library juror for the American Institute of Architects/American Library Association Library Building Awards, the American Library Association/International Interior Design Association biennial Library Building Awards, and *Library Journal*'s "New Landmark Libraries (Academic)" series. A published author and regular presenter at conferences, workshops, and institutes, he is currently principal and owner of 21st Century Libraries Consulting, LLC.

Dr. Martin Halbert is a recognized figure in library innovation and has served as Dean of Libraries at both the University of North Carolina at Greensboro and the University of North Texas. He is also President of the Educopia Institute, an educational nonprofit that advances the well-being of libraries by fostering the advancement of shared information systems and infrastructures, and was one of the founding partners of the U.S. National Digital Preservation Program. Halbert has a PhD in interdisciplinary liberal arts from Emory University; his research examines the future of digital scholarship and research library services. He has served as principal investigator for grants and contracts totaling more than $7 million, funding more than a dozen large-scale collaborative projects among many educational institutions. Halbert has previously worked for Emory University, Rice University, UT Austin, and the IBM Corporation.

* * *

Kelly Brubaker is an accomplished library designer, programmer, and planner with Shepley Bulfinch, an architecture firm recognized internationally for the programming and design of libraries and learning environments. Her recent work includes library and learning commons projects for the University of Minnesota, University of Notre Dame, Virginia Commonwealth University, Atlanta University Center, and Salem State University. Kelly presents and publishes regularly and is actively involved in the American Library Association (ALA) and the Association of College and Research Libraries (ACRL).

Kristi Burns graduated from the University of North Texas with her MLS in May 2016 and has a Graduate Academic Certificate in Advanced Management in Library and Information Agencies. She has worked for the UNT Libraries for over eight years and currently works in the Office of Finance and Administration. There, she serves as the director for hourly employment of one of the largest departments on campus and also serves as the primary contact and mentor for 70 supervisors. In her free time, she assists in set design and strategic initiatives for Cold Fox Films, LLC based in the DFW area.

Summer Cook joined the DIRTT family in 2014 as an Integrated Construction Specialist/Project Liaison. Her 17 years in the commercial construction industry gives her a strong understanding of the challenges clients face when building or renovating their work space. Summer helps clients leverage DIRTT's precise, fully customized manufactured construction and clean, rapid installation to create a space that meets business needs today and tomorrow to accommodate growth. Prior to joining the DIRTT family, Summer spent 13 years working with commercial general contractors assisting clients with the interior finish-out of their space. Her experience over the years has allowed her the ability to work with other construction trades and provide solutions to challenges faced on the job site, which makes her a valuable ally to clients, design teams, and general contractors. Summer is a Texas native, having grown up in North Dallas. She attended Texas Christian University, where she studied marketing and management, receiving a Bachelor of Business Administration from the Neeley School of Business. Summer is married with three children ages 10, 8, and 6 years old.

Elliot Felix founded and leads brightspot, an experience design consultancy that transforms spaces, services, and organizations so that people are better connected to a purpose, a brand, information, and each other. He is an accomplished strategist, facilitator, and sense-maker who has directed projects for leading companies, cultural institutions, and universities, including work with 68 higher education institutions and 42 library projects. Elliot planned three of *Library Journal*'s eight New Library Landmarks and is a frequent keynote speaker on libraries. Solving space, operational, and organizational problems gets him up in the morning. Thinking about the future of work and learning keeps him up late.

Joan K. Lippincott is the Associate Executive Director of the Coalition for Networked Information (CNI), a joint program of the Association of Research Libraries (ARL) and EDUCAUSE. Joan is a widely published author and frequent conference speaker. She serves on the boards of the New Media Consortium (NMC), the journal portal, The Reference Librarian, and the Networked Digital Library of Theses and Dissertations (NDLTD) and on the advisory boards of the *Journal of Learning Spaces* and the NMC's *Horizon Report* for both higher education and libraries. She is past chair of the Association of College & Research Libraries' (ACRL) New Publications Board, and served as a member of the ACRL Information Literacy Competency Standards Review Task Force that produced the Framework for Information Literacy for Higher Education. She has served on the Advisory Boards of the Learning Spaces Collaboratory, the Learning Space Toolkit project, and the EDUCAUSE ELI Seeking Evidence of Impact project. Prior to joining CNI, Joan was a librarian at Cornell, Georgetown, and George Washington universities, and SUNY Brockport. Joan received her PhD in higher education from the University of Maryland, an MLS from SUNY Geneseo, and an AB from Vassar College.

DIRTT Education Director **Betsy Maddox** had an extensive and very successful run in Chicago's design community before joining DIRTT in 2011. As a licensed interior designer, she managed projects in the education, healthcare, and corporate sectors for over 10 years. She joined the team as a sales representative at DIRTT before moving to her current role as DIRTT's education specialist. Betsy is surrounded by educators on the home front; her husband is a high school English teacher, and her mother and mother-in-law are both educators. While she has practical experience designing education spaces, she attributes much of her knowledge to learning by osmosis. Her passion for the convergence of sustainable construction with innovative education spaces to meet new teaching methods is what drives her to help people understand how to leverage DIRTT solutions for students, teachers, and education support staff.

Elizabeth J. Milewicz heads the Digital Scholarship Services department in Duke University Libraries. Her team partners with researchers and students on digital research, teaching, and publishing projects (http://sites.duke.edu/digital) and provides training and consulting in digital approaches to scholarship. She helped to plan and launch a new space for research, called The Edge: The Ruppert Commons for Research, Technology, and Collaboration (http://library.duke.edu/edge), where project teams pursue interdisciplinary, data-driven, and digitally reliant research. Before coming to Duke in 2011, Liz managed two NEH-funded digital humanities projects at Emory University (The Expanded Online Transatlantic Slave Trade Database, http://slavevoyages.org; and African Origins, http://african-origins.org) and worked with the Emory Libraries on a range of digital library initiatives. She earned her doctorate at Emory as well, where she studied the evolving culture, role, and sound of academic libraries.

Susan K. Nutter was the Vice Provost and Director of Libraries at North Carolina State University. Under her leadership, the NCSU Libraries was the first university library to win ACRL's Excellence in Academic Libraries Award, and members of her staff have won nine *Library Journal* "Movers and Shakers" awards in the past twelve years, the most of any academic library. In 2005, Susan received *Library Journal*'s "Librarian of the Year" award.

In January of 2013, the James B. Hunt Jr. Library opened on North Carolina State's Centennial Campus. Designed by Snøhetta, the Hunt Library has been awarded the 2014 Stanford Prize for Innovation in Research Libraries, the 2014 AIA Education Facility Design Award, the 2014 ALA Library Interior Design Award, and the 2013 AIA/ALA Building Award for distinguished accomplishment in library architecture. Recently, Nutter was named the ACRL Academic Librarian of the year, the Hunt Library was named a *Library Journal* New Landmark Library, and the NCSU Libraries received an IMLS National Medal for Library Service from First Lady Michelle Obama.

Parke Rhoads is Principal at Vantage Technology Consulting Group, leading their Library and Academic Technology Design and Consulting practice. In addition to his expertise in academic and information commons technology Parke has served as faculty (Physics and Technology Design) and as Chief Technology Architect for the United Nations, where he developed new technology standards and deployed new archival and collaboration technologies on the global stage.

Architect, master planner, professor, artist, and advocate, **Marie S. A. Sorensen**, AIA seeks out gaps in institutional knowledge, mindset, and process and proactively and interactively collects, structures, and shares designs and insights to change the physical and psychological shape of communities. Marie founded Cambridge, MA–based Sorensen Partners | Architects + Planners, Inc. in 2012 to work with complex knowledge- and mission-driven organizations interested in the possibility of architecture to shape and inspire evolved institutional culture. Sorensen Partners has designed and planned buildings and learning environments for Yale University, Wellesley College, Endicott College, Rowan University, and Benjamin Franklin Institute of Technology.

Shaping the field of academic library planning and design, Marie is convener of the "Knowledge Constellation" research project, bringing together academic librarians and designers to formulate and prototype new physical and digital formats for information discovery. She was keynote speaker at the ACRL New England Chapter Conference in 2015, presenting The History and Future of Collaboration, and is a past presenter at Boston Women in Information. Marie has taught architecture studio, building science, and history at Massachusetts College of Art and Design, Wentworth Institute of Technology, and Norwich University. She is content coordinator of the modern architecture advocacy organization DOCOMOMO-US/New England; contributor to the

Boston Society of Architects' Building Enclosure Council; member of the AIA Massachusetts Government Affairs Committee; past editorial board member of *ArchitectureBoston Magazine*; and has published on the adaptive reuse of industrial buildings and sites. In 2016, Marie was nominated for the American Institute of Architects' Young Architects Award.

Matthew Swift was an Associate Director at brightspot strategy. He is an experienced researcher and strategist whose experience spans management consulting, technology, and design. Matthew believes that understanding people in a more nuanced way provides a powerful frame of reference for reshaping a business or institution.

E-21-97

LIBRARY
WILSON COMMUNITY COLLEGE
902 HERRING AVE.
PO BOX 4305
WILSON, NC 27893